AN INTRODUCTION TO AMPHIBIA

AN
INTRODUCTION TO
AMPHIBIA

By
H.S. Bhamrah
Kavita Juneja

Edited by
Balvinder K.

ANMOL PUBLICATIONS PVT. LTD.
NEW DELHI - 110 002 (INDIA)

ANMOL PUBLICATIONS PVT. LTD.
4374/4B, Ansari Road, Daryaganj
New Delhi - 110 002

An Introduction to Amphibia

First Edition, 1990
Reprint, 1991, 1992, 1994
Second Revised Edition, 2002
ISBN 81-261-0701-4

PRINTED IN INDIA

Published by J.L. Kumar for Anmol Publications Pvt. Ltd., New Delhi - 110 002 and Printed at Mehra Offset Press, Delhi.

Contents

1 **Amphibia: Characters and Classification** 1-23
Characteristics, *Extinct Amphibia, Living Amphibia, Ichthyophis, Uraeotyphlus, Necturus, Proteus, Amphiuma, Triton, Salamandra, Ambystoma, Axolotl Larva, Cryptobranchus, Pipa, Hyla, Siren, Alytes, Bufo, Rhacophorus,*

2 **Rana tigrina** 24-29
Systemic Position; External Features; Sexual Dimorphism

3 **Integument** 30-37
Epidermis; Dermis; Functions of Skin; Coelom and Viscera

4 **Endoskeleton** 38-54
Skull; Vertebral Column; The Appendicular Skeleton

5 **Musculature** 55-61
Principal Body Muscles

6 **Digestive System** 62-75
The Alimentary Canal; Histology: Digestive Glands, Ingestion of Food

7 **Respiratory System** 76-83
Mechanism of Pulmonary Breathing; Physiology of Respiration;

8 **Circulatory System** 84-99
Blood Vascular System; Blood; Lymphatic System

9 **Nervous System** 100-114
Central Nervous System; Peripheral Nervous System; Autonomic Nervous System

10 **Sense organs** 115-126

11 **Urinogenital System** 127-135
Excretory System; Reproductive System

12 **Development of Forg** 136-167
Fertilization; Cleavage; Blastulation; Gastrulation; Larva of Frog; Metamorphosis

13	**Parental Care in Amphibians** Order Anura; Order-Urodela; Order Apoda; Significance	168-175
14	**Neoteny & Paedogenesis** Types of Neoteny; Significance of Neoteny	176-179
15	**Stegocephalia** Features of Stegocephalia; Affinities of Stegocephalia	180-184
16	**Origin and Evolution of Amphibia** Piscine Ancestores; Evolution of Amphibia; The Modern Amphibia	185-192
17	**Courtship and Mating in Amphibians**	193-204
	Index	205-208

Preface

We feel pleasure in bringing out the second revised edition of the present book on the instance of our learned teachers. Besides rectifying the errors of first edition, new material is added here and there in the light of recent development and researches in the field.

This text is designed to approach the morphology, anatomy, physiology and development of the *Amphibia* in a coherent way since it is most natural for a student in studying the architectural elements of an animal body in the quest to know how they function. This text intends, therefore, to enable the student, through his own natural appetency, to correlate form and function so that he possesses for subsequent work in either anatomy or physiology a firm foundation for a real edifice of knowledge.

The book features both a text and a laboratory guide. It deals with the structures and physiological phenomena of each system. Origin, adaptative radiation and other general topics are also dealt in details. It is hoped that this book will not only meet the requirement of Indian students but will also be useful as a guideline to the teachers in their teaching.

There can be no claim to originality except in the manner of treatment and much of the information has been obtained from the books and scientific journals available in different libraries.

We express our thanks to our friends and colleagues whose constant inspiration have initiated them to bring out this book.

The authors are also grateful to Dr. J. Bahadur, Professor and Head, School of Studies in Zoology, Jiwaji University Gwalior, Dr. A.K. Pandey, Professor & Head, Vikram University, Ujjain for their valuable suggestions.

All the constructive criticisms and suggestions for improvement from learned teachers and scholars are welcome.

H.S. Bhamrah
Kavita Juneja

1

Amphibia : Characters and Classification

There is no doubt that the amphibians have sprung up from fish-like ancestors and that in turn given rise to reptlies. Thus amphibian consequently hold a very important intermediate position. The term *Amphibia* was coined by *Linnaeus* although he kept both, the amphibians as well as some reptiles in this particular class. Later on naturalists and taxonomists put the amphibians particularly in this class, although the characteristic features of the old amphibians and those of recent are little more different. Followings are the characteristic features of recent amphibians.

CHARACTERISTICS

1. Amphibians may be aquatic, terrestrial or both.
2. These are cold-blooded (*poikilothermous*) animals. Their body temperature is variable and most of them undergo *hibernation* during winter. Some undergo *aestivation* during summer.
3. The shape of body is variable, it may be depressed or cylindrical and divisible into head, neck, trunk and tail or into head and trunk.
4. The skin is thin, moist, glandular and devoid of exoskeleton.
5. Four pentadactyl limbs are supported by girdles. The apodans are without limbs.
6. The median fin when present is not supported by fin-rays.
7. There is a pair of nostrils, which open into the buccal cavity. They are provided with valves to exclude water.
8. The teeth are alike (*homodont*), *acrodont* and *polyphyodont*.
9. Endoskeleton is largely bony or ossified. Skull is *dicondylic* i.e. possesses two occipital condyles for the attachment to the vertebral column. Ribs, if present, are not attached to sternum.
10. Alimentary canal opens into *cloaca*.
11. Heart is three-chambered i.e. two atria and a ventricle. Sinus-venosus and truncus arteriosus are present.
12. The red blood corpuscles are oval and nucleated.

13. Respiration by gills, skin and lungs.
14. The ear-drum or *tympanum* is external and is connected to the internal ear by *columella auris.*
15. Eyes are provided with movable lids and tear glands to clean and protect them in air.
16. Brain has smooth cerebral hemispheres and the cerebellum is poorly developed.
17. There are ten pairs of cranial nerves.
18. Kidneys are *mesonephric* and provided with persistent nephrostome.
19. Sexes are separate. The gonads are paired. Gonoducts open into the cloaca.
20. Fertilization is generally external, sometimes internal.
21. Mainly oviparous. Eggs are mesolecithal and are covered with gelatinous covering. They are laid in water.
22. Development is indirect i.e. through a larval stage which undergoes metamorphosis.

Classification

The classification followed here is given by *G.K. Noble* (1931).

EXTINCT AMPHIBIA

The extinct amphibian are placed under three orders.

Order-1. Labyrinthodontia

1. Distributed from Carboniferous to the Triassic period.
2. These were crocodile or salamander-like amphibians.
3. The skull was completely roofed over with bones. The number of bones in the skull were more than those of recent forms.
4. The teeth were enlarged and with greatly folded dentine in both the jaws.
5. All the vertebrae consist of neural arches and intercentra. Further in all the forms except in stereospondyle, a pre-ossiifed pleurocentrum is present.

Order Labyrinthodontia is divided into three sub-orders on the basis of difference in the vertebrae.

Sub-order-I. Embolomeri

1. Distributed from lower Carboniferous through Permian.
2. The centra of vertebrae were double i.e. the intercentrum and pleurocentrum form a complete ring and the neural arch was attached to one or both of them.

3. The occipital condyl was single or tripple.
4. The palate was well ossified.

Examples : *Palaeogyrinus, Eogyrinus.*

Sub-order-II. Rhachitomi

1. They were distributed from Permian to Triassic periods.
2. Each vertebra consist of a half-moon shaped intercentrum and one or two pairs of pleurocenra.
3. Occipital condyl was tripple.
4. The inter-pterygoid cavities wider then Embolomeri. An otic notch occured.

Example: *Eryops*

Sub-order-III. Stereospondyli.

1. They were distributed in the early Triassic period.
2. The centrum found almost entirely of the intercentrum. The pleurocentrum being rudimentary or absent.
3. Two occipital condyles were present.
4. The inter-pterygoid cavities increase in size.

Examples : *Capitosaurus. Cyclotosaurus* etc.

Order-2. Phyllospondyli

1. They were distrubuted in Carboniferous to Permain period.
2. They were small, salamander-like amphibians.
3. The vertebrae were tubular with the notochord and spinal cord lying in one cavity.
4. The centrum was represented by the thick floor of each vertebral ring.
5. The transverse processes were well marked with short ribs.
6. Cartilaginous pubis and coracoid.
7. Three pairs of gills in long larval life resembles the urodeals.

Example : *Ichthyostega.*

Order-3. Lepospondyli

1. They were distrubuted from Carboniferous and Permian periods.
2. Each vertebrae was composed of a single piece. The neural arch continued with centrum.
3. The ribs articulating with column intervertebrally. In some cases there was a secondary shift of the ribs to the side of vertebra.

This order is divided into four sub-orders.

Sub-order I. Adelospondyli

1. The neural arch was joined by sutures to the centrum which had a distinct form. A pair of depressions penetrating the ventro-lateral surface of each vertebra.
2. The skull had incompletely roofed skull.

   Example : *Lysorophus*

Sub-order-II. Aistopoda

1. These were limbless and long-bodied animals of Carboniferous period.
2. Elongated skull
3. Snake-like body with as many as 100 vertebrae.
4. Ribs were forked and transverse processes were distinct.

   Example: *Ophiderpeton, Aistopod*

Sub-order-III. Nectridia

1. Distributed in the upper Carboniferous period.
2. One form was superficially snake-like and limbless (Sauropleura).
3. *Diplocaulus* had a huge triangulr head and small limbs.
4. Skull developed an extraordinary armament formed by the outgrowth of the tabulars. Cranium which was largely unossified.
5. Coracoids were separate.

   Examples : *Diplocaulus* and *Sauropleura*

Sub-order-IV. Gastrocentrophori

These were salamander-like Lepospondyli, their relation to other sub-orders is not well defined.

LIVING AMPHIBIA

Order-4. Gymnophiona or Apoda

1. The animals are aberrant blind, worm-like, limbless, Tropical Amphibia-with a very short tail.
2. The body is usually grooved transversely, and in the grooves are often series of minute *scales*.
3. The eyes are lid-less and sometimes covered by cranial bones.
4. Between the eyes and nostrils is present a tentacle which is protrusible.
5. Males possess a protrusible copulatory organ.
6. Fertilization is internal.
7. Development of eggs is internal in *Typhlonectes* (viviparous) or external (from large-yolked eggs which are laid in burrows) as in *Rhinatrema.*

8. The fossils are unknown and living animal is rarely seen.
   Examples : *Typhlonectes, Rhinatrema, Uraeotyphlus* and *Ichthyophis.*

Order-5. Caudata or Urodela

1. Body with distinct head, trunk and tail.
2. Paired limbs are present.
3. The skull is very much reduced.
4. Their larvae, if aquatic, resemble their parents and there is no conspicuous metamorphosis. Caudata is divided into five sub-orders.

Sub-order.I. Cryptobranchoidea

1. Body is depressed, the skin is soft and flabby.
2. Gills are absent in adult.
3. Eyelids are absent.
4. The angular is free and not fused with pre-articular.
5. The spine of premaxilary is short and does not separate the nasals.
6. Fertilization is external. The cloacal glands are reduced.
   Examples : *Cryptobranchus, Megalobatrachus* etc.

Sub-order-II. Ambystomatoidea

1. The angular is fused with pre-articular in lower jaw.
2. The second epibranchial is lost.
3. The premaxillary spine is elongated.
4. Fronto-squamosal arch is absent in skull.
5. Vertebrae are amphicoelous.
6. Internal fertilization.
   Examples : *Ambystoma, Rhyacotriton* etc.

Sub order III. Salamandroidea

1. Teeth are present on the roof of palate well behind the internal nares.
2. Fronto-squamosal arch is present.
3. Eyelids are present or absent.
4. Vertebrae are amphicoelous.
5. Fertilization is internal, usually viviparous.
   Examples : *Salamandra, Amphiuma, Triton,* etc.

Sub-order IV. Proteida

1. Eyelids are absent.
2. Permanent larval forms with external gills.
3. Cartilaginous skull without maxillae.

4. Tail is provided with a fin.
5. Permanently aquatic.

   Examples : *Proteus, Necturus*

Sub-order-V. Meantes

1. Body is slender eel-like.
2. The adults are permanent larvae.
3. Three pairs of external gills are present.
4. Angular is fused with pre-articular bone in lower jaw.
5. Only the fore-limbs are present.
6. Jaws with horny covering.
7. Fertilization is external.

   Examples : *Siren* and *Pseudobranchus.*

Order-6. Anura or Salientia

1. The body is short, broad comprising only head and trunk. the tail is absent in adults.
2. Eyes are large with eyelids.
3. Middle ear is generally present.
4. Hind-limbs are much larger than fore-limbs.
5. Feet are webbed for leaping and swimming.
6. Vocal cords are present.
7. Skull is thin without a solid roof.
8. Ribs are reduced or absent.
9. Oviparous, fertilization is external.
10. Development indirect through a larval stage which is very different from adult. Order-Anura is divided into five sub-orders.

Sub-order-I Amphicoela

1. Vertebrae are amphicoelous.
2. Though the tail is absent yet the tail muscles are present.
3. Fertilization is internal.

   Examples : *Ascaphus, Leiopelma.*

Sub-order-II. Opisthocoela

1. Vertebrae are opisthocoelous.
2. Free ribs are present either in larva or adult.
3. Tongue and tympanum are absent.
4. Eustachian tubes open into pharynx by a single aperture.

   Examples : *Pipa, Alytes, Xenopus, Bombinator.*

Sub-order. III Anomocoela

1. Vertebrae are procoelous.
2. Free ribs are absent.
3. There are eight pre-sacral vertebrae, and fused with urostyle.
4. Skin is rough.

   Examples : *Megalophyrs, Pelobates, Scaphiopus.*

Sub-order IV. Procoela

1. Vertebrae are procoelous.
2. Ribs are absent.
3. Urostyle articulates with the last vertebra by two condyles.
4. Maxillary teeth are absent.

   Examples : *Bufo, Hyla, Rhinoderma* etc.

Sub-order V. Diplasiocoela

1. First seven vertebrae are procoelous.
2. Eighth vertebra is amphicoelous.
3. The sacral vertebra is a acoelous bearing two condyles posteriorly for the attachement with urostyle.
4. Ribs are absent and pectoral girdle is fused with sternum.

   Examples : *Rana, Rhacophorus.*

ICHTHYOPHIS

Phylum	-	Chordata
Group	-	Vertebrata
Subphylum	-	Gnathostomata
Class	-	Amphibia
Order	-	Gymnophiona or Apoda
Genus	-	*Ichthyophis*

1. It is a burrowing animal found in moist soil near ponds and commonly known as 'caecilian'.
2. It is carnivorous feeds on worms and small invertebrates which it finds underground.
3. The body is slender, eel-like measuring about 15-20 cm long.
4. The skin is moist and has ring-like folds containing minute dermal scales embedded deep in it.
5. Slime glands and squirt glands are present in the skin. Squirt glands produce irritating fluid.
6. Eyes are very small and covered by opaque skin. Mouth is fairly large. Tympanum is absent.

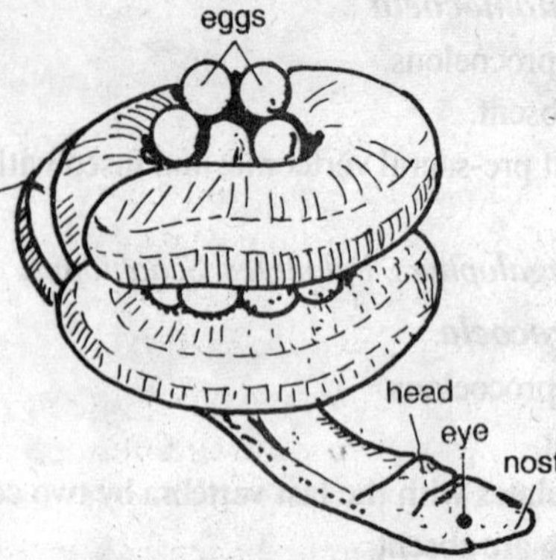

Fig. 1.1. *Ichthyophis.*

7. The limbs and girdles are absent.
8. A sensory tentacle is situated in a groove between nostrils and eyes on each side.
9. Respiration through lungs. Right lung is elongated while the left lung is reduced.
10. The cloaca is terminal, hence the tail is absent.
11. Cloaca is reversible in male to act as a copulatory organ.
12. Fertilization is internal.
13. Eggs are laid in wet burrow. The mother shows *parental care*. She coils round the egg mass till they are hatched.
14. The tadpole larva with three pairs of external gills, a pair of gill-slits, better developed eyes and a compressed tail bearing tail-fin.
15. Larva undergoes metamorphosis.
16. It is found in India and Sri Lanka.

URAEOTYPHLUS

Phylum	-	Chordata
Group	-	Vertebrata
Sub-phylum	-	Gnathostomata
Class	-	Amphibia
Order	-	Gymnophiona or Apoda
Genus	-	*Uraeotyphlus*

1. It is a burrowing animal in soft mud and commonly known as 'caecilian'.
2. Body is elongated, eel-like, dark green, brown or black dorsally and white ventrally.

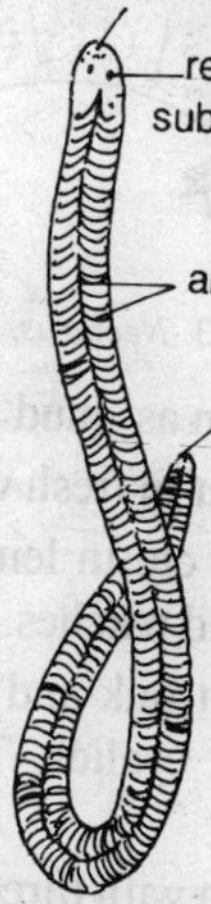

Fig. 1.2. *Uraeotyphlus*.

3. Body surface is wrinkled and giving the appearance of segmentation. Minute cycloid scales are embedded in the skin.
4. The eyes are non-functional, indistinct and covered by opaque skin.
5. Tympanum, tympanic cavity and columella are absent.
6. Mouth is terminal but the anus is subterminal.
7. A sensory tentacular apparatus is present in a groove of maxilla between eye and nostril.
8. Tail is extremly short.
9. Limbs are absent.
10. It feeds on worms i.e. carnivorous.
11. The copulatory structures are very short.
12. Oviparous. The animals show *parental care*.
13. It has been reported from India, Malaya, South Africa and South America.

NECTURUS

Phylum	-	Chordata
Group	-	Vertebrata
Sub-phylum	-	Gnathostomata
Class	-	Amphibia
Order	-	Urodela or caudata
Sub-order	-	Proteida
Genus	-	*Necturus*

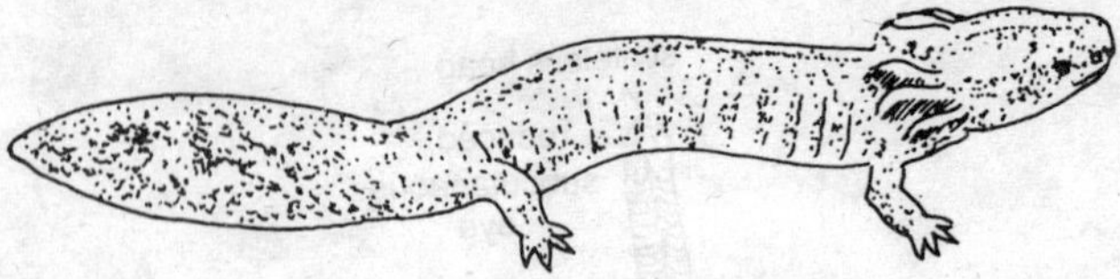

Fig. 1.3. *Necturus.*

1. *Necturus* is commonly known as 'mud puppy' or 'water dog'.
2. It is an aquatic animal present in fresh water rivers and lakes.
3. Body attains a size of 30-40 cm in length. Skin is smooth, slimy, brown with blackish spots and patches.
4. Body is divisible into head, trunk and tail. Head is depressed and contains small eyes without eyelids. Tympanum is absent. Skull cartilagenous.
5. It is permanent neotinic larva with three pairs of bushy red coloured external gills and two gill-slits behind the head.
6. Lungs are present but respire through external gills.
7. Limbs are short and weak, provided with four digits only. First diet is lost. Limbs are used for crawling on the land.
8. Tail is compressed and provided with tail fin.
9. Lateral line system is present.
10. Breeding season is autumn. Female lays about 18-180 eggs in nests in May or June. Hatching takes place within 38-63 days. Nests are guarded by females. Larva matures in 6 years to full size.
11. It is found in North America and Yougoslavia.

PROTEUS

Phylum	-	Chordata
Group	-	Vertebrata
Sub-phylum	-	Gnathostomata
Class	-	Amphibia
Order	-	Urodela or Caudata
Sub-order	-	Proteida
Genus	-	*Proteus*

1. It is commonly known as 'cave salamander'.
2. It is a cave dwelling salamander found in deep caves and underground streams.
3. It feeds on small crustaceans.

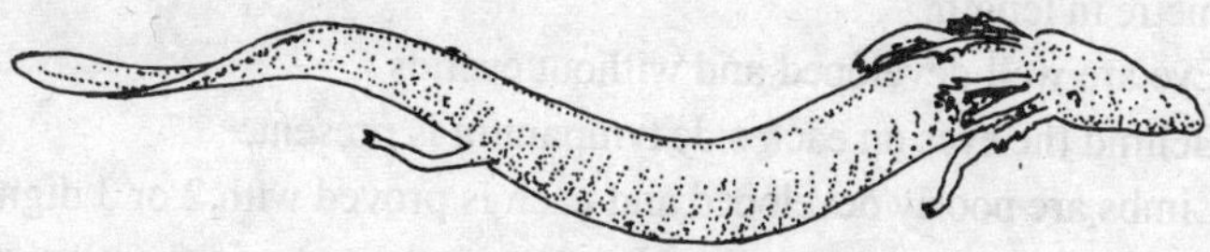

Fig. 1.4. *Proteus.*

4. Elongated, eel like body about 25 cm in length, eyes deeply sunken without eye-lids. Skull cartilaginous.
5. Limbs are poorly developed with three digits in fore-limbs and two digits in hind-limbs.
6. Three pairs of external gills (carmine-coloured), and two pairs of gill slits are present. Lungs are also present.
7. Tail is compressed with a caudal fin. It is the only organ of locomotion.
8. Both the jaws have teeth. Maxillaries are absent. Premaxillaries, vomers and mandibles are toothed.
9. They are distributed in South-eastern Europe, Germany and Austria.

AMPHIUMA

Phylum	-	Chordata
Group	-	Vertebrata
Sub-phylum	-	Gnathostomata
Class	-	Amphibia
Order	-	Urodela
Sub-order	-	Salamandroidea
Genus	-	*Amphiuma*

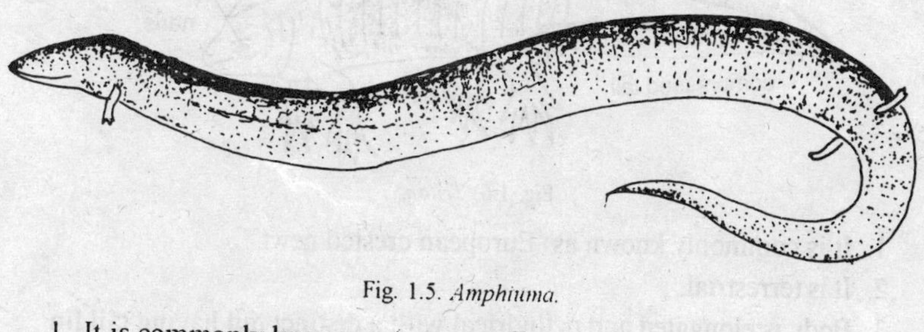

Fig. 1.5. *Amphiuma.*

1. It is commonly known as 'congo eel'.
2. It is commnly found in swampy medows and rice fields.
3. Carnivorous. feeds on molluscs. cray fishes and small fishes.

4. Body is covered with black and smooth skin and measures about one metre in length.
5. Eye are well developed and without eyelids.
6. Behind the eyes on each side tympanum is present.
7. Limbs are poorly developed and each is proved with 2 or 3 digits.
8. Gill clefts are two in number. Largest erythrocytes in these animals about 80 μ in diameter.
9. Oviparous, eggs are laid in water. Female shows *parental care*, she coils round the eggs till they hatch.
10. They are found in American swamps, muddy water, burrows etc.

TRITON

Phylum	-	Chordata
Group	-	Veretbrata
Sub-phylum	-	Gnathostomata
Class	-	Amphibia
Order	-	Caudata
Sub-order	-	Salamandroidea
Genus	-	*Triton*

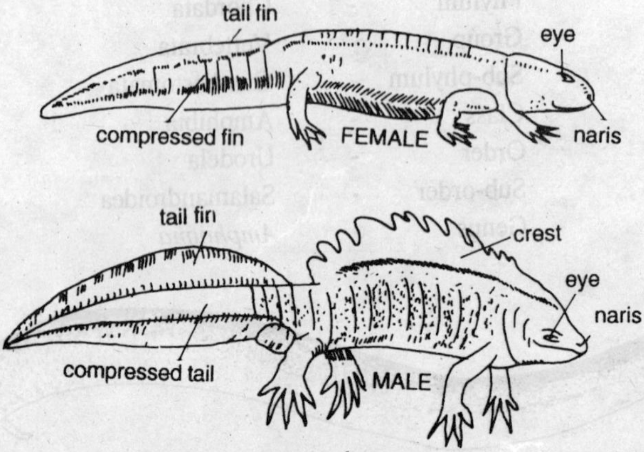

Fig. 1.6. *Triton.*

1. It is commonly known as 'European crested newt'.
2. It is terrestrial.
3. Body is elongated and cylindrical with a distinct tail having tail fin with fin rays.
4. Head is conical and compressed. Mouth is wide. Nostrils are small. Eyes are small and provided with upper and lower eyelids.

5. Tympanum is absent.
6. Limbs are well developed; forelimbs possess four digits each. Hind limbs with five digits etc.
7. Gills are absent in adult, respiration by means of lungs and skin.
8. Exihibits sexual dimorphism. Male possesses a dorsal median crest on the back and becomes brilliantly coloured in breeding season.
9. The larva possesses three pairs of external gills which are lost in the adult.
10. Found in the U.S.A. from California to Southern Alaska and Europe.

SALAMANDRA

Phylum	-	Chordata
Group	-	Vertebrata
Sub-phylum	-	Gnathostomata
Class	-	Amphibia
Order	-	Urodela
Sub-order	-	Salamandroidea
Genus	-	*Salamandra*

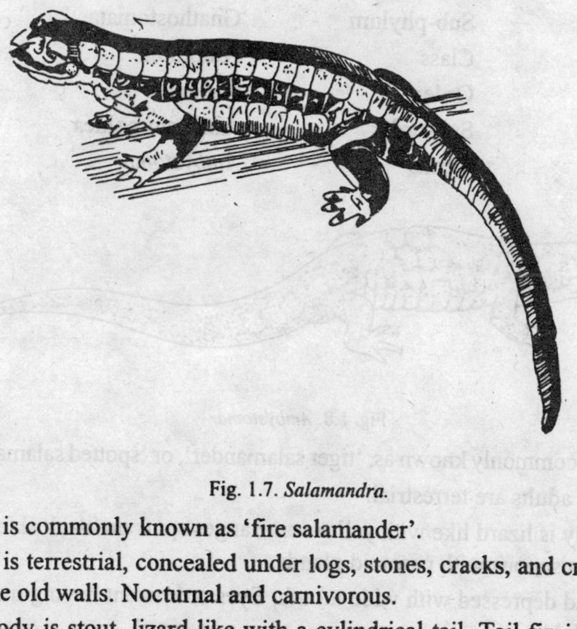

Fig. 1.7. *Salamandra.*

1. It is commonly known as 'fire salamander'.
2. It is terrestrial, concealed under logs, stones, cracks, and crevics of the old walls. Nocturnal and carnivorous.
3. Body is stout, lizard-like with a cylindrical tail. Tail fin is absent. Males measure 12-15 cm in length. Females are longer than males.

4. Brilliantly coloured with irregular patches of yellow colour on black body.
5. Head contains eyes and nostrils. Eyes are provided with movable eye-lids. The large parotoid glands are present behind the head.
6. Skin smooth and slimy. Cutaneous glands secrete poisonous fluid.
7. Gills and gill clefts are absent in adults.
8. Teeth are present on both the jaws.
9. Limbs well developed. Fore limbs possess four digits and hind limbs five digits.
10. Some forms like *S. maculosa* are viviparous. The eggs developed in oviducts. Larvae with gills which are shed before hatching during metamorphosis.
11. Undergoes hibernation.
12. Found in shady places in Europe, Syria and Algeria.

AMBYSTOMA

Phylum	-	Chordata
Group	-	Vertebrata
Sub-phylum	-	Gnathostomata
Class	-	Amphibia
Order	-	Caudata
Sub-order	-	Ambystomoidea
Genus	-	*Ambystoma*

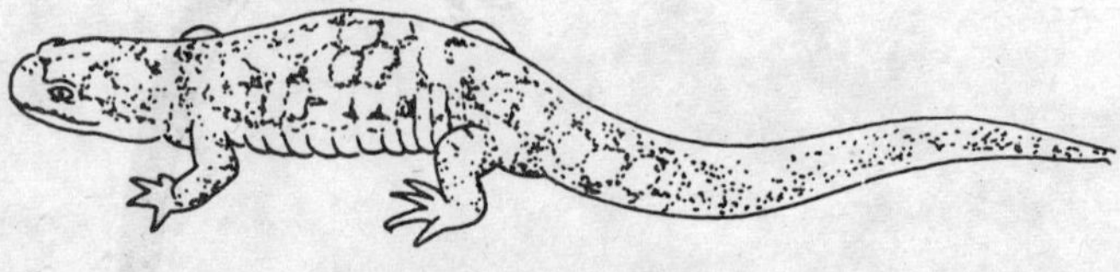

Fig. 1.8. *Ambystoma.*

1. It is commonly known as, 'tiger salamander', or 'spotted salamander'.
2. The adults are terrestrial.
3. Body is lizard like with yellow or oranges spots on black skin. Skin is poisonous with parotoid glands.
4. Head depressed with wide mouth. Eyes prominent having movable eyelids.
5. External gills and tail fin are absent.

6. Limbs are well developed. Fore-limbs have four digits each ; and hind-lirnbs have five digits each.
7. Neck with a prominent gular fold.
8. Sexes are separate. Fertilization internal. Eggs are laid in water and develop into Axoloti larvae.Axolotl is the excellent example of neoteny.
9. They are found in North America, Central Mexico and the U.S.A.

AXOLOTL LARVA

Phylum	-	Chordata
Group	-	Vertebrata
Sub-phylum	-	Gnathostomata
Class	-	Amphibia
Order	-	Urodela
Sub-order	-	Ambystomoidea

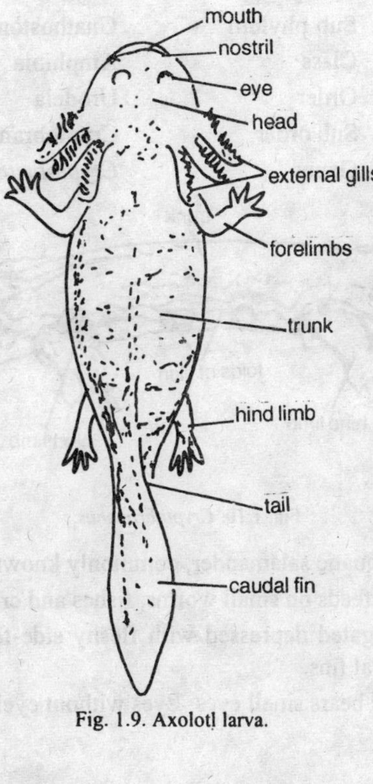

Fig. 1.9. Axolotl larva.

1. It was previously considered as adult and called *Siredon*. Later it was found to be a larva of *Ambystoma*, commonly known as 'serpent of water'.
2. Body stout with laterally compressed tail. Tail bears tail fin or caudal fin without fin-rays.
3. Three pairs of crimson coloured external gills and four pairs of gill-slits are also present.
4. Limbs are well-developed.
5. It becomes sexually mature and lays eggs. This phenomenon is known as *paedogensis* or *neoteny*
6. It retains larval characteristics throughout the life and generally does not metamorphose into adult due to lack of iodine in water. Metamorphosis can be induced by injecting thyroid injection into axolotl larva.
7. This is found in mountain lakes of Mexico and Central America.

CRYPTOBRANCHUS

Phylum	-	Chordata
Group	-	Vertebrata
Sub-phylum	-	Gnathostomata
Class	-	Amphibia
Order	-	Urodela
Sub order	-	Cryptobranchoidea
Genus	-	*Cryptobranchus*

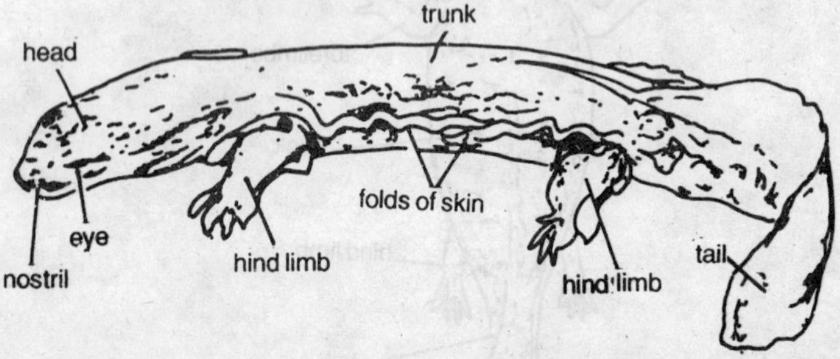

Fig. 1.10. *Cryptobranchus.*

1. It is a giant aquatic salamander, commonly known as 'hell bender'.
2. Carnivorous, feeds on small worms, fishes and crustaceans.
3. Body is elongated depressed with fleshy side-folds of skin. Tail contains caudal fins.
4. Head is broad bears small eyes. Eyes without eyelids.

5. External gills absent but epibranchialis are present.
6. First gill-cleft or spiracle remains open and acts as excurrent opening for the water taken into the mouth during buccal respiration.
7. Lateral line organs are well developed.
8. Limbs are well developed with four digits in each fore-limbs and five digits in each hind limbs.
9. Fertilization is external. Female lays about 300 eggs; laid in gelatinous sac pulled out into two long rosary-like strings. Larva hatches in November and takes several years to mature.
10. It is commonly found in Eastern Asia, Japan and New Yark.

SIREN

Phylum	-	Chordata
Group	-	Vertebrata
Sub-phylum	-	Gnathostomata
Class	-	Amphibia
Order	-	Caudata
Sub-order	-	Meantes
Genus	-	*Siren*

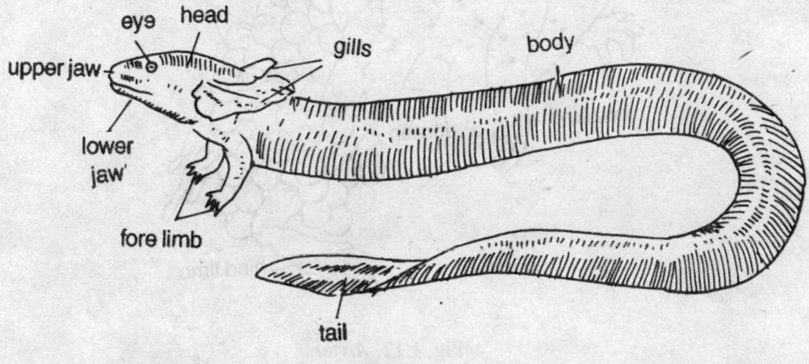

Fig. 1.11. *Siren.*

1. It is commonly known as 'mud eel' found in the burrows, muddy ditches and ponds.
2. Body is slender. elongated and measures 75 cm in length.
3. Skin soft. slimy and without scales.
4. Head is conical with small eyes and nostrils. Eyes without eyelids.
5. Fore-limbs are short with four digits each. Hind-limb are absent. Tail is provided with caudal fin.

6. Three pairs of external gills and one pair of gill-slits are present.
7. Teeth absent in both the jaws. Jaws covered with horny sheaths.
8. Cloacal glands are absent. Fertilization is probably external. It is a neotenic form as larva does not undergo complete metamorphosis.
9. *Siren* is found in the U.S.A. chiefly in Indiana Florida, Virginia and Texas.

ALYTES

Phylum	-	Chordata
Group	-	Vertebrata
Sub-phylum	-	Gnathostmata
Class	-	Amphibia
Order	-	Anura or Salientia
Sub-order	-	Opisthocoela
Genus	-	*Alytes*

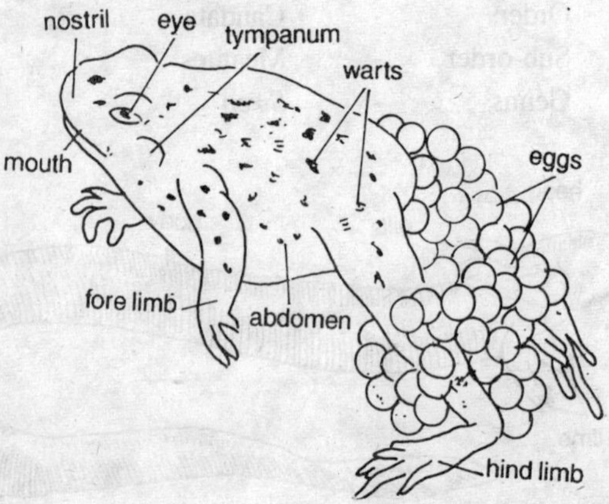

Fig. 1.12. *Alytes*.

1. It is commonly known as 'mid-wife toad'.
2. Body measures 5-8 cm in length and divisible into head and trunk.
3. Body surface is dry and warty, brownish or greenish in colour.
4. Head contains large tympanum and protruding eyes. Eyelids are movable and a vertical pupil.
5. Tongue rounded or disc-shaped and non protrusible.
6. Males are without vocal sacs.
7. Upper jaw possesses teeth. Adults have ribs.

8. The limbs are well developed, fingers are free, toes are feebly webbed.
9. Fertilization and eggs deposition external.
10. Parental care is shown by males. A male carries eggs on its back and thigh. When the larvae are ready to hatch, it shifts to the nearest pond to release the progeny.
11. It is found in European countries.

PIPA

Phylum	-	Chordata
Group	-	Vertebrata
Sub-phylum	-	Gnathostomata
Class	-	Amphibia
Order	-	Anura
Sub-order	-	Opisthocoela
Genus	-	*Pipa*
Species	-	*americana*

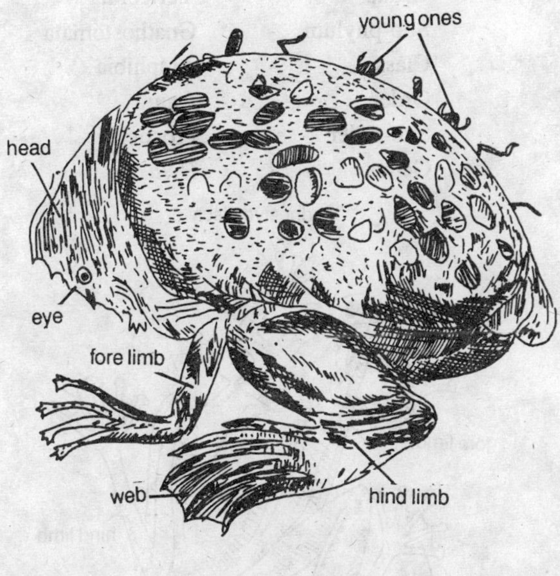

Fig. 1.13. *Pipa americana.*

1. It is commonly known as 'surinam' toad.
2. It is an aquatic form.
3. Body has shabby appearance and measures 18 cm in length. Skin papillated and with poison glands.

4. Head is triangular and depressed, and bears a number of short irregularly shaped flaps and tentacles on the upper lip, infront of the eyes and at the angles of mouth.
5. Eyes are small without eyelids and have a circular pupil.
6. Tongue and teeth are absent.
7. Tympanum absent.
8. Limbs are well developed. The fingers are slender and free each ending into a four rayed star. These tips bear sensory papillae. Toes are fully webbed.
9. Female shows parental care. The skin of back becomes soft and spongy in breeding season. It forms pocket-like structures. The male places the fertilized eggs in these pockets. An operculum or lid is also formed over each pocket. The young ones develop in these pockets.
10. It is found in South America.

HYLA

Phylum	-	Chordata
Group	-	Vertebrata
Sub-phylum	-	Gnathostomata
Class	-	Amphibia
Order	-	Anura
Sub-order	-	Procoela
Genus	-	*Hyla*

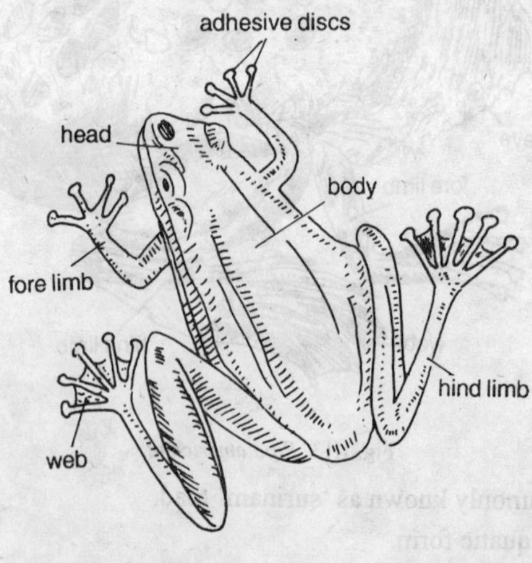

Fig. 1.14. *Hyla*.

1. It is commonly known as 'tree frog'.
2. It is arboreal in habit living on trees and rocks. It feeds on insects.
3. It has about 5 cm long body with smooth green skin. Body divisible into head and trunk.
4. Eyes are well developed with horizontal pupil.
5. Tympanum has well distinct voice often loud.
6. Limbs are long and slender. Fingers are free but toes are webbed. All the digits have flat, circular adhesive discs at the tip.
7. They can change their colour according to their environment.
8. Skin of belly and throat contains hygroscope glands which help the animal in adhering with leaf, twig or stem.
9. A species of *Hyla faber* shows parental care. The female digs up mud of shallow pond, and makes small nurseries and eggs are laid there. The larvae after hatching go into submerged water.
10. It is commonly distributed in India, China, U.S.A., Africa and Canada.

BUFO

Phylum	-	Chordata
Group	-	Vertebrata
Sub-phylum	-	Gnathostomata
Class	-	Amphibia
Order	-	Anura
Sub-order	-	Procoela
Genus	-	*Bufo*

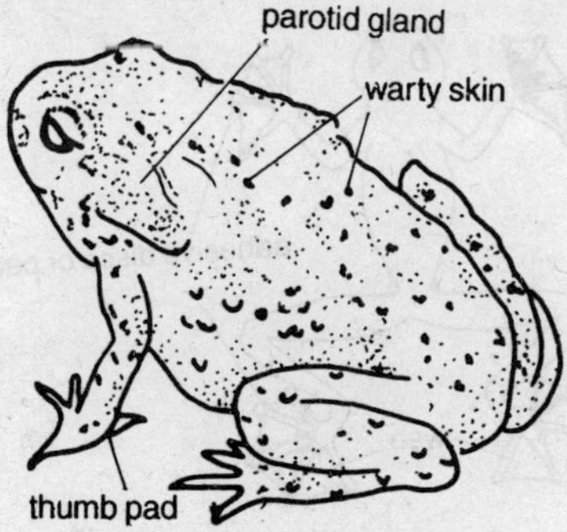

Fig. 1.15. *Bufo*.

1. It is commonly known as 'toad'.
2. It is terrestrial, nocturnal, hiding under stones or in burrows in day. It feeds on worms, insects etc.
3. Body is divisible into head and trunk. The skin is rough, dry and warty with more poison glands than the mucous glands.
4. Behind the eyes there is a pair of large parotoid poison glands. Tympanum is circular.
5. Teeth are absent.
6. Hind-limbs are short. Toes are provided with horny tips and poorly developed webs.
7. Tongue pear-shaped and thicker in front, free behind but not bifid. It is protrusible.
8. It breeds in water during rainy season.
9. It hibernates during winter.
10. Eggs are pigmented and laid in gelatinous string. Tadpole larva undergoes metamorphosis. Young toad matures in many years.
11. It has worldwide distribution.

RHACOPHORUS

Phylum	-	Chordata
Group	-	Vertebrata
Sub-phylum	-	Gnathostomata
Class	-	Amphibia
Order	-	Anura
Sub-order	-	Diplasiocoela
Genus	-	*Rhacophorus*

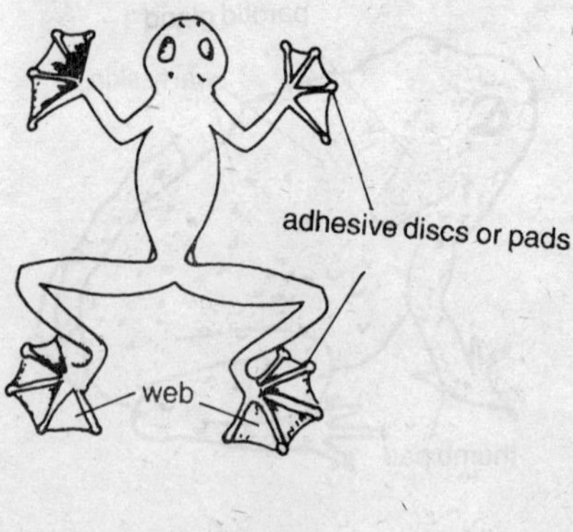

Fig. 1.16. *Rhacophorus*.

1. It is commonly known as 'flying frog'.
2. It is arboreal living on trees.
3. Body is slender, divisible into head and trunk.
4. Head broad and somewhat conical. Eyelids and tympanum are present.
5. Limbs elongated and contain well-developed webs in digits which also bear adhesive pads at tips.
6. It can glide thruogh the air for a considerable distance at its webs.
7. It has power of rapid colour changing.
8. It is active at dim-light (crepuscular).
9. It lays eggs in a nest of gelatinous foam in shallow water pools and rice-fields. Tadpoles when ready, drop into water.
10. They are found in India, Japan, Africa and Medagascar.

Revision Questions

1. Give an outline classification of class Amphibia.
2. Mention distinguishing characters of class Amphibia and classify it upto orders giving suitable examples.
3. Classify modern Amphibia upto orders giving characteristic features and suitable examples.
4. Write short notes on : (a) *Hyla,* (b) *Ichthyophis,* (c) Axolotl larva, (d) *Salamandra.*

2

Rana tigrina

Amphibians are the first vertebrates who have adapted themselves for life on land to some extent. They pass some of the time of their life cycle in water, and some on land (Gr., *amphi*=both or dual; *bios*= life). The term Amphibia was given by *Linnaeus*.

Rana tigrina is the most common and largest frog of India. It is commonly known as 'bull frog of India' because of its loud voice and large size.

SYSTEMIC POSITION

Phylum	-	Chordata
Group	-	Vertebrata
Sub-phylum	-	Gnathostomata
Class	-	Amphibia
Order	-	Anura
Sub-order	-	Diplasiocoela
Genus	-	*Rana*
Species	-	*tigrina*

Habitat

Frogs in general are found in fresh water lakes, rivers, ponds, ditches etc. and moist land. They live near water mainly for two reasons-to keep the skin moist for cutaneous respiration, and to escape enemies by jumping in water. Moreover, during breeding reason the eggs are laid in water.

Habits

It rests on land by keeping its short angular fore-limbs upright and the hind limbs folded by the side of body giving *squatting posture*. In the water it swims actively by alternating flexing and extending its hindlimbs. During swimming the webs, between the toes, are pushed against the water and thus carry the animal forward.

The frogs are carnivorous and feed on living insects, worms, molluscs and tadpoles which are caught by throwing out the extensible tongue coated with sticky mucous

The animals are *cold blooded* or *poikilothermal*. The body temperature does not remain constant. They undergo *hibernation* during winter and *aestivation* during summer. Frogs burry in the soft damp bottom mud for protection. During hibernation or aestivation the pulmonary respiration is stopped while cutaneous respiration through damp skin alone is sufficient. Feeding is also stopped, it consumes the reserve food stored in the form of fat bodies.

The frogs, generally, breed in rainy reason. They come out from their hidden places and start crocking. Crocking is a characteristic sound produced by forcing air from lungs over vocal cords into mouth cavity and back again. Male frogs crock more loudly than females. Male frogs crock to attract the female frogs for breeding or copulation. Pairing is called *amplexus* which lasts for several days. The eggs are laid in water, fertilization is external. There is no *parental care*. Life history includes a larval form known as *tadpole*.

Once a month during active season, the skin of frog is moulted as thin sheets or small shreds. The skin castings are eaten up by the frog. Frogs can change the colour of its skin, very slowly, to match with that of the surroundings. This type of protective colouration is known as *camouflage*.

Frogs have many natural enemies such as snakes, herons, mangoose, turtle and man. To escape from these enemies frog tries to jump into water.

Economic Importance

It is a beneficial animal as it feeds on insects which may be harmful to the crops. It is used, in laboratory, for dissections by the students all over the world. The muscular legs of frogs are used as a food by men. It is used as fish-bait.

EXTERNAL FEATURES

Shape and size

The body of frog is perfectly streamlined which is most suited for aquatic life. It is somewhat pointed anteriorly but rounded posteriorly. It measures about 18 cm in length and 5-8 cm in width.

Skin and colour

The skin of frog is smooth, moist and slimy without any scale. It remains attached to the underlying muscles at certain places. Skin of back and dorso-lateral folds or thickening called *dermal plicae*. It is olive-brown with irregular, dark patches and a light median streak or *vertebral line* (from tip of snout to the cloacal opening) on the dorsal surface. The skin on the ventral side is pale-yellow. The skin is kept moist and slimy by the secretion of mucous glands present in the integument.

Divisions of body

The body is divisible into two parts only - the head and trunk. Neck and tail are absent in frogs.

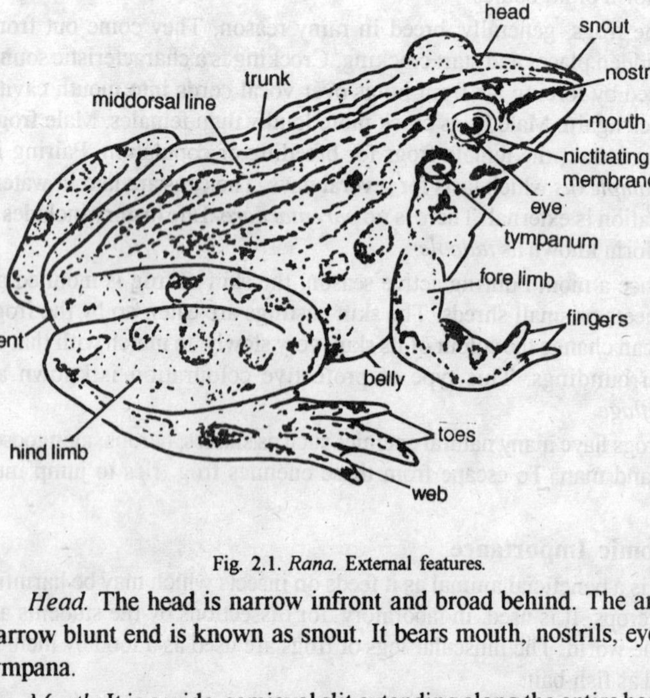

Fig. 2.1. *Rana.* External features.

Head. The head is narrow infront and broad behind. The anterior narrow blunt end is known as snout. It bears mouth, nostrils, eyes and tympana.

Mouth. It is a wide, semioval slit extending along the entire border of the head. The mouth is bounded by upper and lower lips which cannot move and are stationary. These lips are formed by the skin which is turned in over the jaws.

External nares. There are two small apertures or external nares on the dorsal side of the snout and serve in respiration. They open into the olfactory sacs.

Eyes. Two very large. spherical and protruding eyes are situated dorso-laterally on the top of head. The frog overcomes the absence of neck with their help, since the eyes are situated at the highest part of the body the frog can see all around without moving the body. The eyes are provided with three eye-lids-*upper eye lid, lower eye lid* and *nictitating membrane*. The upper eyelid is thick and fixed hence immovable while the lower eyelid is thin semi transparent and freely movable. The third eyelid or nictitating membrane is thin, transparent and freely movable. It is prolongation of lower eyelid. Nictitating membrane covers the eyeball and protects it during swimming and keeps it moist in air.

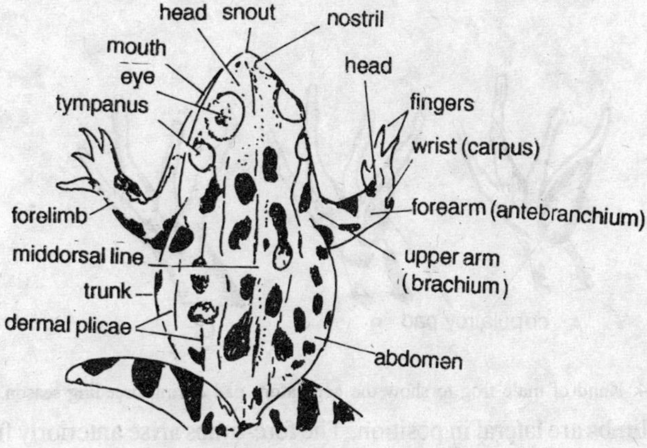

Fig. 2.2. *Rana*. External features in dosal view.

Tympanum. On either side of head, a little below the eye, is a prominent circular patch of tightly stretched skin known as *tympanum* or *eardrum*, that receives round waves.

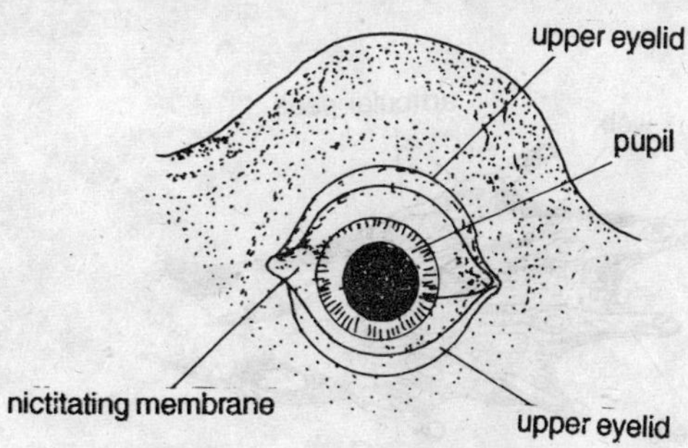

Fig. 2.3. Frog. Eye.

In front of the eyes, in the middle line of body, there is a light coloured rounded patch known as *brown spot.* It represent the vestigial pineal eye or third eye. In male frogs, a pair of wrinkled *vocal sacs* are found on the lower side of buccal cavity below the mouth. The vocal saces raise the pitch of the sound during crocking thus act as resonators.

Trunk. The trunk lies behind the head. Its back is raised in the middle as a characteristic sacral prominence or *hump.* It bears two pairs of limbs and a terminal and median *cloacal aperture.* It is a common aperture for the exit of faecal matter, urine and the male and female gametes (sperms and ova).

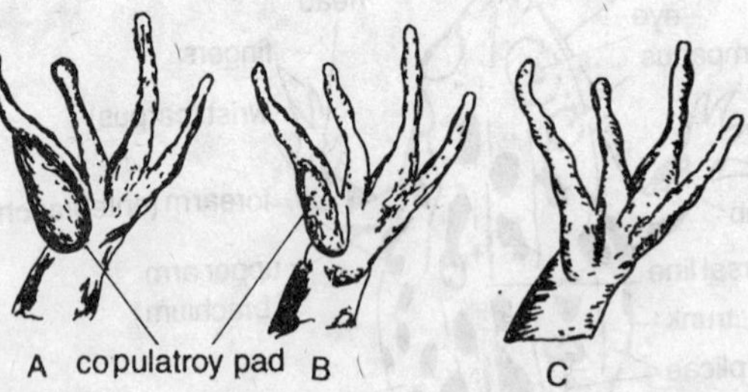

Fig. 2.4. Hand of male frog to show the copulatory pad during breeding season.

The limbs are lateral in position. The fore-limbs arise anteriorly from the trunk just behind the head. Each fore limb is composed of three parts the upper arm or *brachium,* the forearm or *antebrachium* and hand or *manus.* The hand bears four digits which are without claws. In the male frog, the inner finger of each hand has at its base a dark rough-swelling known as *nuptial* or *copulatory* or *amplexusary pad.* Normally the nuptial pads appear merely as rough patches but during breeding season, these

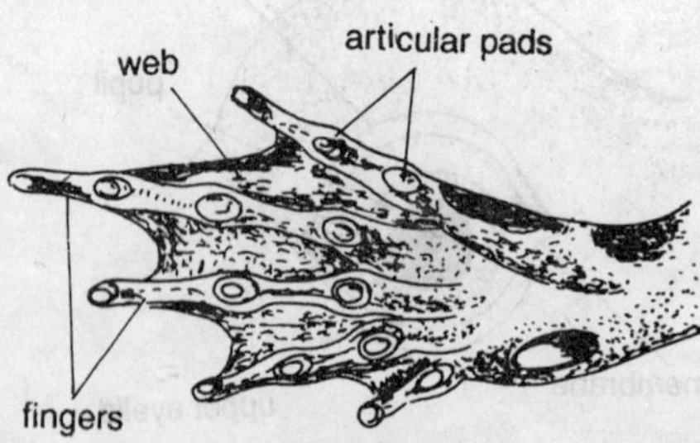

Fig. 2.5. Foot showing web and perhallux.

become very thick and sticky. They are used for grasping the female in amplexus.

The hind-limbs are much longer and powerful than the fore-limbs. Each is divisible into three parts- *a thigh,* a long middle *shank* and a *foot* or *pes.* The foot further differentiated into *ankle*, *metatarsus* and five *toes.* The toes are joined together by webs which are thin folds of skin. All the toes have small *articular pads* at the joints on underside. A rudimentary sixth digit is also present internal to the base of typical first toe termed *hallux.* The sixth digit is known as *prehallux.* The digits are without claws.

SEXUAL DIMORPHISM

The males and females can be distinguished from one another due to some differences. These are as follows:

1. The males are smaller than females. Their colour is dark.
2. Only the males possess a pair of ventro-lateral wrinkled *vocal sacs* for croaking.
3. The fore limbs in male possess swollen copulatory or nuptial pads on inner side. During breeding season they become very thick and for grasping the female during amplexus.

3

Integument

The integument is the outer covering of the body and is commonly referred to as the *skin*. It is continuous with the mucous membrane lining of the eye lids, mouth, nostrils, and the opening of the rectum and urogenital organs. The primary function of skin is to cover and protect the tissue lying beneath it. Since this is the part of the body which comes in contact with the environment. It is abundantly supplied with sensory nerve endings which are affected by environmental stimuli. Besides serving the function of protection and covering, in frog, the skin also serves as a respiratory organ. The skin is kept moist to serve efficiently the respiratory function. The skin is, therefore, tough, slimy, moist and attached to underlying muscles at intervals by connective tissue. The spaces which are left between the skin and muscles are filled with the *lymph* and are called the *sub-cutaneous lymph sinuses*. The muscular layer is covered internally by a thin peritoneum.

The integument of frog consists of two regions the *epidermis* and *dermis*.

EPIDERMIS

The epidermis is the outer, non-vascular, region of skin composed of several layers of cells. It is differentiated into an innermost layer of columnar cells, known as *stratum Malpighii* or *stratum germinativum*, and outermost several layers of dead, keratinized squamous cells known as *stratum corneum*. The cells of germinating layer divide mitotically and produce cells which pass outwards. During this process these cells gradually become flat and their protoplasm is changed into a horny substance, the *keratin*. Keratin is insoluble in water thus form a protective water-proof outer covering for the body. By the time they reach the surface of the epidermis, they become extremely thin and nearly dead. These cells form the *stratum corneum*, which is cast off periodically in patches.

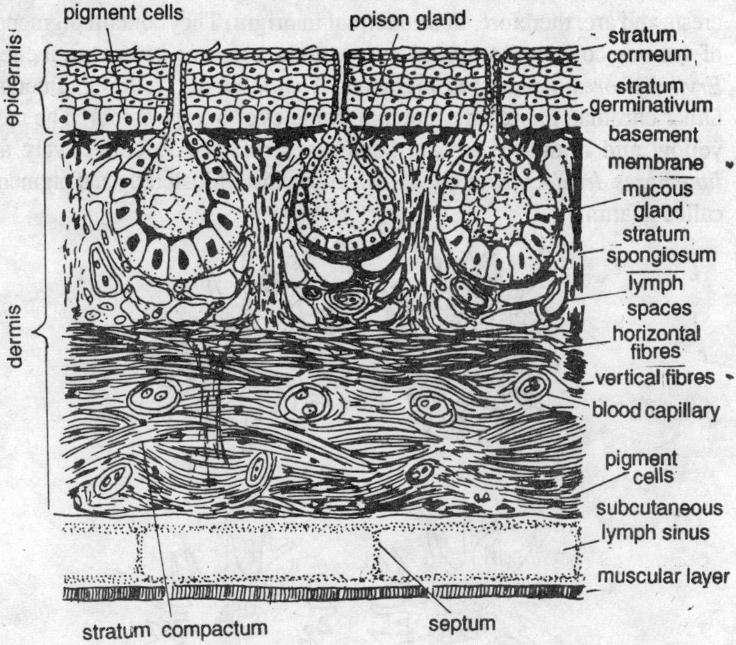

Fig. 3.1. *Rana.* V.S. of skin.

DERMIS

The dermis is the inner, thick, vascular region of the integument. It is differentiated into two zones.: (A) *Stratum spongiosum* and (B) *Stratum compactum*

(A) Stratum spongiosum

It is an outer looser layer. Its upper part is often more compact than the remainder of this layer. Blood vessels, lymph spaces, nerves, glands and pigment cells (chromatophores) are abundant in this layer.

(a) Blood-vessels

The amphibian skin is an important organ of respiration, thus the dermis is supplied with an unusually large number of blood vessels.

(b) Pigment cells or Chromatophores

The ability of the skin to change colour so as to blend in with the environment is related to the chromatophores which are present. for the most part. beneath the stratum germinativum in the dermis. Each chromatophore is highly branched cell. Its shape is not constant. sometimes wander into the epidermis. In lower forms these are derived from neural crests and are, therefore, of ectodermal in origin. They contain pigments of various colours. *Melanophores* contain black or brown pigments. *Erythrophores* contain red pigments. *Xanthophores,* yellow pigments. Other chromatophores may contain granules of orange colour. The red, yellow and orange types are sometimes referred to collectively as *lipophores. Irridocytes* or *guanophores* contain whitish reflected pigment called guanin.

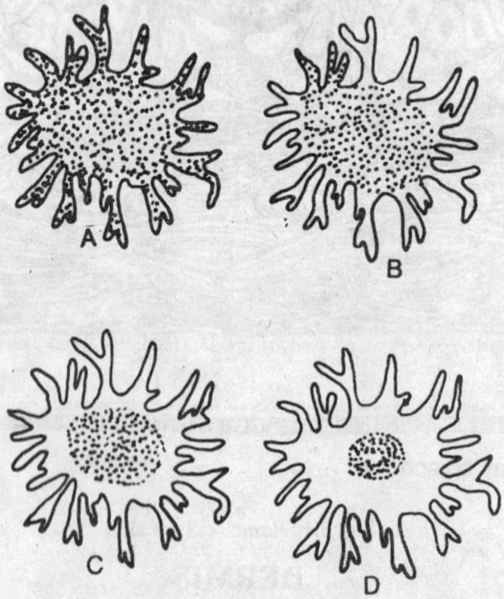

Fig. 3.2. *Rana.* Chromatophore.

When the pigment granules are dispersed throughout the cell, it displays the greatest amount of colour. When the granules becomes concentrated about the nucleus only a small spot of colour is visible. Various colours may be produced by combinations and blending of chromatophores bearing different kinds of pigment granules and by various degrees of dispersion of the granules. The back-ground colour of pigment in the cells of stratum germinatvum is also of importance in producing any effect. The ability of change colour is known as *metachrosis.* Changes are probably mediated, for the most part, by impulse, reaching the brain from the eyes. Thus there are two methods of control the changing of colour-*nervous* and *endocrine*. Hormone *epinephrin* from adrenal gland brings about concentration of pigment and the *intermedian* hormone from intermediate lobe of the pituitary gland brings about its dispersion.

(c) Cutaneous glands

In frog the skin is an important respiratory organ, it must be kept moist so that exchange of gases may take place between the surface capillaries and the surroundings. In these forms the large number of skin glands, that are present, aid in keeping the skin moist. These glands are usually simple saccular structure, formed by infoldings of stratum germinativum of the epidermis. Their bulb like expansions lie in the stratum spongiosum of the dermis, although they arise from epidermis. Their secretion is first accumulated in the cavity of gland, then, it carried by narrow neck and poured out on the surface of body through a minute pore. The cutaneous glands are of two types:

(i) *Mucous glands* and (ii) *Poison glands.*

(i) Mucous glands. These are more numerous and smaller than poison glands. They are present all over the surface of the body but are more abundant in some parts than in others. They secrete mucous and this secreted mucous on the skin is very useful in many ways. It helps in cutaneous respiration and keeps the skin slimy due to which the enemies of frog can not hold it so easily. It also helps in keeping the body of frog cool.

(ii) Poison glands. These are large, less numerous and they are not evenly distributed over the surface of skin. In many species their number is higher on the dorsal side of body and hind-limbs. The secretion of these glands is whitish fluid which is said to have a burning taste. *Hyla,* a tree frog, gives off a poisonous secretion so strong that when the animal is handled the poison causes inflammation of the skin. The poison glands, in the skin, are thus an adaptation for protection. In toads and salamanders the *parotid glands,* which lie on the neck, are actually masses of poison glands.

(iii) Sticky glands. These tubular glands are less common. Simple tubular sticky glands are found on the copulatory pads of the male frog and toads. Their secretion helps in grasping the female during copulation. In *Hyla,* they are found in the adhesive discs, their secretion helps in clinging to the surface over which the tree frog walks.

(B) Stratum compactum

It is composed of dense layer of connective tissue which comprises vertical and horizontal fibres of connective tissue (collagen fibres). Glands are absent but blood vessels, lymph capillaries, nerve fibres, few pigment cells, elastic fibres and unstriped muscle fibres are present.

Below the dermis lies a thick muscular layer which is separated from skin by a sub-cutaneous connective tissue. The sub-cutaneous connective tissue consists of two layers - a layer beneath the skin contains guanophores (white pigment cells) and lying on ventral side of the body; and other layer overlying the muscle layer. A number of septa connect the two layers of sub-cutaneous connective tissue. These septa are separated from each other by *sub cutaneous lymph sinuses.* The muscle layer is internally lined with parietal peritoneum or coelomic epithelium. All the structures from epidermis to coelomic epithelium constitute the body wall.

FUNCTIONS OF SKIN

The integument or skin is a very versatile organ, since it performs so wide a range of functions that it may be quite appropriately termed as "Jack of all trades". The functions are summarized below :

1. Protection. It provides protection in many ways :

(a) *From mechanical injuries.* The skin serves to protect the visceral organs from external shocks, pressure, frictions etc.

(b) *From the micro-organisms.* It checks the entry of harmful micro-organisms like bacteria, fungi, parasitic worms etc. Thus the body is protected against the harmful effects of micro-organisms.

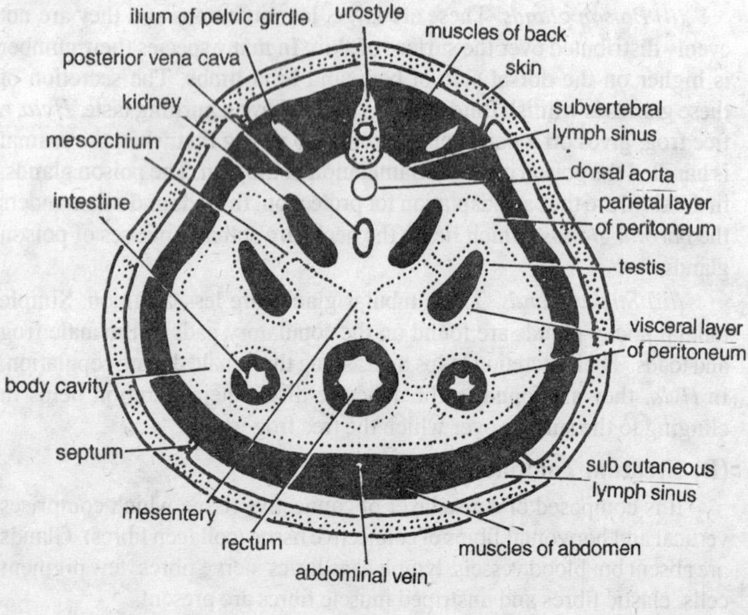

Fig. 3.3: *Rana.* T.S. Through abdominal cavity.

(c) *From the enemies.* The colour of skin is important in this respect. The colour may conceal the animal in the environment thus it is protected from its enemies. The melanin pigment also protects the visceral organs from the ill-effects of ultra-violet rays.

(d) *From the loss of water.* Stratum corneum forms a water-proof convering so that it prevents the loss of water from visceral organs and thus it protects the body from dehydration.

2. It helps in locomotion. Wing membrane of flying frogs and web in the feet of frogs are the folds of skin that helps in propulsion or locomotion.

3. It forms the efficient respiratory surface. The thin, moist and rich vascularized skin serves an important respiratory organ besides the lungs. Such a respiration is very important during aestivation and hibernation.

4. Absorption of water. The animal absorbs its required amount of water through general body surface into cutaneous blood capillaries.

5. Role of mucous glands. The glands secrete mucous which helps in respiration, keeps the body slimy due to which enemies cannot hold it easily. Besides it prevents the frog from drying. The evaporation of mucous and water keeps the body cool (regulation of body temperature).

6. Role of poison glands. The secretion of these glands causes inflammation of the skin to its enemy and protects the animal from its enemies.

7. Role of sticky glands. The secretion of these glands helps in grasping the female during reproduction.

8. Reception of stimuli. The skin is a tactile organ. It is sensitive to touch, pressure, pain, temperature etc. and responds to external stimuli.

9. Removal of microorganisms. Due to periodic moulting of stratum corneum, the microorganisms that tend to accumulate upon body surface are removed.

10. Role in hatching. The skin of tadpole larva produces certain hatching enzymes which dissolve the egg membrane so that the hatching of larva takes place.

11. It contributes in sexual selection. Brilliant shades of skin plays a valuable role in sexual selection.

12. Role in skeleton formation. The dermal bones or membrane bones are formed by the ossification of dermis in some parts of the body, particularly in the head.

13. Healing of wounds. The skin has a great power of regeneration and helps in rapid healing of wounds.

14. Formation of teeth. The teeth are developed partly from epidermis and partly from dermis.

COELOM AND VISCERA

The body wall encloses a spacious cavity, the *coelom.* It is situated in the trunk. It contains most of the *internal organs* or *viscera.* The cavity is filled with a colourless and viscid, lymph-like *coelomic fluid.* A thin,

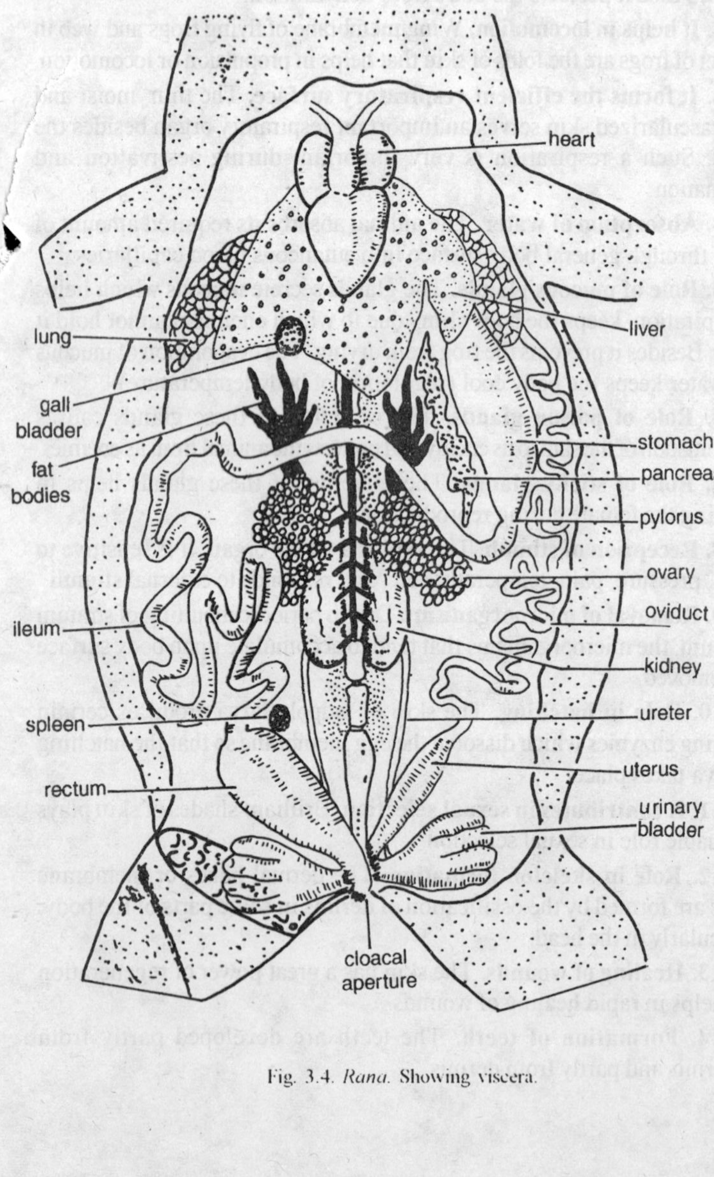

Fig. 3.4. *Rana.* Showing viscera.

transparent membrane of mesodermal origin, the *peritoneum,* lines the body cavity called *parietal peritoneum* and also covers the internal organs, the *visceral peritoneum.*

The coelom is divided into two completely separated parts - an anterior small *pericardial cavity* that encloses the heart and posterior large *pleuro-peritoneal* or *perivisceral cavity* which contains all the remaining internal organs except the kidneys.

In *abdominal cavity*, the drosal part of parietal peritoneum is separated from dorsal body wall by a large subvertebral lymph sinus. The parietal and visceral peritonea of right and left sides converge together in mid-dorsal axis of body beneath the subvertebral lymph sinus forming a thin two layered *dorsal mesentary.* Through the mesentary nerves and blood vessels are connect to the organs and the alimentary canal and other organs are properly suspended in the coelom. The alimentary canal is connected to the adjacent organs by *omenta.* Similarly organ to organ ligamentous connections are called *septa.*

4

Endoskeleton

The endoskeleton of frog is composed of bones and cartilages. In the tadpole (early stage of development) the skeleton is made up of cartilage only, but in adult the skeleton is greatly replaced by the bones called

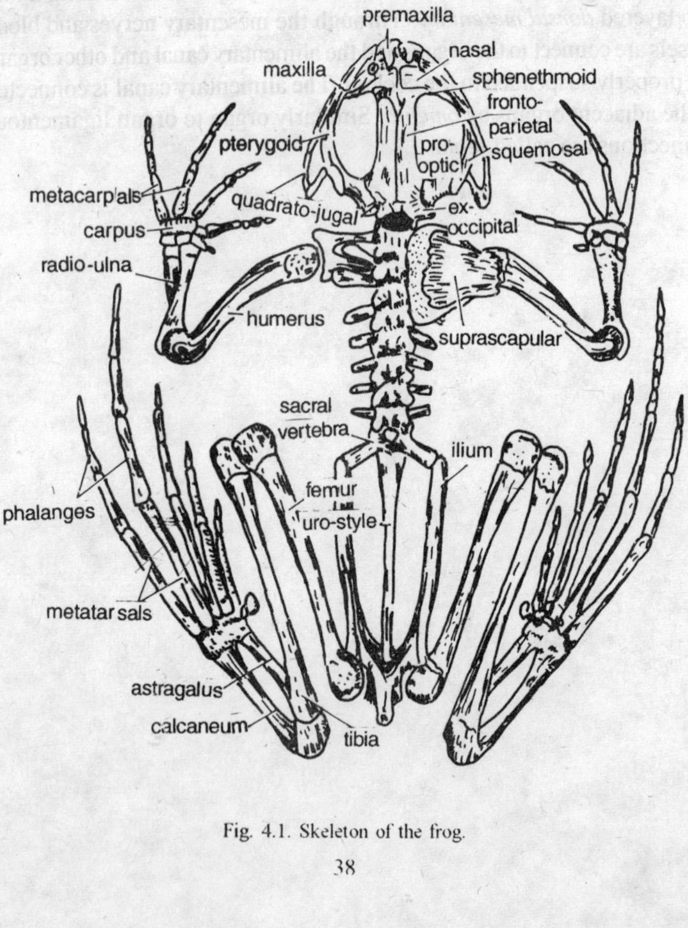

Fig. 4.1. Skeleton of the frog.

cartilage bones or *replacing bones.* Bones are also formed from epidermis or dermis where there was no pre-existing cartilage. Such bones are called *dermal bones* or *membrane bones.* At certain places the cartilage is impregnated by calcium salts and it becomes hard, such a cartilage is called *calcified cartilage.*

Like in other vertebrates, the endoskeleton is divided into two parts -an *axial skeleton* comprising the skull and vertebral column, and the *appendicular skeleton* includes the bones of limbs and the girdles.

SKULL

The skull consists of three parts :

1. Cranium
2. Sense capsules and
3. Visceral skeleton.

1. Cranium

The cranial region of skull is long, rectangular and hollow. It encloses the brain hence also known as brain-box. Posteriorly, a large aperture, the *foramen magnum,* is found in it, through which the spinal cord comes out. Two irregular bones, the *exoccipitals,* lies on either side of foramen. These bones are cartilaginous and form the posterior wall of cranium.

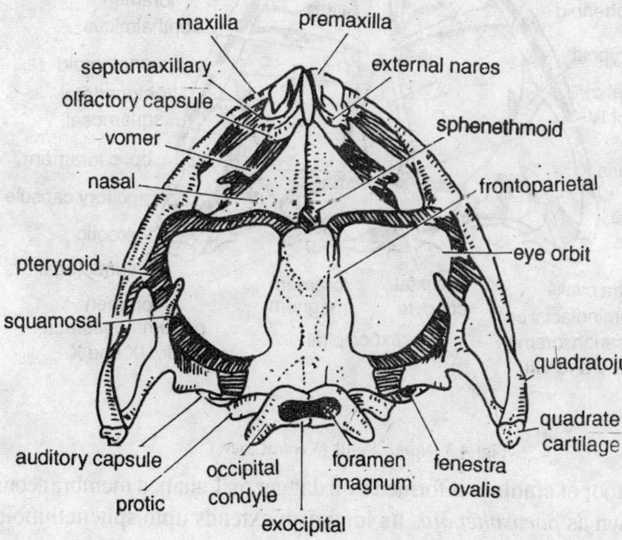

Fig. 4 2. *Rana.* Skull (Dorsal view).

Each occipital bears an oval projection known as *occipital condyle.* The occipital condyles articulate with the two anterior concavities of atlas vertebra. Supra-occipital and basioccipital are absent. The roof of cranium is formed by *frontoparietals.* These are membraneous bones. They are long flattened, broad and paired. In tadpole, the frontal and parietals occur separately but in adult they are fused to form a single bone. Anteriorly the two bones slightly diverge so as to expose a small diamond-shaped area of the sphenethmoid. Anteriorly the frontoparietals articulate with the nasals and posteriorly with the prootic and exoccipitals. The *sphenethmoid* is tubular cartilaginous bone. It is dorsally covered by the frontoparietals and nasals but ventrally by the parasphenoid. It is divided into two regions by the transverse partition, the anterior region is ethmoidal and the posterior is sphenoidal region. The anterior region is further divided into right and left parts, by a longitudinal partition, in which olfactory sacs lodge. In the sphenoidal region the fore-brain lodges.

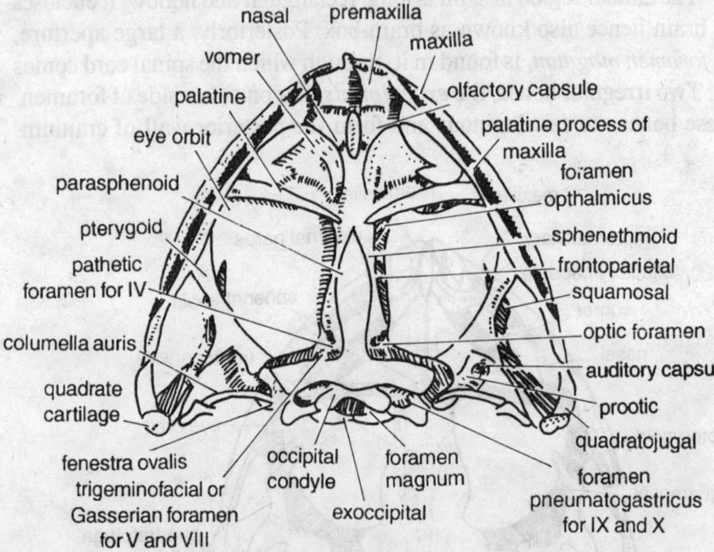

Fig. 4.3. *Rana.* Skull (Ventral view).

The floor of cranium is formed by a dagger or T shaped membraneous bone known as *parasphenoid.* Its long arm extends upto sphenethmoid anteriorly whereas its short arms are attached to the auditory capsules posteriorly.

The cranium is perforated by several small apertures, the *foramina* to provide passage to cranial nerves and blood vessels.

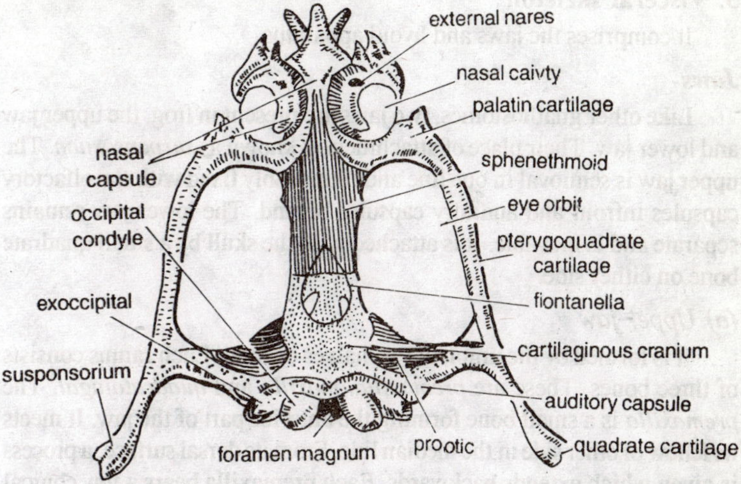

Fig. 4.4. *Rana.* Cartilages and cartilage bones of skull.

2. Sense capsules

The sense capsules include a pair of *auditory capsules,* enclosing the organs of hearing and a pair of *olfactory capsules* enclosing the organs of smell.

(i) Auditory capsules

They are situated on the sides of exoccipitals posteriorly. These are cartilaginous. The anterior part and roof of each capsule is formed of *prootic.* The outer wall of each capsule has an aperture, the *fenestra ovalis.* In the fenestra ovalis fits a thin cartilaginous plate, the *stapedial plate.* A rod shaped bone, the *columella auris* is attached to this plate and extends outwards to meet the *tympanic membrane.*

(ii) Olfactory capsules

The olfactory capsules are situated anterior to the cranium and are joined with it They are irregular, mainly composed of cartilage. Their posterior parts are ossified and form the ethmoidal region of sphenethmoid. Both the capsules are separated from each other by a vertical partition. the *mesethmoid.* Each capsule opens out by external naris and into the buccal-cavity by internal naris. On the dorsal side there is a membrane bone, the *nasal* and on the ventral side is a smaller triradiate bone the *vomer.* Vomer possesses vomerine teeth on the posterior side.

3. Visceral skeleton

It comprises the jaws and hyoid apparatus.

Jaws

Like other gnathostomes, two jaws are present in frog, the upper jaw and lower jaw. Their place of attachment is known as *suspensorium.* The upper jaw is semioval in out-line and immovably fixed with the olfactory capsules infront and auditory capsules behind. The lower jaw remains separate and is movable. It is attached with the skull by a small quadrate bone on either side.

(a) Upper jaw

It is formed by the union of two halves or rami. Each ramus consists of three bones. These are *premaxilla, maxilla* and *quadratojugal.* The *premaxilla* is a small bone forming the anterior part of the jaw. It meets its fellow of other side in the median line. From its dorsal surface, a process is given which extends backwards. Each premaxilla bears a few conical teeth in two rows along its anterior lower edge. On outer side it meets the maxilla of its side.

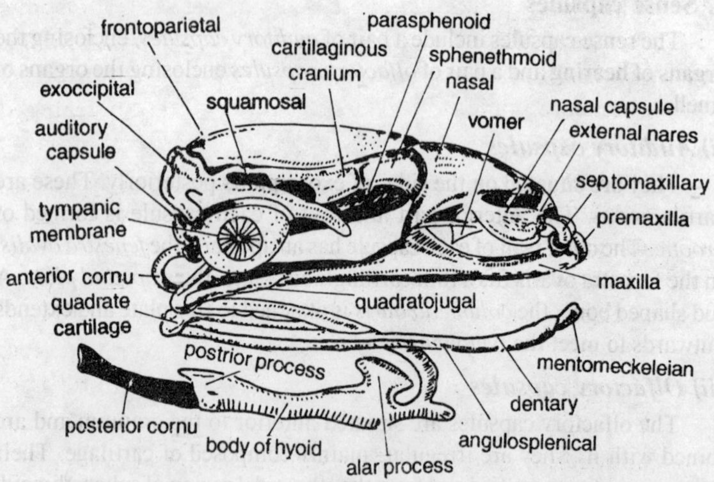

Fig. 4.5. *Rana.* Lateral view of skull with hyoid and lower jaw.

Maxilla is a long, thin curved bone lying behind the premaxilla. Its anterior end is broad and the posterior end is narrow. It also bears teeth on the lower edge. Maxilla is connected behind with quadratojugal while it articulates at about the middle of its length with palatine and anterior limb of pterygoid.

The *quadratojugal* is a small slender bone with a characteristic comma-like (,) shape. It lies behind the maxilla and forms the posterior part of outer margin of upper jaw. These bones have no teeth.

The upper jaw is attached to the cranium with the help of three bones. These are the *squamosals, pterygoids* and *palatines.* Each squamosal is a large, hammer-shaped or 'T' shaped bone forming the dorsal part of the posterio-lateral border of the orbit of its side. The anterior limb of 'T' or head remains free whereas the posterior short limb is attached to the auditory capsule and prootic and the third with the cranium. There is a large space left between the maxilla and the cranium, the space is known as *orbit* in which the eye is situated.

Pterygoids. These are 'Y' shaped bone or triradiate membrane bones. These are present ventral to squamosal attached, laterally to posterior end of cranium. Its anterior ray is attached to the outer end of palatine and maxilla, second ray is attached to auditory capsule and the third process is attached to quadrate.

Palatines. These are slender, rod-like membrane bones lying horizontally to form the ventral part of anterior border of eye orbit. It connects the anterior side of cranium with the middle of maxilla.

(b) Lower jaw

Lower jaw or mandible is semi-oval in outline. It is made up of two halves or rami. Both the ramus are attached anteriorly by a ligament and

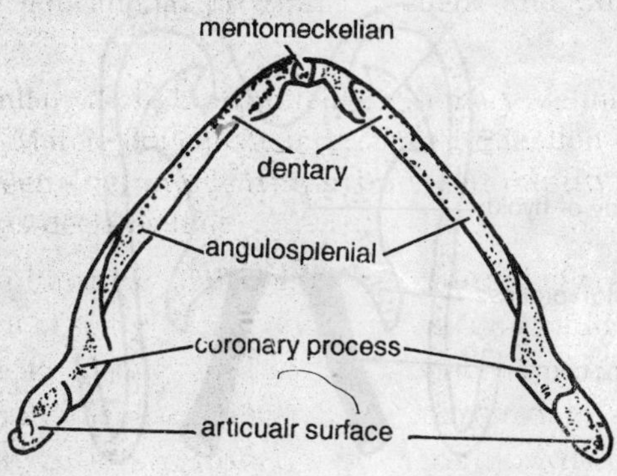

Fig. 4.6. *Rana.* Lower jaw.

movably articulate behind with the upper jaw. Each ramui consists of a core of *Meckel's cartilage* surrounded by an anterior *mentomeckelian, dentary* and *angulosplenial* on the outer side.

Mentomeckelian. It is a small cartilage bone at the anterior side of each ramus. Both the mentome-ckelians medially join together at the tip of the arch by symphysis.

Dentary bones. These are relatively short and dagger-shaped covering the outer surface of anterior portion of Meckel's cartilage. Their anterior ends extend upto mentomeckelian bone whereas posterior ends closely applied to the outer side of angulosplenial bones.

Angulosplenial. These are long and somewhat curved rod-like membrane bones. Each bone is composed of two parts an anterior end tapering while its posterior end bears a condyle or knob-like articular surface for the quadrate of skull. Just infront of articular surface, the angulosplenial sends upwards a small coronary process.

The teeth are absent in the lower jaw.

Hyoid apparatus

The branchial skeleton which consists of hyoidean and branchial arches that supports the gills of tadpole larva become reduced and modified into hyoid apparatus during metamorphosis. It is situated in the floor of buccal cavity and provides surface for the attachment of tongue. The hyoid apparatus is composed of- a thin membraneous, shield-like *body* and four pairs of processes (the anterior and posterior cornua).

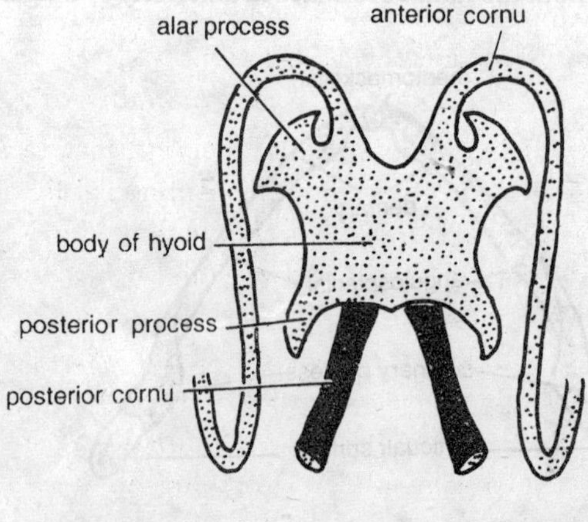

Fig. 4.7. *Rana.* Hyoid apparatus.

Body of hyoid. It is the main part of apparatus. It is broad, flattened and squarish cartilaginous plate. The four corners of the plate are expanded wing-like processes—the *alar processes* infront and *posterior processes* behind.

Anterior cornua. Arise from the anterior side of body of hyoid are a pair of long slender and rod-like cartila-ginous processes known as anterior cornua. They first run forwards and then, abruptly turn backwards and upwards to articulate with the auditory capsule of their sides.

Posterior cornua. From the posterior side of the body of hyoid, a pair of short, stout, straight and ossified processes arise known as posterior cornua. They run one on either side of glottis to provide support to the larynx.

VERTEBRAL COLUMN

The vertebral column or backbone is formed by a number of small bones called as *vertebrae,* articulating one behind the other in a linear

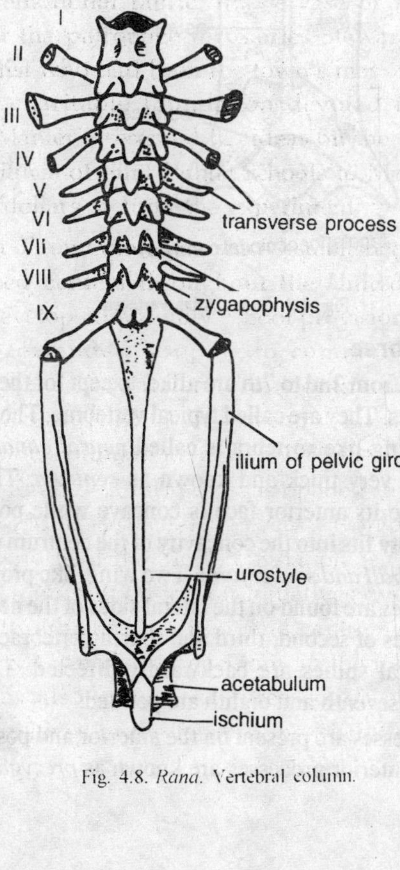

Fig. 4.8. *Rana.* Vertebral column.

series. It encloses and protects the spinal cord. Vertebral column is comparatively short in the absence of tail. It is formed of ten vertebrae. First nine are ring-like and termed as vertebrae while the last one is long, rod-like and termed as *urostyle*.

1. Atlas vertebra

It is the first vertebra of back bone. It is very small, ring-like bone. The centrum and neural spine are reduced. Transverse processes and prezygapophyses are absent. Anterior face of centrum bears a pair of large, oval and somewhat concave articulate facets for articulation with occipital condyles of skull. Postzygapophyses are present on the posterior margin of neural arch.

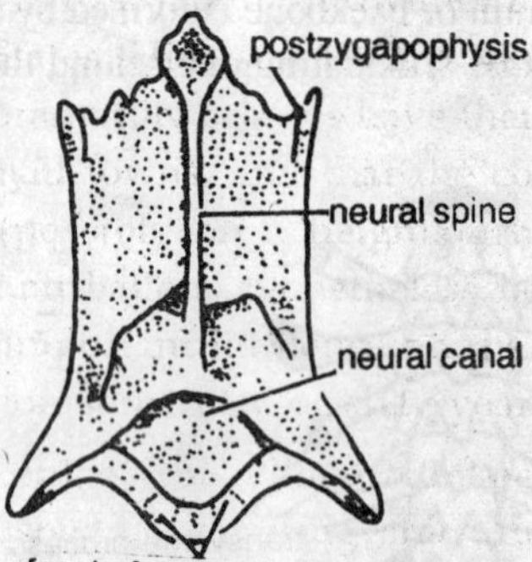

Fig. 4.9. *Rana.* Atlas vertebra.

2. Typical vertebrae

The vertebrae from 2nd to 7th are alike, except for the angle of their transverse processes. They are called typical vertebrae. The circular space surrounded by a ring-like vertebra is called *neural canal.* The ventral part of vertebra is very thick and known as *centrum.* The centrum is *procoelous* because its anterior face is concave while posterior face is convex. Its convexity fits into the concavity of the centrum of the vertebra behind, forming a *ball and socket joint*. Two wing-like projections called *transverse processes* are found on the lateral sides of the neural arch. The transverse processes of second, third and fourth vertebrae are large and broad. Their neural spines are backwardly directed. The transverse processes of sixth, seventh and eighth are pointed.

A pair of processes are present on the anterior and posterior faces of neural arch. The anterior processes are known as *prezygapophyses* and the posterior as *postzygapophyses.* The prezygapophyses face upwards and inwards, the postzygapophyses face downwards and outwards. The pre-and post-zygapophyses articulate with each other in the successive vertebrae. Between the neural arches of every two vertebrae, there is a pair of spaces called *intervertebral foramina.* The spinal nerves come out through these foramina.

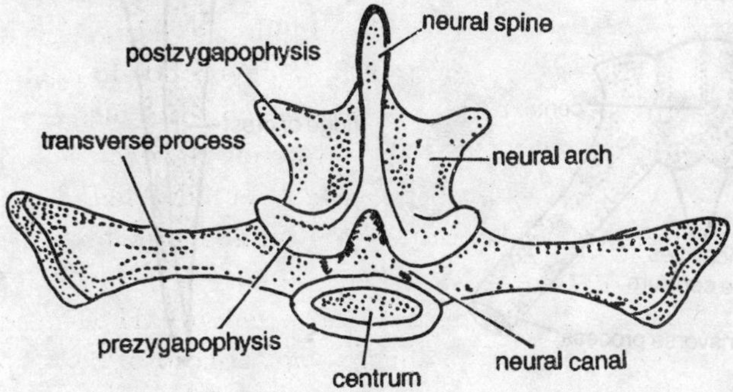

Fig. 4.10. *Rana.* Typical cervical.

3. The eighth vertebra

The centrum is *amphicoelous* i.e. concave at both the ends. The transverse processes of this vertebra are narrow, pointed and directed straight upwards.

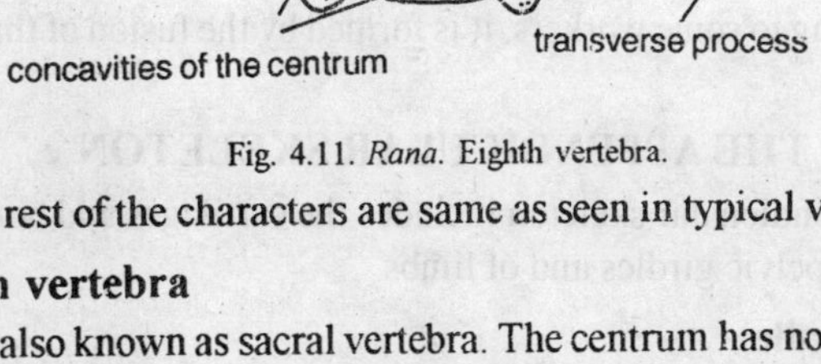

Fig. 4.11. *Rana.* Eighth vertebra.

The rest of the characters are same as seen in typical vertebra.

4. Ninth vertebra

It is also known as sacral vertebra. The centrum has no cavity such a vertebra is known as *acoelous.* The centrum is having one convexity on anterior side and two convexities on posterior side. The convexities fit into two corres-ponding cavities of urostyle. The transverse processes

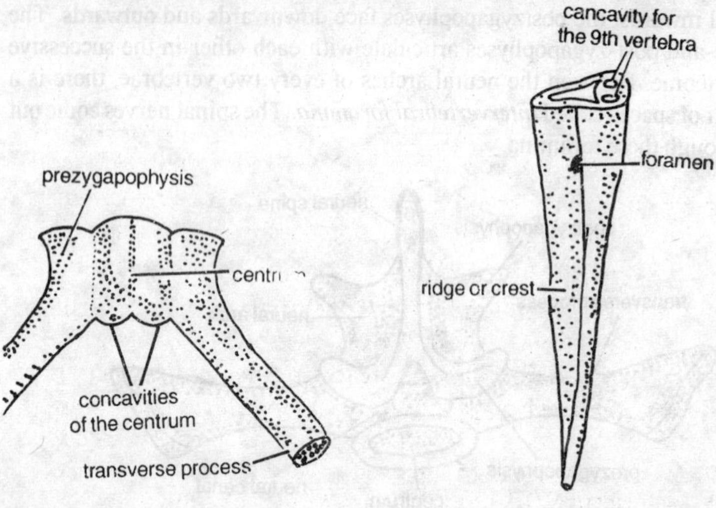

Fig. 4.12. *Rana*. Ninth and tenth vertebrae.

are longest, thickest and strongest. These processes articulate with the ilia bones of the pelvic girdle. The postzygapophyses are absent. Neural spine is directed forwards.

5. Urostyle

It is as long as the rest of vertebral column. It is slender, tapering bone bears a thin vertical ridge along the upper side. The base has a pair of concavities at the anterior end for the articulation with the ninth vertebra. The anterior part of the ridge contains the *neural canal* for the terminal portion of spinal cord. A short distance behind the front end of urostyle, there is a pair of minute lateral pores for the exit of tenth pair of cranial nerves.

According to some workers, it is formed by the fusion of three sacral vertebrae.

THE APPENDICULAR SKELETON

The appendicualar skeleton includes the cartilages and bones of the pectoral and pelvic girdles and of limbs.

Pectoral girdle

The pectoral girdle is embedded in the body wall at the anterior end of the trunk, where it braces the fore-limbs. The basic pattern consists of two sets of elements, replacing bones and membrane bones. The chief replacing bones are the *coracoid, scapula* and *suprascapula* whereas the *clavicle* is the membrane bone.

The pectoral girdle is made up of two similar halves, one on either side of the body. On the ventral side they are united with each other. Their union is known as *symphysis*. On the dorsal side both are separate and are bound to the vertebral column by muscles and ligaments. Each half is made up of above said bones and can be differentiated into a dorsal *scapular part* and ventral *coracoid part.* The scapular part consists of a *suprascapula* which is a large, spatula shaped flattened bone and forms the dorsal part of each half. The free margin consists of hyaline or plain cartilage and is wider and thinner. The remaining part of scapula is bony and is attached with a smaller and rectangular bone, the *scapula* on ventral side. The scapula is flattened but considerably thicker and stronger. Its inner anterior angle is produced forward into a short *acromian process.*

The coracoid part is pierced by a wide oval space called the *coracoid fontanelle* or *foramen.* The fontanelle is bounded behind by a stout 'T' shaped *coracoid* and in front by a narrow transverse strip, the *precoracoid. Clavicle,* a slender bone, overlies the precoracoid anterioventrally. Another strip, the *epicoraciod* occurs along the inner side of the precoracoid and the coracoid. Two epicoracoids are closely applied to each other in mid-ventral line. A depression, the *glenoid cavity,* is present on the posterior side, at the junction of scapular and coracoid parts, for the articulation with the head of humerus.

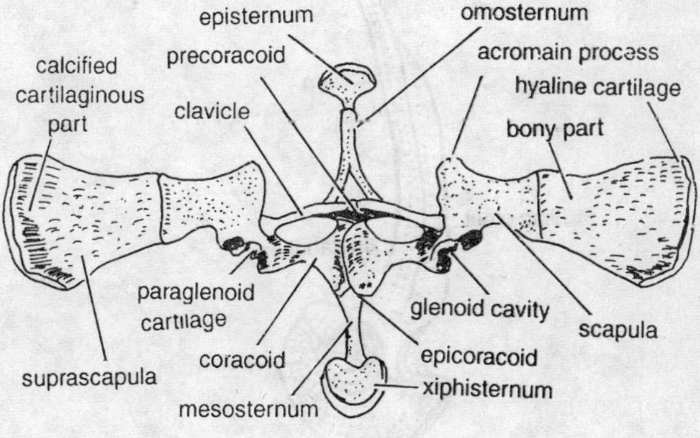

Fig. 4.13. *Rana.* Pectoral girdle and sternum.

Sternum

Due to absence of ribs in frog, the sternum articulates with pectoral

girdle. It lies in the mid-ventral line intimately connected between the two halves of pectoral girdle. It is composed of four parts :

The *episternum* is a flat, circular and cartilaginous disc lying on omosternum.

The *omosternum* is a 'Y' shaped bone. Anteriorly it is attached to episternum and the two arms rest upon the clavicles of pectoral girdle posteriorly.

The *mesosternum* is a cartilaginous rod which is united infront with the epicoracoids of pectoral girdle.

The *xiphisternum* is a terminal, circular plate of cartilage which forms the posterior part of sternum.

Pelvic Girdle

Like pectoral girdle, the pelvic girdle is embedded in the body wall and serves to brace the appendages i.e. hind-limbs.

It is situated in the posterior part of trunk and consists of two halves or *os innominata* which are separated anteriorly but are fused posteriorly to form a median vertical disc. Their union is called as *symphysis*. Thus a 'V' shaped structure is formed. The median disc possesses a prominent cup-like depression, the *acetabulum,* on lateral sides. The acetabulum is for the articulation with the head of femur.

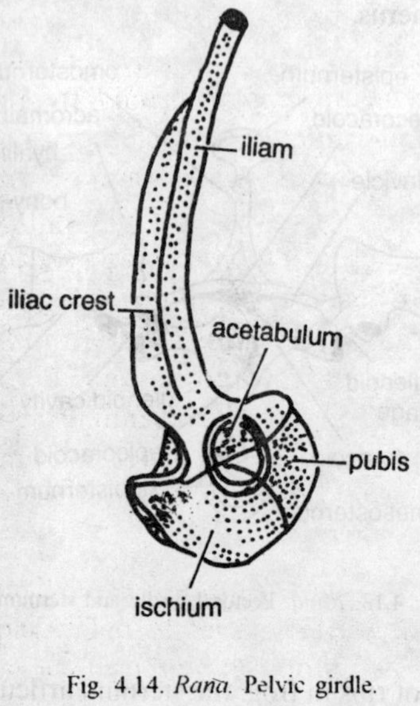

Fig. 4.14. *Rana.* Pelvic girdle.

Each os innominatum is made up of three cartilaginous bones, the *ilium, ischium* and *pubis* which share the median disc and the acetabulum.

1. *Ilium.* It is a long, rod-like bone forming one arm of the girdle. Posteriorly, it becomes flattened, joins its fellow of the other side at an *iliac symphysis.* It is dorsally produced into a prominant vertical ridge the *iliac crest.* The crest provides insertion to certain muscles. It extends forward in the form of an arm to articulate with the transverse process of 9th vertebra.

2. *Ischium.* It is relatively large and triangular piece of bone and is fused with its fellow of the other side at *ischial symphysis.* It forms the posterior one-third of the disc and acetabulum.

3. *Pubis.* It is much reduced, triangular piece of bone fused with the pubis of other side by *pubic symphysis.* It forms about one-sixth of ventral part of disc and the acetabulum.

Bones of Fore Limbs

The fore-limb is divided in three regions : 1. Upper arm or brachium, 2. Fore-arm or antebrachium, 3. Hand or manus.

1. Upper arm or brachium

It contains only one bone i.e. *humerus.* It has a proximal *head* which fits into the glenoid cavity of the pectoral girdle. The head is almost a

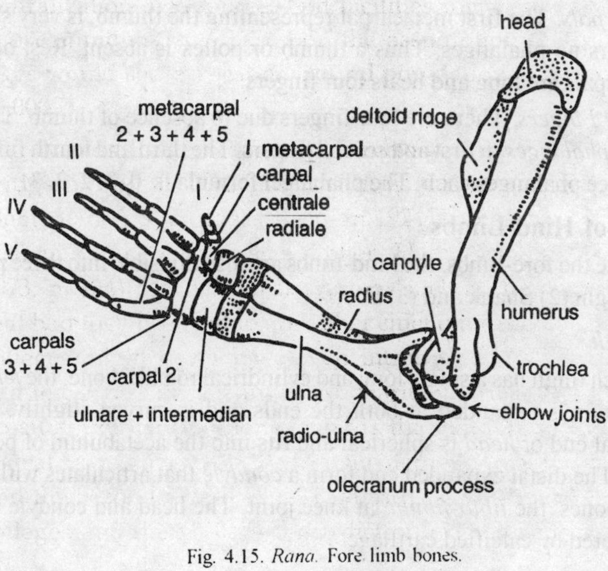

Fig. 4.15. *Rana.* Fore limb bones.

spherical and smooth caped by a thin layer of calcified cartilage. Below the head is a long *shaft* with *deltoid ridge* which is continued up to the proximal half of the shaft. The distal end has a prominent rounded ball-like *condyle* or *capitulum.* On either side of the condyle there is a *ridge* or *trochlea.*

2. Antebrachium or fore-arm

It has two bones, the *radius* infront and *ulna* behind, but these are fused together into a single bone, *radio-ulna.* The fusion is clearly seen in the distal half of the bone. The proximal end of radio-ulna articulates with the distal end of humerus and forms the elbow joint. Ulna is extended backwards as an *olecranon process.* This process bears a notch which is known as olecranon notch. The condyle of humerus fits into the notch.

3. Manus or hand

The hand is composed of three parts (i) wrist, (ii) palm and (iii) fingers.

(i) Wrist. Each wrist or carpus has six bones known as *carpals*. These are arranged in two rows of three carpals each. In the proximal row the bones are-*radiale, intermedium* and *ulnare.* Radiale lies infront of radius and ulnare infront of ulna. In the distal row these carpals are known as the *trapezium, trapezoid* and *capitatohamatum.* The third carpal is obviously formed by fusion of three carpals.

(ii) Palm. There are five bones in the palm which are called *metacarpals.* The first metacarpal representing the thumb, is very small and bears no phalanges. Thus a thumb or pollex is absent. Rest of the metacarpals are long and bears four fingers.

(iii) Fingers. There are four fingers due to absence of thumb. There are two *phalanges* in first and second fingers. The third and fourth fingers bear three phalanges each. The phalangel formula is, 0, 2, 2, 3, 3.

Bones of Hind-Limbs

Like the fore-limbs, the hind-limbs are also divisible into three parts : (i) Thigh, (2) Shank and (3) Foot.

1. Thigh

Each thigh has a single long and cylindrical rod like bone, the *femur.* The femur is expanded at both the ends and is curved slightly. The proximal end or *head* is spherical and fits into the acetabulum of pelvic girdle. The distal expanded end form a *condyle* that articulates with the shank bones, the *tibio-fibula,* at knee joint. The head and condyle both are covered by calcified cartilage.

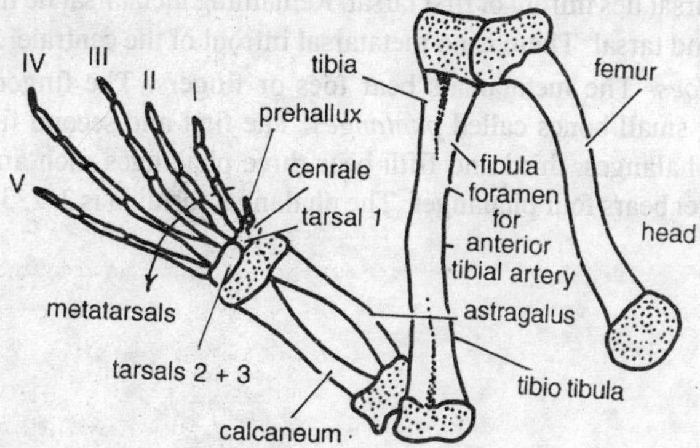

Fig. 4.16. *Rana*. Hindlimb bones.

2. Shank

The shank is supported by two bones, inner *tibia* and outer *fibula*. The tibia and fibula are firmly fused together, forming a somewhat flattened and curved bone, the *tibiofibula.* Its proximal end articulates with the distal end of femur and forms knee-joint. The distal end articulates with the bones of ankle. A poorly developed *cnemial crest* is present in a short proximal part of tibia. A nutrient foramen is present for the passage of blood vessels in the middle region.

3. Foot

It is divisible in three parts :

(i) Ankle, (ii) Sole and (iii) Toes.

(i) *Ankle.* The ankle or tarus is exceptionally elongated and has five *tarsal* bones which are arranged into two rows. The proximal row has two large bones united together at both the ends but widely separated in the middle. These are called *astragalus* or *tibiale* lies infront of tibia and *calcaneum* or *fibulare* infront of fibula. The astragalus is a curved and thinner while calcaneum is longer and thicker. The fused ends are covered with calcified cartilage forming *epiphyses* or *articular surfaces*. The distal row consists of three bones -a small *centrale* infront of astragalus. a small *first tarsal* by the side of centrale. and a large *compound tarsal* infront of calcaneum. It is formed by the fusion of second. third and fourth distal tarsals. Fifth tarsal is lacking.

(ii) *Sole.* It contains five large and stout bones the *metatarsals.* The first metatarsal lies infront of first tarsal. Remaining metatarsal lie infront of compound tarsal. There is no metatarsal infront of the centrale.

(iii) *Toes.* The metatarsals bear toes or fingers. The fingers are containing small bones called *phalanges.* The first and second fingers bear two phalanges, third and fifth bear three phalanges each and the fourth finger bears four phalanges. The phalangal formula is 2, 2, 3, 4, 3.

5

Musculature

The main function of the muscular system is to bring movement of structures present in the body of an organism and locomotion. This is possible as a result of coordination between skeleton and muscles. Muscles may be classified in accordance with any number of critaria-location, structure, function, embryonic origin, shape or any other useful criterion. On the basis of distribution and function the muscular system is composed of three types of muscle-fibres-*smooth*, *cardiac* and *striated*.

The smooth muscles are also known as *unstriped* or *involuntary* muscles. There is no control of the will power of animal on these muscles. Their fibres are mostly occur in the wall of alimentary canal, genital organs, blood vessels, urinary bladder and various ducts. In the alimentary canal they are arranged in circular or longitudinal manner.

The cardiac muscles found in the heart, are involuntary in action but stripped in structure. They keep on working throughout the life of the animal.

The striped muscles are also known the *skeletal muscles* or *voluntary muscles*. The muscles are under the control of the will power of the animal and they function when the animal wishes. These occur in the body wall and the limbs. A frog has 200 voluntary muscles.

A striped muscle consists of numerous bundles of muscle fibres which are arranged parallel to each other called *fasciculi*. Fibres of each fasciculus are bound together by a fibrillar connective tissue, called *endomycium*. All fasciculi of a muscle are bound together by a connective tissue termed *perimycium* which also forms a sheath around each fasciculus. Similarly, the whole muscle itself is covered by a connective tissue sheath called *epimycium*. Two opposite ends of a voluntary muscle are usually connected to bones directly or by means of *tendons* which are inelastic connective tissue cords.

The end which is attached to the immovable bone is called the *origin* and that which is attached to the movable bone is known as the *insertion* end.

On the basis of their action, the muscles are classified as follows :

1. *Flexor*. These muscles bend the parts of the body. Example : *biceps brachii*. It brings the fore-arm towards the upper arm.
2. *Extensors*. They extend or straighten a limb. Example : *tricaps brachii*.
3. *Adductor*. One part of the body is pulled and brought near other part with the help of these muscles. Example : *latissiumus dorsal* muscle.
4. *Depressors* : Any part of body is lowered by these muscles. Example : *depressor mandibulae* which lowers down the lower jaw.
5. *Abductors* : Some part of the body is moved away from the other with the help of these muscles. Example : *deltoideus*.
6. *Elevators*. These muscles help in lifting the part of the body. Example : *masseter*, which lifts the lower jaw to close the mouth.

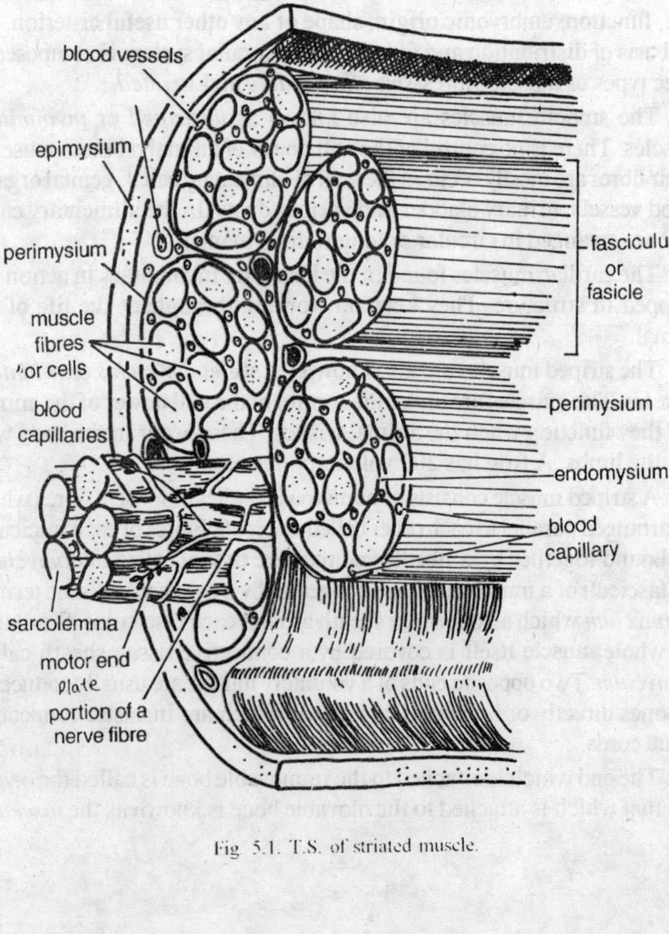

Fig. 5.1. T.S. of striated muscle.

7. *Rotators*. These muscles rotate the organs. Example : *pyriformis*. It raises and rotates the thigh.
8. *Constrictors*. The diameter of any opening is reduced or closed with the help of these muscles. Example : *sphincter* muscles.
9. *Dilators*. These muscles enlarge any opening.
10. *Supinators*. The upper side of any organ is turned downwards with the help of these muscles.

PRINCIPAL BODY MUSCLES

Head muscles

On the ventral side of the head, there is a *mylohyoid* or *sub-maxillary muscle* which forms the floor of the buccal cavity. Its origin is from the medial surface of the lower jaw and remain inserted into longitudinal connective tissue septum in throat between two mylohyoids. The muscle helps in swallowing the food and elevates the throat in breathing. Dorsally, on the head, is situated a *temporalis muscle*. It is originated from pro-otic bone of the skull and is inserted into the angulosplenial bones of lower jaw. It elevates the lower jaw to close the mouth.

A *depressor mandibulae* arises from the dorsal surface of the supra scapula and converging down to be inserted into the angle of lower jaw. It is an depressor muscle which lowers down the lower jaw to open the mouth. The *masseter* muscle arises from the quadrato-jugal and inserted into the outer surface of lower jaw. It elevates the lower jaw so that the mouth is closed. It also stratches tympanum.

Sternohyoids originate from dorsal side of coracoid and sternum and inserted into ventral surface of hyoid by means of tendon. They depress the throat during breathing.

Hypoglossus arise from the bony posterior cornua of the hyoid. Both meet infront of the larynx to be inserted into the tongue. They help in withdrawal of tongue. The *geniohyoid* originated from the lower jaw and inserted into the tongue and protrudes it.

The *pterygoideus* arises from the side of the skull to be inserted into lower jaw. It is an elevator.

The eye muscles are six in number they are *recti* and *oblique*. In addition there are *levator bulbi*, a thin sheet lying between the mouth cavity and the eye ball causing the eye-ball to bulge out; and *retractor bulbi* arising from the parasphenoid and inserted into the eye ball with the set of recti muscles embressing the optic nerve.

Trunk muscles

Rectus abdominis is a large muscle which covers the ventral mid-line from sternum to the pubis. It is separated into two bundles situated on either side of the middle line. This muscle supports abdomen and flexes the back.

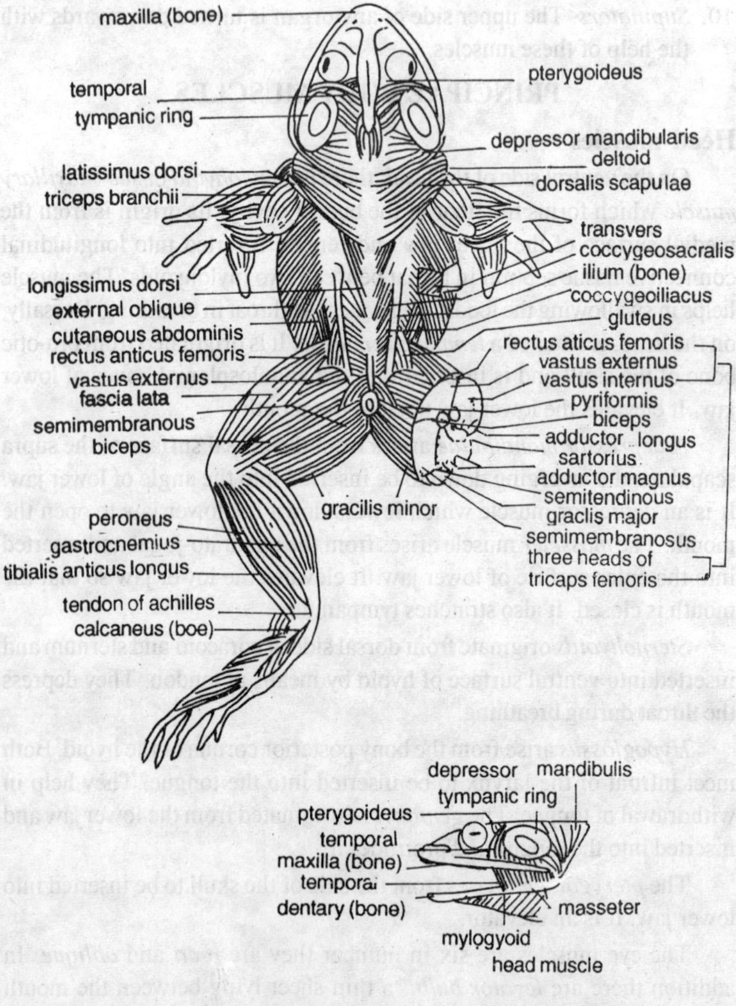

Fig. 5.2. *Rana*. Muscle. Dorsal view.

Oblique externus is originted from the connective tissue of back and ilium and inserted into linea alba (a white line of connective tissue present in mid-ventral line). It supports the abdomen, reduces abdominal cavity in breathing to compress the lungs.

Transversus abdominis originating from the ilium and vertebrae and inserted into the tibio-fibula and sternum. They constrict the abdomen.

Longissimus dorsai originate from the posterior end of the skull and dorsal surface of backbone and it is inserted into urostyle and ilium. It helps in the elevation of head and extends the back.

Coccygeoiliacus and *coccygeosacralis* arise from the lateral sides of urostyle. The former inserted into the ilium and latter into sacral vertebra.

Fore-limb muscles

An important muscle is the *deltoideus* which is originated from the clavicles, precoracoid, omosternum and scapula. It is inserted into the

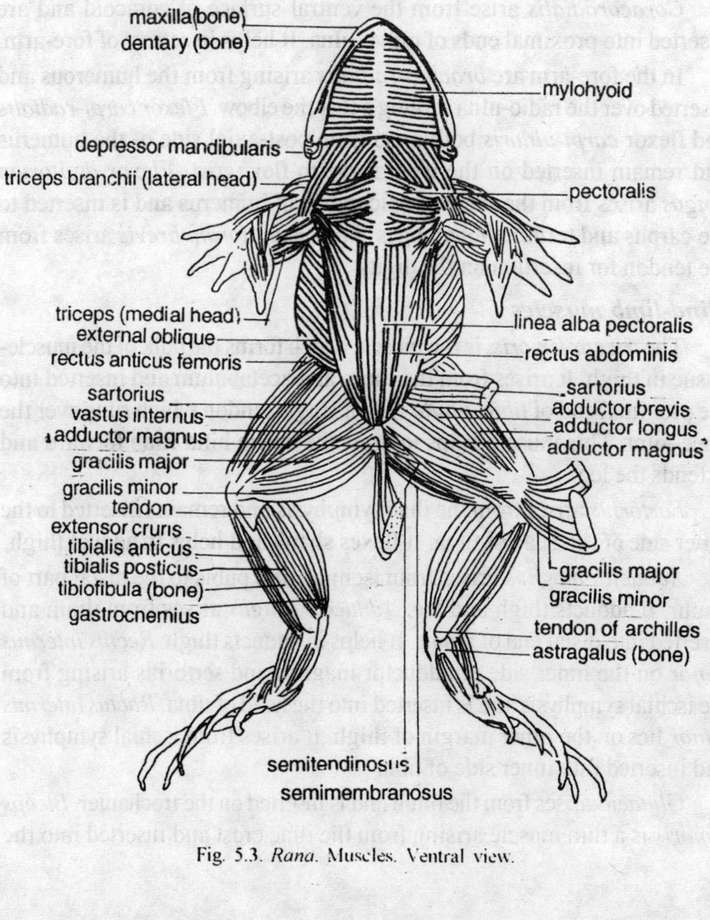

Fig. 5.3. *Rana*. Muscles. Ventral view.

deltiod ridge of humerus bone. It helps in the pushing forwards the arm by its contraction. The *biceps* arise from the omosternum and epicoracoid and is inserted into the radio-ulna. It bends the fore-arm. *Triceps brachii* arise from the base of scapula and shaft of humerus and remain inserted into the proximal end of radio-ulna just below the elbow joint.

Latissimus dorsi is a large, powerful muscle. It arises from the base of scapula and shaft of humerus and inserted into the radio-ulna. By its contraction it brings the arm upwards and backwards.

The *pectoralis* muscle is broad and flat. It arises from the sternum and fascia of rectus abdominis and remains inserted into the deltoid ridge of humerus. This is a powerful adductor muscle of the upper arm.

Dorsalis scapulae. arise from the scapula and suprascapula and inserted into the proximal end of humerus. It helps in extending the arm.

Coracoradialis arise from the ventral surface of coracoid and are inserted into proximal ends of radio- ulna. It helps in retract of fore-arm.

In the fore-arm are *brachio-radialis* arising from the humerous and inserted over the radio-ulna serving a flex the elbow. *Flexor carpi-radialis* and flexor *carpi-ulnaris* both arise from post-axial side of the humerus and remain inserted on the wrist serve to flex wrist. *Flexor digitorum longus* arises from the -medial epicondyle of humerus and is inserted to the carpus and terminal phalanges. *Flexor digitorum brevis* arises from the tendon for insertion on the digits.

Hind-limb muscles

The *triceps femoris*, is the muscle which forms the bulk of the muscle-tissue in thigh. It arises from the ilium and acetabulum and inserted into the proximal end of *tibio-fibula* with a single tendon which runs over the knee-joint. This muscle helps to draw the entire hind limb forward and extends the leg.

Sartorius arises from the iliac symphysis and remains inserted to the inner side of the head of tibia. It flexes shank and helps in adduct thigh.

Adductor magnus arises from ischium and pubis to the distal part of femur. It adducts thigh and leg. *Adductor longus* arises from ilium and inserted into distal end of femur. It helps in adducts thigh. *Rectus internus major* on the inner side of adductor magnus and sertorius arising from the ischial symphysis and is inserted into the head of tibia. *Ractus internus minor* lies on the inner margin of thigh. It arises from ischial symphysis and inserted into inner side of tibia.

Glutaeus arises from the ilium and is inserted on the trochanter. *Biceps femoris* is a thin muscle arising from the iliac crest and inserted into the distal end of femur and the head of tibia. *Semi-membranous* arise from ischium and inserted into proximal end of tibio-fibula. It helps in flexing shank and extending thigh. *Pyriformis* arises from the urostyle and is inserted into the femur.

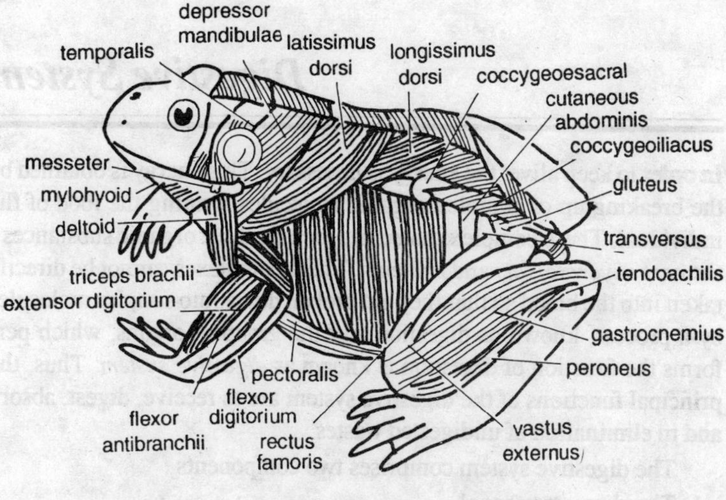

Fig. 5.4. *Rana.* Lateral view of superficial muscles.

Semitendinous, a double headed muscle arises from the ischium and inserted into the tibia. *Adductor brevis* lying beneath the adductor muscle magnus. It arises from pubic and ischial symphysis and is inserted on the femur. *Pectineus* arises from the pubic symphysis and is inserted in the proximal part of femur. *Iliopses* arises from the ilium is inserted into the femur. *Obturator* arises from ischial symphysis and is inserted into the head of femur close to glutaeus.

Gastrocnemius arises from distal end of femur and inserted into toes. It extends foot and helps in flexing shank. *Tibialis posticus* arises from the tibia and is inserted into astragalus by means of a tendon. *Tibialis anticus* arises by a thin tendon from lower end of femur and inserted into astragalus and calcaneum. *Extensor tarsi* arises by a long tendon from the condyle of femur and is inserted into the tibia. *Peroneus* arises from the distal end of femur and is inserted into the tibia and calcaneum.

6

Digestive System

In order to keep alive, the energy is necessary. This energy is obtained by the breaking up of complex organic molecules forming the food of the individual. These complex molecules include three organic substances - the *carbohydrate, fats* and *proteins.* These complexes cannot be directly taken into the blood so that they are broken down into simpler molecules by a process, known as digestion and the group of organs, which performs the function of digestion is known as *digestive system.* Thus, the principal functions of the digestive system are to receive, digest, absorb and in elimination of undigested wastes.

The digestive system comprises two components :

I. The alimentary canal.

II. The digestive glands.

I. THE ALIMENTARY CANAL

The alimentary canal is a tube, seldom straight and often tortuously coiled and can be differentiated into following zones :

I. The ingressive zone.

II. Progressive zone.

III. Degressive zone.

IV. Egressive zone.

I. Ingressive Zone

The ingressive zone consists of :

(a) Mouth and (b) Buccal cavity.

(a) Mouth

The mouth is relatively wider, semioval slit. It extends along the entire margin of head. It is bounded by upper and lower lips which are covered with inturn skin. The upper jaw is fixed while the lower jaw can move up and down to close or open the mouth. Mouth leads into a large dorsoventrally flattened chamber, the *buccopharyngeal cavity.* Its anterior part is known as buccal cavity and posterior as pharynx.

(b) Buccal Cavity

The buccal cavity is lined with ciliated columnar epithelial cells contains goblet cells which secrete mucous for the lubrication of food material.

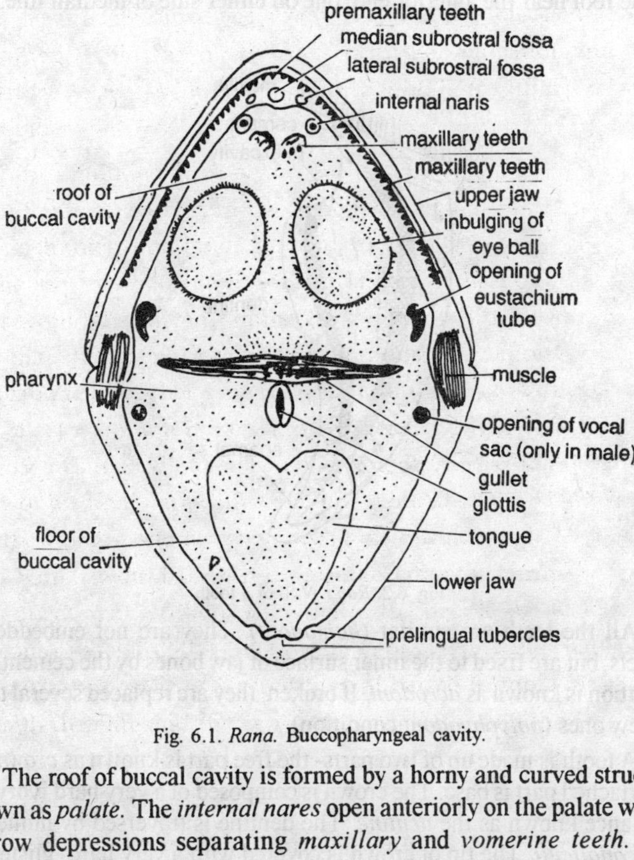

Fig. 6.1. *Rana.* Buccopharyngeal cavity.

The roof of buccal cavity is formed by a horny and curved structure known as *palate.* The *internal nares* open anteriorly on the palate within narrow depressions separating *maxillary* and *vomerine teeth.* The maxillary teeth and vomerine teeth are present one on each side of the median line of the palatal surface and internal to the internal nares. There are three shallow pits situated near the tip of upper jaw within the maxillary teeth, one of them is *median subrostral fossa* and two are *lateral subrostral fossae.* These help to close the mouth firmly during respiration.

Behind the vomerine teeth, on the roof of buccal cavity, there are two large pale oval areas known as the *bulgings of eye balls.* The play a part in swallowing.

Teeth

The teeth are present only in the upper jaw. There are two types of teeth on the basis of their location (i) the *maxillary* teeth, occur in a single row along the margin, and (ii) the *vomerine* teeth, present in two patches on the roof near the anterior end, one on either side of median line.

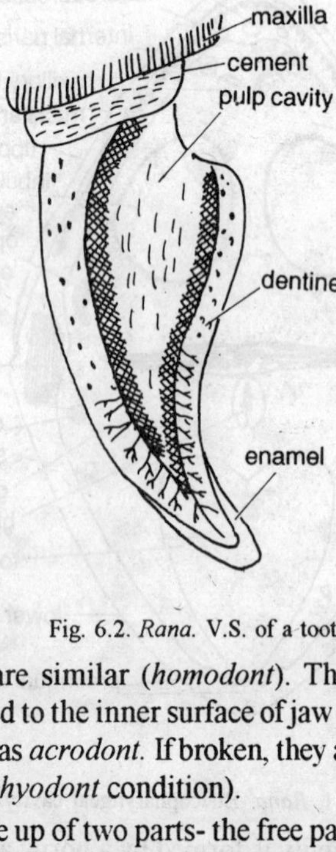

Fig. 6.2. *Rana.* V.S. of a tooth.

All the teeth are similar (*homodont*). They are not embedded in sockets, but are fixed to the inner surface of jaw bones by the cement, this condition is known as *acrodont.* If broken, they are replaced several times by new ones (*polyphyodont* condition).

A tooth is made up of two parts- the free part is known as *crown* and the attached part is base. The crown is composed of a very hard ivory like substance known as the *dentine.* The dentine is traversed by numerous fine *canaliculi.* The tip of crown is covered with a very hard. glistening substance. the *enamel.* The tooth is hallow and contains a cavity known as *palp cavity.* This cavity contains connective tissue. blood-vessels and nerve endings. The odontoblast cells provide new material for the growth of tooth. The base is derived from the bone.

Tongue

The floor of buccal cavity is occupied by a fleshy tongue attached anterio-ventrally to the hyoid apparatus from the front of lower jaw. The tongue is oval, flattened, narrow anteriorly but bifid posteriorly. The tongue is always covered with mucous hence sticky. It has the power of protrusion. During protrusion it passes along the palatal depression of the *intermaxillary glands* collecting a mucoid secretion on lingual surface. The protrusion is brought about by pair of *genioglossus muscles,* which, arise from the lower jaw and are inserted in the tongue. The withdrawal is brought by a pair of *hyoglossus muscles.* These muscles arise from the posterior cornua of the hyoid to the root of tongue. The tongue helps in capturing the prey. Taste buds are present on the papillae of the tongue.

II Progressive Zone

It includes, *pharynx, oesophagus* and *stomach.*

(a) Pharynx

The pharynx bears, on its roof, two openings known as openings of *eustachian tubes* which connect the middle ears with pharynx and help in keeping the air pressure equal on both the sides of the tympanic membrane. In the angles of the lower jaw, pharynx bears a pair of *openings of vocal sacs,* these are of blue colour and are found only in male frog. In the middle of the floor, there is a vertical slit called *glottis* which carries air to the lungs. Pharynx abruptly tapers behind to lead into oesophagus through *gullet.*

(b) Oesophagus

The oesophagus is that portion of the alimentary canal immediately following the pharynx. At its other end it joins the stomach. It is extremely short. The lining of oesophagus is ciliated which swept small food particles on to the stomach. Secretory cells in the oesophageal epithelium of the frog are reported to secrete *propepsin,* which, however, is ineffective until it reaches the stomach. In the presence of hydrochloric acid it is converted into *pepsin* which helps in digestion.

(c) Stomach

The stomach is basically a dilation of the digestive tract for the temporary storage of food. It lies on the left side of body cavity attached to the dorsal body wall by a mesentery known as *mesogaster.* The end of the stomach which connects to the oesophagus is nearer the heart and, therefore, is called *cardiac stomach*. The *pyloric stomach* is the narrower lower part and connects to the intestine. At the junction of two lies a *pyloric valve.* In frog the stomach is slightly curved. Two faces, the lesser and greater curvatures are thus formed. The lesser curvature is actually ventral and the greater curvature is dorsal side. The expansion at the cardiac end of the stomach, formed by the greater curvature, is sac-like and known as fundus which is absent in frog. A *cardiac valve* is also present at the junction of oesophagus and cardiac stomach. The cardiac and pyloric valves consist of rings of muscles in the wall of stomach.

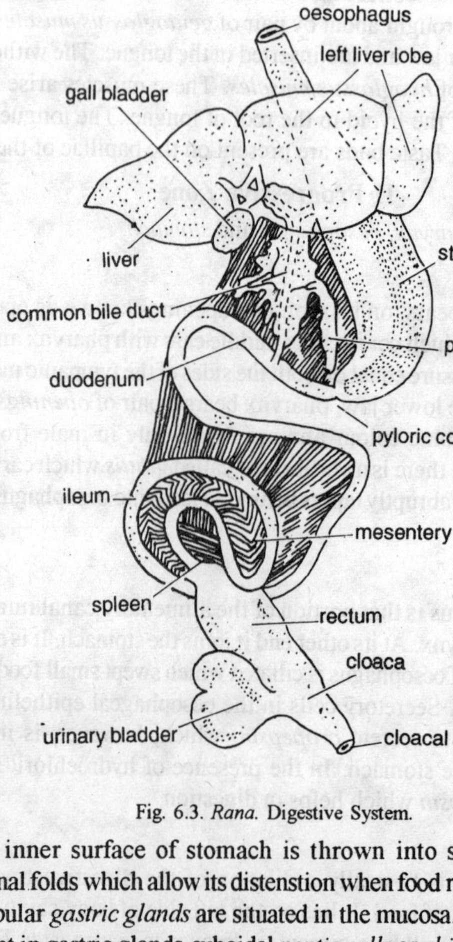

Fig. 6.3. *Rana.* Digestive System.

The inner surface of stomach is thrown into several prominent longitudinal folds which allow its distension when food reaches there. Many small, tubular *gastric glands* are situated in the mucosa. Two types of cells are present in gastric glands-cuboidal *peptic cells* or *chief cells* that secrete enzyme; and ovoid *oxyntic cells* that secrete hydrochloric acid. These glands open into lumen of stomach by *gastric pits* situated in mucosa.

III. Degressive Zone

It includes *small intestine*. It is long, coiled and narrow tube about 30 cm long. It remains attached to the dorsal body wall by mesenteries. It is differentiated into two parts - the part of small intestine which immediately follows the stomach is called *duodenum* which receives the hepato-pancreatic duct from liver and pancreas. The remaining part of small intestine is known as *ileum*. Duodenum runs forwards parallel to the stomach forms a 'U' with stomach and remains attached to the latter by *gastro-duodenal omentum*. The inner lining is thrown into numerous transverse folds called *valvulae conniventes* which increase area of secretion and absorption. The ileum is the longest part of small intestine and is coiled. Its lining is also thrown into longitudinal folds.

The small intestine devoid of true villi, definite glands and crypts as seen in higher chordates.

IV. Egressive Zone

It includes only *large intestine* or the *rectum*. It is a short, wide tube measuring 4 cm in length. It runs back and opens into cloaca by *anus*. The anus is guarded by *anal sphincter*.

Cloaca. It is a small sac-like structure which receives the digestive system and urinogenital system. It opens out side by the *cloacal aperture* or *vent* situated at the posterior end of the trunk between the hind-limbs.

HISTOLOGY

Each part of alimentary canal consists of four layers from inner to outer side :

(1) Mucosa, (2) Sub mucosa, (3) Muscular layer and (4) Serosa.

1. Mucosa

It is the innermost part and made up of three layers-inner-*columnar epithelium*, middle *lamina propria* and outer *muscularis mucosa*. The columnar epithelial cells rest on a basement membrane. Lamina propria consists of a thin sheet of reticular connective tissue. It contains blood-capillaries, lymph vessels and nerves. the muscularis mucosa is made up of thin layer of unstriped muscle-fibres.

2. Sub-mucosa

It is present outside the mucosa. It is composed of dense connective tissue with white and yellow fibres. It is vascular in nature.

3. Muscular layer

It surrounds the submucosa and composed of unstriped muscle fibres. The muscle fibres are of two types - inner *circular muscle fibres*, and outer *longitudinal muscle fibres*. The lumen of alimentary canal becomes narrow by the contraction of longitudinal muscle fibres and widen by the contraction of circular muscle fibres.

4. Serosa

This is the outermost layer and made up of visceral peritoneum (a thin sheet of connective tissue and squamous epithelium).

Histology of Oesophagus

Its histology is similar to that of described above. The mucosa invaginates into the sub-mucosa to form branched glands. The columnar cells are ciliated. Goblet cells that secrete mucous are also present.

The muscularis mucosa is absent.

The visceral peritoneum is absent.

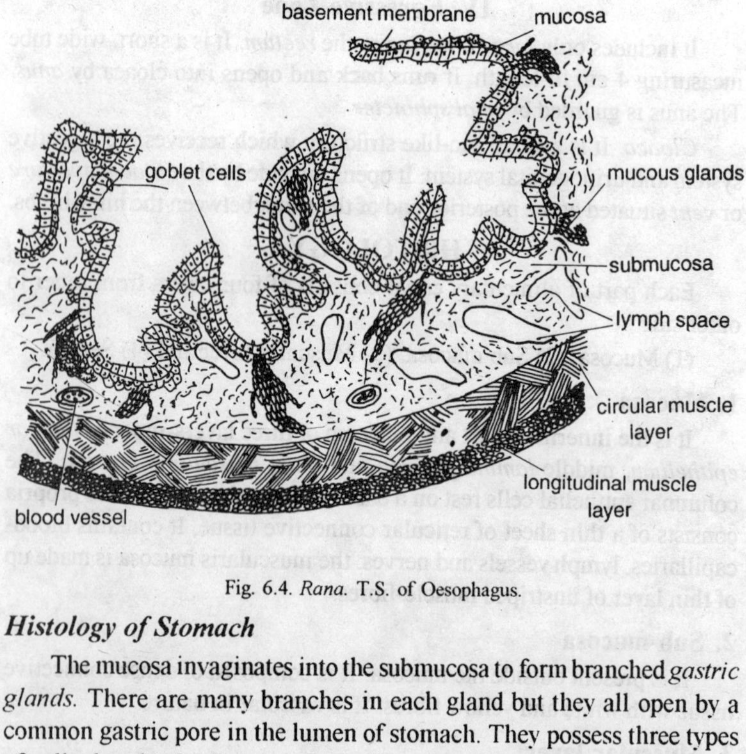

Fig. 6.4. *Rana.* T.S. of Oesophagus.

Histology of Stomach

The mucosa invaginates into the submucosa to form branched *gastric glands.* There are many branches in each gland but they all open by a common gastric pore in the lumen of stomach. They possess three types of cells the *chief cells* or *peptic cells* secrete enzyme; the *oxyntic cells* secrete hydrochloric acid and *goblet cells*- that secrete mucous.

The muscularis mucosa is well developed.

Muscular layer is very thick particularly the circular muscle fibres.

Histology of Duodenum

The mucosal membrane is disposed in transverse folds. It possesses only mucous secreting cells - the *goblet cells, enzymes* secreting cells called *Paneth cells* and undifferentiated argentaffin cells.

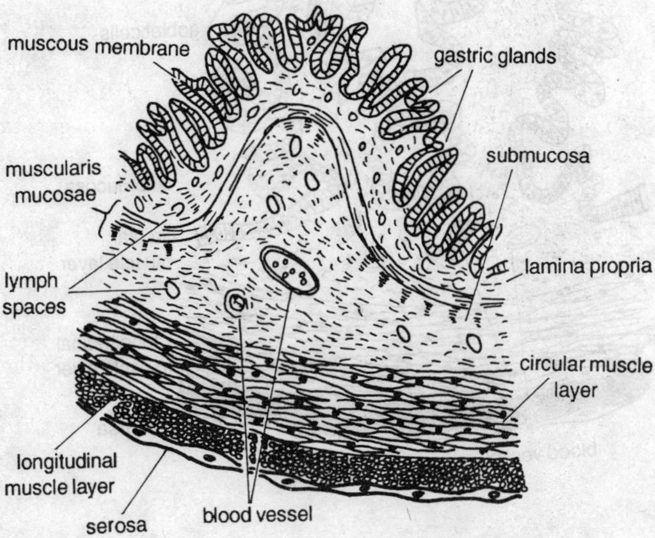

Fig. 6.5. *Rana.* T.S. of Stomach.

A plexus of nerve cells and fibres is present in the sub-mucosa known as *sub-mucous plexus of Meissner*.

The muscular layer is well-developed and comprises of inner circular muscle fibres and outer longitudinal muscle fibres. Between the two muscle layers lies a network of nerve fibres and cells, known as *sympathetic myenteric plexus of Auerbach*.

Histiology of Rectum

Its histology is similar to that of small intestine instead of transverse folds it possesses longitudinal folds. Goblet cells are present throughout the rectum in columnar epithelial cells.

II. DIGESTIVE GLANDS

There are four types of digestive glands-

(1) Liver. (2) Pancreas. (3) Gastric glands and (4) Intestinal glands.

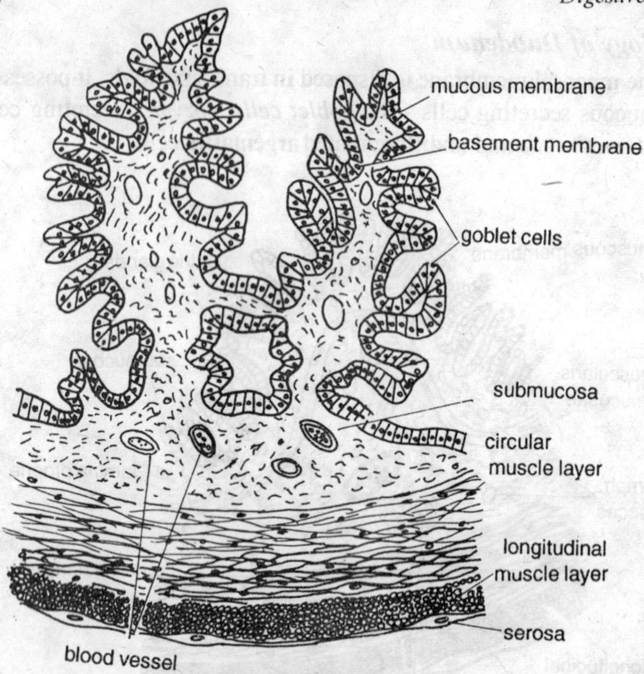

Fig. 6.6. *Rana.* T.S. of Duodenum.

1. Liver

The liver is one of the most important organ and is the largest gland present in body. It is large, dark-red gland present in the anterior body suspended by mesentery. The liver is made of two lobes, a *right lobe* and a *left lobe.* The left lobe is larger and covers the greater part of stomach. The left lobe is further sub-divided into two lobes, on the dorsal side, at the junction of two lobes of liver, there lies a thin walled, greenish, spherical sac known as *gall bladder.* Liver secretes *bile* which is brought to gall bladder, for storage, by means of three ducts. These ducts arise from the three different lobes of the liver and are joined together into a *cystic duct.* The duct of gall bladder or *bile duct* passes through the pancreas to open into the doudenum. In its way the duct receives *pancreatic ducts* from pancreas. Thus the duct which opens into the duodenum is, therefore, called the *hepato-pancreatic duct.*

Histologically, the liver consists of small lobules which are closely placed to each other. These lobules are made up of polygonal cells, each with a prominent nucleus and glycogen granules. There are spaces between

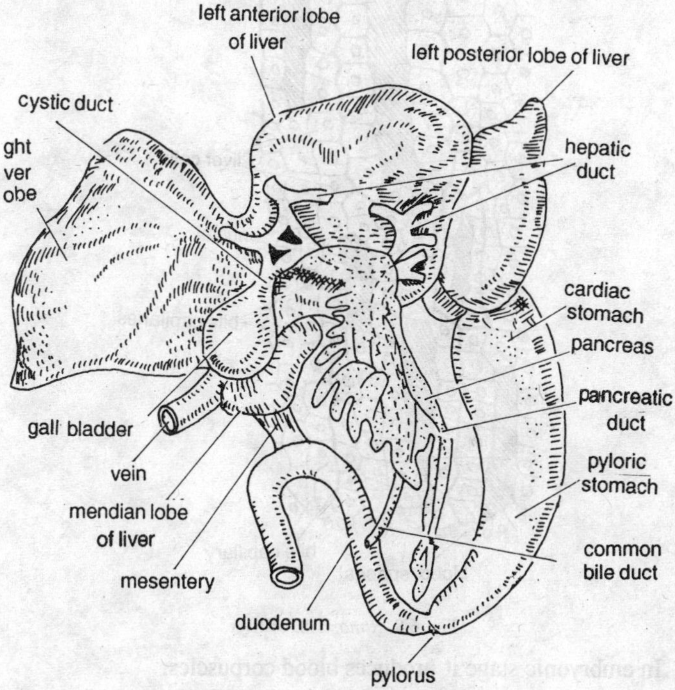

Fig. 6.7. *Rana*. Digestive glands.

lobules which have connective tissue, hepatic duct, blood sinuses and blood capillaries. The blood sinuses receive blood from hepatic portal vein and the hepatic artery which is ultimately empty into the hepatic vein. Bile capillaries are distributed among the cells of lobules. These capillaries unite to form ducts and these ducts form the cystic duct.

Actually, the liver is not a digestive gland as it does not secrete any enzyme that helps in digestion. It only secretes bile which is formed by the destruction of red blood corpuscles, which helps in the digestion of fats.

Functions of Liver. The liver performs following functions.

1. It secretes bile that helps in digestion of fats.
2. It stores excessive sugar in the form of glycogen. At the time of deficiency it converts glycogen into glucose for utilization. Thus it maintains a sugar level in blood.
3. Ammonia. which is harmful (formed during deamination of amino acids) is changed into urea.

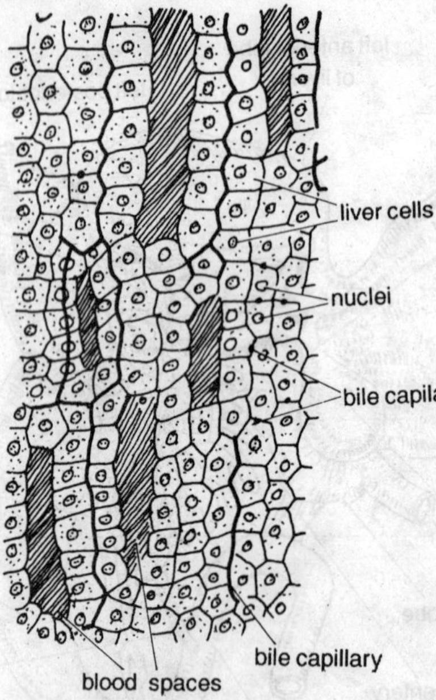

Fig. 6.8. *Rana.* T.S. of liver.

4. In embryonic stage it produces blood corpuscles.
5. The red blood corpuscles are degenerated in the liver.
6. The liver manufactures *heparin* which does not allow the blood to clot in blood vessels.
7. It produces prothrombin and fibrinogen which are important proteins in blood clotting.
8. The bacteria that have come into the blood are destroyed in the liver. Thus it has phagocytic action.
9. It stores inorganic salts of copper and iron.
10. As a result of chemical reactions, a toxic substance prussic acid is formed, which is converted into non-toxic potassium sulpho-cyanide by liver.
11. Certain excretory products are also eliminated and discharged with the bile into the intestine.
12. It helps in the formation of vitamin-A from carotene.

2. Pancreas

It is an irregular, elongated, whitish gland situated in a thin mesentary between the stomach and duodenum. It produces pancreatic juice which is carried into bile duct through several *pancreatic ducts,* and finally poured into duodenum by a common hepatopancreatic duct.

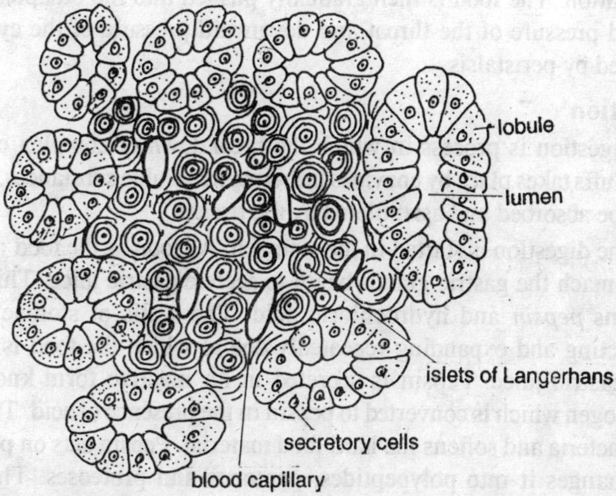

Fig. 6.9. *Rana.* T.S. Pancreas.

Histologically, the pancreas is composed of a large number of *acini* or *lobules.* Each lobule is lined with columnar epithelial cells. The lobules are held together by connective tissue. In the connective tissue are present blood vessels, nerve endings, lymph vessels etc. From each louble a minute ductule arises and the ductules unite to form the pancreatic ducts. The latter open into the bile-duct. Irregularly dispersed among the acini are masses of small cells, known as *islets* of *Langerhans.* They are present in the connective tissue. They are without any lumen and form *endocrine glands* which produce hormones.

3. Gastric Glands

These are microscopic and present in stomach, secrete gastric juice.

4. Intestinal glands

These are also microscopic present in small intestinel secrete intestinal juice.

INGESTION OF FOOD

Frog is a *carnivorous* animal. It feeds on various insects. spiders, snails etc. Small prey is captured with the tongue. Whenever an insect lies near the mouth of frog. the tongue is flicked out and striken at the insect. The insect thus adheres to the sticky tongue which returns through the mouth to the pharynx. The escape of insect is prevented by backward curvature of maxillary and vomerine teeth. The prey is swallowed without mastication. The food is then gradually pushed into the oesophagus by upward pressure of the throat and downward pressure of the eyeballs, followed by peristalsis.

Digestion

Digestion is process in which the breakdown of complex organic food-stuffs takes place by enzymes into simpler soluble substances, which could be absorbed and assimilated by the tissues.

The digestion is started in the stomach. As soon as the food reaches the stomach the gastric glands begin to secrete gastric juice. This juice contains *pepsin* and hydrochloric acid. The walls of stomach start contracting and expanding repeatedly due to which the food is mixed with gastric juice. Pepsin is secreted in an inactive form known as pepsinogen which is converted to pepsin in the presence of acid. The acid kills bacteria and softens the hard food material. Pepsin acts on proteins and changes it into polypeptides, peptones and proteoses. The food becomes semiliquid and is known as *chyme*. Food remains about two to three hours in the stomach. The chyme now passes into the duodenum through the pyloric valve. The acidic medium is changed into alkaline medium due to *bile juice*. The pancreatic juice contains *trypsin, amylopsin* and *steapsin*. Trypsinogen is converted into trypsin by *enterokinase* which is secreted by duodenum. Trypsin acts on proteins and converts into dipeptides. Amylopsin converts starch into maltose. Steapsin changes emulsified fats into glycerol and fatty acids.

In the duodenum intestinal juice is mixed with food. The intestinal juice contains - *Erepsin* converts polypeptides into amino acids; *maltase* convertes maltose to glucose ; *sucrase* converts sucrose to glucose and fructose lactose converts lactose to glucose and glactose; and *lipase* splits fats into fatty acids and glycerols.

Absorption

The complex molecules are converted into simpler molecules during digestion. Their absorption takes place through the walls of small intestine. The longitudinal folds and villi of intestine provides greater surface area for absorption. The exact mechanism of absorption is not well known but osmotic force and other factors seem to play a part. Amino acids, glucose, fructose, water, mineral salts diffuse through the mucosa into the blood capillaries and through hepatic portal vein they go into the liver. Fatty acids and glycerol pass into lymphatic capillaries or lacteals which are present in the longitudinal folds and so into the veins.

Assimilation

Utilization of absorbed food by the body tissue is termed as assimilation. Assimilated glucose is mostly used in catabolism for energy production. Excessive sugar is converted into glycogen and is stored in liver and muscles. Fatty acids and lipoproteins are mostly used in synthesis of triglycerides phospholipids and cholesterol. It is utilized for storage or for the formation and repair of cell membrane, organelles of cells or for the synthesis of steroids and hormones. Aminoacids are utilized in protein synthesis. Water is used as solvent. Salts are used in the synthesis of complex molecules. Vitamins act as co-enzymes.

Egestion

Digestion and absroption of food is completed in small intestine. The undigested food material is pass on to the rectum by peristalsis of small intestine. In the rectum the undigested food material is stored and converted into faecal matter. At intervals the faecal matter passes into the cloaca and egested out through cloacal aperture.

7

Respiratory System

The respiratory system functions chiefly in the exchange of oxygen and carbon dioxide between the organism and its environment. Every living cell of an organism consumes oxygen which is necesary for *catabolism* (a phase of metabolism) for the liberation of heat and other forms of energy along with the production of carbon dioxide. This end product of metabolism, unless removed from the cell acts as a poison which is harmful to protoplasm. Thus removal of carbon dioxide is as essential as the supply of oxygen. To fulfil this requirement some parts or organs of the body are set aside specially for the exchange of gases from the surrounding. Such an organ is known as *respiratory organ* and the surface where exchange of gases occur is known as *respiratory surface.* Blood and lymph are the carrier of gases from respiratory surface to the tissues.

Frog lives in water as well as on land (amphibious) thus the respiration is aquatic as well as aerial. The adult frog has three modes of respiration *cutaneous respiration, buccopharyngeal respiration* and *pulmonary respiration.*

1. Cutaneous Respiration

The cutaneous respiration takes place with the help of integument or skin. It is thin and kept moist by mucous secreted by the mucous glands of skin. The mucous always holds a thin film of water between itself and the skin surface. The skin is ideal for exchange of gases because there is no thick layer of kertain and scales over it, as well as it is richly supplied with blood vessels.

Cutaneous respiration goes on without any effort on the part of frog. The oxygen, dissolved in water film, diffuses into the blood capillaries present in dermal region and combines with haemoglobin to form oxyhaemoglobin. The oxyhaemoglobin then conveys the oxygen to the tissues. Likewise carbon dioxide is diffused out in the water film. By cutaneous respiration about 30% of their total oxygen is taken inside.

The cutaneous respiration is most important of the three types of respiration viz. cutaneous, buccopharyngeal and pulmonary respirations found in frogs. It takes place all the time, in water as well as on land. This is the only type of respiration when the animal is submerged in water or during hibernation or aestivation to conserve food.

2. Bucco-phryngeal respiration

As the heading indicates, such a respiration takes place in bucco-pharyngeal cavity. Like the skin, the mucosa of bucco-pharyngeal cavity is also idially suited for exchange of gases. It removes more carbon dioxide than the pulmonary respiration. It communicates with the exterior by a pair of short passage called *respiratory tracts.* Air comes in or goes out through these tracts.

The respiratory tracts consist of a pair of *external nares* which lie on the snout just above the mouth. They open into the *nasal chambers* which are situated in olfactory capsules of skull. Through a pair of *internal nares,* the nasal chambers open into bucco-pharyngeal cavity. The internal nares are present on the roof of the cavity anteriorly. The lining of bucco-pharyngeal cavity is kept moist by mucous and it is highly vascular.

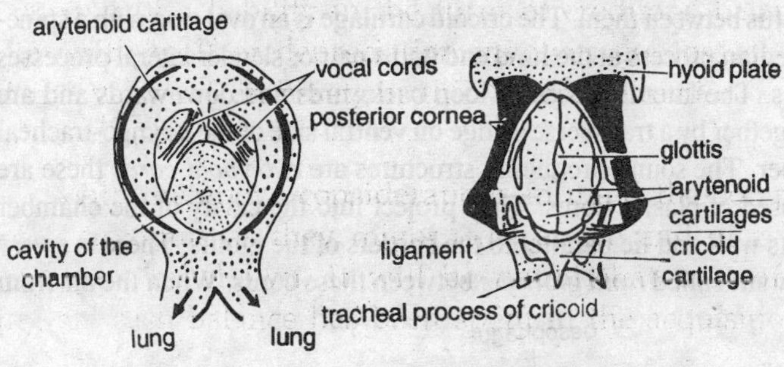

Fig. 7.1. *Rana.* Laryngotracheal chamber.

During bucco-pharyngeal respiration, the mouth, gullet and glottis remain closed, but the external nares remain open. The floor of bucco-pharyngeal cavity is lowered powerfully by means of a set of muscles known as *sternohyal muscles.* These muscles arise from the dorsal surface of the caracoid and clavicle and inserted into the ventral surface of hyoid apparatus. By lowering the bucco-pharyngeal cavity becomes enlarged reducing the pressure of air in it so that fresh air rushes into the cavity through the respiratory tract. Raising of the floor of bucco-pharyngeal cavity is brought about by contraction of another set of muscles, the *petrohyal muscles.* One end of these muscles inserted upon the sides of hyoid apparatus and the other end of these muscles inserted upon the auditory capsules of respective sides near squamosal. This reduces the bucco-pharyngeal cavity and raises the pressure of air in it above that of the atmopshere. Thus the deoxygenated air is expelled through the external nares. During this process the external nares always remain open.

3. Pulmonary respiration

The pulmonary respiration takes place in the lungs. Air enters or leaves the lungs through respiratory tract.

The respiratory tract starts from external nares and comprises the nasal passage, internal nares, bucco-pharyngeal cavity. Through a slit-like opening the glottis, which is present in pharynx, the cavity leads into the *laryngo-tracheal chamber.* It also performs the function of sound production. It is formed by the union of larynx and trachea. The trachea is absent in frog and in place laryngo-tracheal chamber is present. The walls of this chamber are supported by a pair of cartilages which are known as *arytenoid cartilages* and a *cricoid cartilage.* The arytenoid cartilages are semilunar in shape. They lie in the cricoid ring and enclose the glottis between them. The cricoid cartilage is an oval ring with a spine-like median process at the hind end and a pair of slender lateral processes at sides. The lateral processes loop backwards and downwards and are join together by a transverse bridge on ventral side of the laryngo-tracheal chamber. The sound producing structures are two *vocal cords* these are composed of elastic fibres. They project into the cavity of the chamber from its wall and lie parallel to the borders of the glottis. There is a very narrow slit called *rima glottidis* between these cords. When the air from

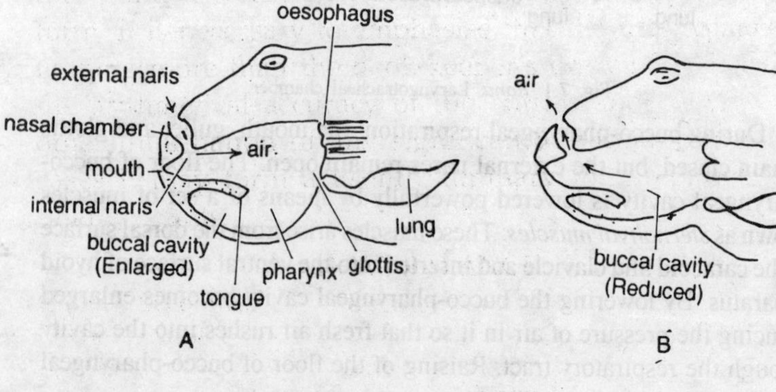

Fig. 7.2. *Rana.* Buccopharyngeal respiration.

lungs passes through rima glottidis then the vocal cords vibrate quickly producing the crocking sound which can be increased or decreased by the tension of vocal cords.

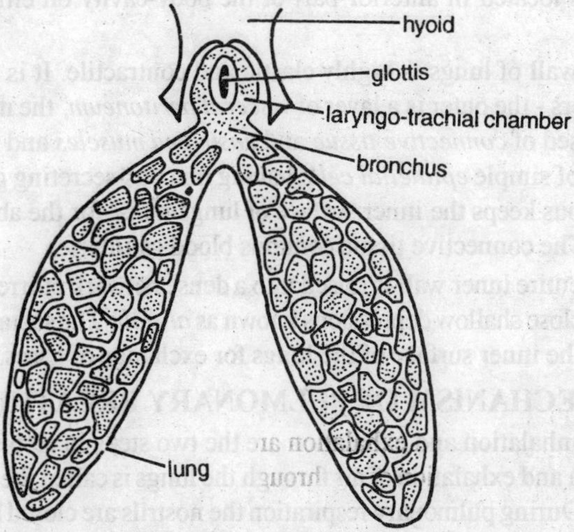

Fig. 7.3. *Rana.* Lung.

The male frog has a pair of *vocal sacs* which open into bucco-pharyngeal cavity. When they distended increase the volume of sound several times.

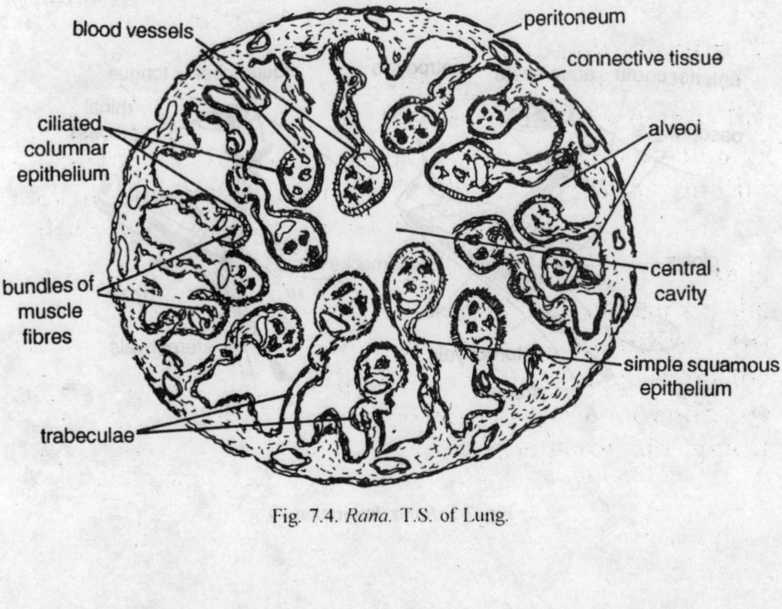

Fig. 7.4. *Rana.* T.S. of Lung.

The laryngo-tracheal chamber opens into the lungs by a pair of very small tubes, the *bronchi*.

The lungs are a pair of elongated, pear-shaped, pinkish sac-like structures located in anterior part of the body-cavity on either sides of heart.

The wall of lungs is highly elastic and contractile. It is made up of three layers - the outer is a layer of *visceral peritoneum*, the middle layer is composed of *connective tissue* and *unstriped muscles* and the inner is made up of simple *epithelial cells* having mucous-secreting goblet cells. The mucous keeps the inner surface of lungs moist for the absorption of oxygen. The connective tissue contains blood capillaries.

The entire inner wall is raised into a dense network of irregular *septa* which enclose shallow depressions known as *alveoli*. The septa and alveoli increase the inner surface of the lungs for exchange of gases.

MECHANISM OF PULMONARY BREATHING

The inhalation and exhalation are the two steps in respiration. The inhalation and exhalation of air through the lungs is called the ventilation of lungs. During pulmonary respiration the nostrils are closed by a special pad, the *tuberculum prelingulae*, which are present on the anterior angle of the lower jaw and are supported by mentomeckelian bone.

Inspiration

It is the intake of air from atmosphere into the lungs. The throat is lowered by the contraction of the *sternohyal muscles*. Due to lowering of

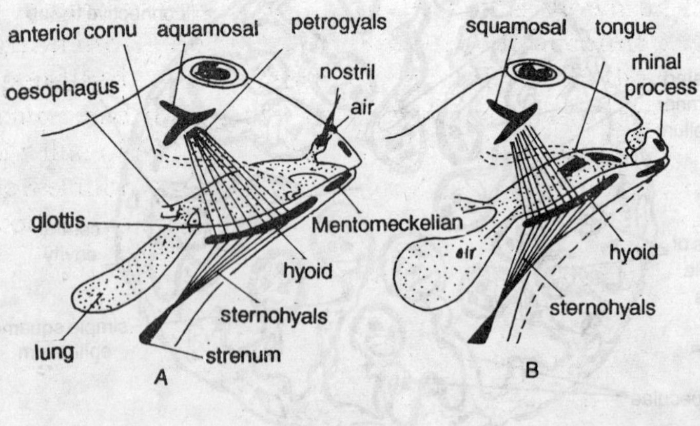

Fig. 7.5. *Rana.* Inspiration.

throat, the bucco-pharyngeal cavity is enlarged. This reduces the pressure of air in it. The air rushes into the bucco-pharyngeal cavity through the respiratory tracts. The passage of air from surrounding into the bucco-pharyngeal cavity is known as *aspiration.* After that the lower jaw fits more tightly against the upper jaw, pressing the mentomeckelian bone. Contraction of tuberculum prelingule rises the mentomeckelian bone which pushes the premaxillae apart, causing the septomaxillaries to move and block the external nares. By the contraction of *petrohyal muscles* the floor of bucco-pharyngeal cavity is raised due to which the cavity becomes smaller and the pressure on the air, present in it, increases considerably. The air forces open the glottis and passed into the lung through laryngo-tracheal chamber and bronchii because the external nares and gullet are closed.

Expiration

Inhaled air is retained in lungs for sometime to exchange of gases. Now the throat is again lowered by sternohyal muscles contraction creating a partial vaccum in the bucco-pharyngeal cavity. The air in lungs open the glottis and comes into the bucco-pharyngeal cavity. The emptying of lungs is brought by the contraction of lung muscles aided by the contraction of pectoralis and abdominal muscles. At the same time the tuberculum prelingulae relaxed so that the mentomeckelian bone and the upper and lower jaws are brought to normal position thus the external nares are opened. By the contraction of petrohyal muscles the throat is raised and the air goes out due to reduction in volume of bucco-pharyngeal cavity.

The pulmonary respiration is not a common method of respiration. It occurs when the animal leads an active life on land, in the search of food or when actively breeding, its oxygen requirement is increased only then pulmonary respiration takes place. Otherwise, the most common methods of respiration are cutaneous and bucco-pharyngeal.

PHYSIOLOGY OF RESPIRATION

The air from atmosphere enters the lungs and fills the alveoli during inspiration. The alveoli are highly vascular structures. These are richly supplied with blood capillaries formed from the pulmonary veins and arteries. The oxygen diffused into the blood across the moist respiratory surface and combines loosely with a respiratory pigment, the *haemoglobin* (present in red blood corpuscles) to form an unstable compound, the *oxyhaemoglobin.* Similarly carbon dioxide diffused out into the lungs from blood capillaries across the respiratory surface. A similar exchange takes place during cutaneous and bucco-pharyngeal respirations. The oxygenated blood distributes the oxygen to various tissues of the body. The oxyhaemoglobin breaks up into its components, the oxygen for the use of tissue and haemoglobin is reduced. The transportation of oxygen from respiratory surface to the tissues and of carbon dioxide from tissues to the respiratory surface is known as *external respiration.*

$$\underset{\text{(Haemoglobin)}}{Hb_4} + \underset{\text{(Oxygen)}}{4O_2} \rightarrow \underset{\text{Oxyhaemoglobin}}{Hb_4O_8}$$

The oxygen is utalized by the tissue for the oxidation of food-stuff to obtain energy. The end product of oxidation are carbon dioxide, water with liberation of energy. This process is known as *internal respiration* or *tissue respiration.*

Glucose and glycogen are the food-stuffs which are generally used for oxidation. Glycogen is first converted to glucose and then glucose into water, carbon dioxide and energy.

$$C_6H_{12}O_6 + 6O_2 \rightarrow 6O_2 + 6H_2O + \text{Energy (686 Kcal/mole)}$$

The release of energy and liberation of carbon dioxide in the tissue is not a simple process. It takes place through many chemical reactions in the presence of specific enzymes. It will be too much to describe all the reactions taking place in tissue respiration. In brief, within each cell glucose is first metabolized to pyruvic acid and then, if oxygen supply is there, to carbon dioxide and water. It is when hydrogen atoms are combined with oxygen that most of energy is released in cell. By storing energy in the molecules of adenosine triphosphate (ATP), cell can utalize its energy for various activities.

Transportation of carbon dioxide

As a result of tissue respiration carbon dioxide is formed. Which is toxic in higher concentration. It must be eliminated from the body. Three methods are employed for its transportation to the lungs.

(i) *As carbonic acid.* It dissolves in the water of plasma so as to form carbonic acid. It is very toxic to the animal. With circulation of blood it is brought to the lungs. Only 10% of carbon-dioxide combines with water.

$$CO_2 + H_2O \rightarrow H_2CO_3 \text{ (Carbonic acid).}$$

(ii) *As carbamino compound.* About 10% of carbon dioxide is transported as carbamino compounds. It combines directly with the amino groups ($-NH_2$) of haemoglobin to form *carbaminohaemoglobin.*

$$CO_2 + Hb\,NH_2 \rightarrow \text{HbNHCOOH (Carbaminohaemoglobin).}$$

(iii) *As bicarbonates.* About 80% of carbon dioxide is transported by this method. Here carbon dioxide forms bicarbonates in plasma as well as in blood corpuscles. As carbon dioxide enters the blood corpuscles from tissues, it combines with water to form carbonic acid (H_2CO_3) which dissociates to H^+ and HCO_3^- diffuses into plasma and forms sodium or potassium bicarbonate with sodium (Na^+) or potassium ions (K^+).

$$Na^+ + HCO_3^- \rightarrow NaHCO_3 \text{ (sodium bicarbonate)}$$
$$K^+ + HCO_3^- \rightarrow KHCO_3 \text{ (Potassium bicarbonate)}$$

Liberation of carbon dioxide in lungs

Thus carbon dioxide is carried to lungs in the form of carbonic acid, carbamino compounds and bicarbonates. Due to a higher tension of carbon dioxide in lung capillaries than the lung alveoli, carbondioxide is given off from blood into the alveoli as :

(i) $\underset{\text{(Carbonic acid)}}{H_2CO_3} \xrightarrow{\text{carbonic anhydrase}} H_2O + CO_2$

(ii) $\underset{\text{(Carbaminohaemoglobin)}}{Hb\ NHHCOOH} \xrightarrow{\text{Increase oxyhaemoglobin}} \underset{\text{(Haemoglobin)}}{HbNH_2} + CO_2\uparrow$

(iii) $\underset{\text{(Sodium bicarbonate)}}{2NaH\ CO_3} \xrightarrow{\text{Acidity due to oxyhaemoglobin}} \underset{\text{(Sodium carbonate)}}{Na_2CO_3} + H_2O + CO_2$

8

Circulatory System

The circulatory system or *blood vascular system* including heart, blood vessels and blood; and *lymphatic systems* including lymph vessels and lymph. The blood carries oxygen collected in the respiratory system, nutrients from the digestive system, hormones from endocrine glands, waste products of metabolism be removed in suitable excretory organs. Lymph channels collect interstitial tissue fluid not taken up by the bloodstream and emulsified fats absorbed in the small intestine and pour into the large venous channels of the blood vascular system.

BLOOD VASCULAR SYSTEM

The blood vascular system includes the heart, blood vessels and blood.

Heart

External Structure

The heart appears to be a conical muscular structure lying in the midventral line at the level of fore-limbs. It is reddish contractile structure enclosed in a double walled thin bag known as *pericardium*. The outer layer is known as *parietal layer* and the inner which is closely applied to heart is *visceral layer*. Between two layers is a space, the *pericardial cavity*, filled with a protective and lubricating fluid, the *pericardial fluid*. The pericardial fluid prevents desiccation of the heart and protects it from external shocks.

Although the heart is five chambered but conventionally, the heart is taken to comprise of *auricles*, the *ventricle* only. On this basis, the heart is three-chambered in frog;other two chambers, the *sinus venosus* and *truncus arteriosus* are also directly connected with auricles and ventricle.

A small and faint, longitudinal interauricular furrow is well distinct which divides the auricle into right and *left auricles* or *atria*. The ventricle is a undivided part. The sinus venosus is large, triangular, thin walled structure situated on the dorsal side of heart. The sinus venosus opens into right auricle. Three large veins, two *precavals* and a *post caval* open into sinus venosus. The truncus arteriosus is a small, thick walled and cylindrical in structure lying in ventral side of right auricle. Anteriorly it splits into *right* and *left aortic arches.*

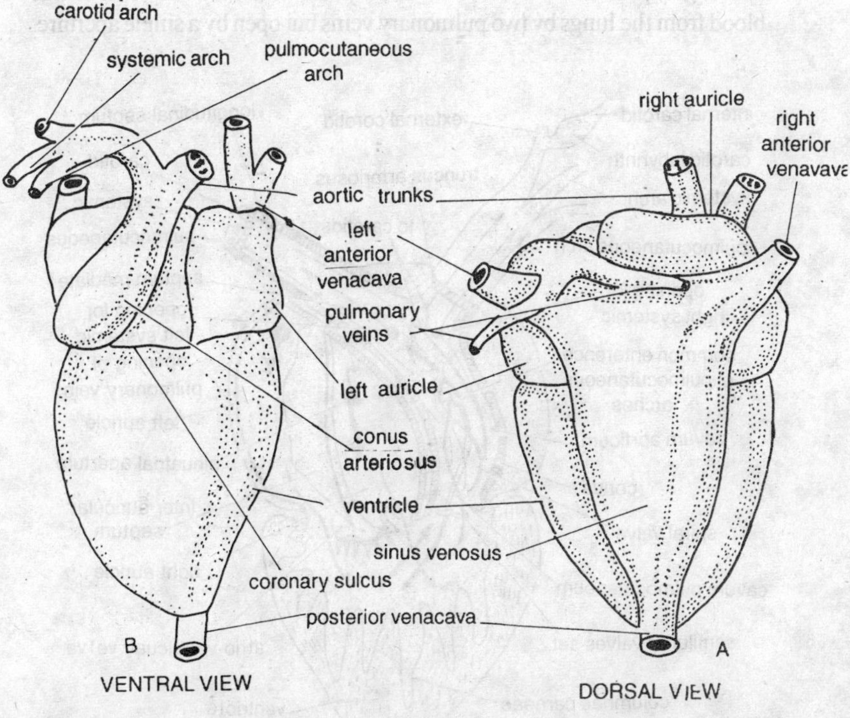

Fig. 8.1. *Rana.* External feature of heart, A—Dorsal view and B—Ventral view.

Internal Structure

The heart wall is composed of three layers-the outer most is *epicardium* composed of visceral pericardium;inner *endocardium* composed of a thin epithelial membrane having some smooth muscle fibres and many blood vessels covering the cavities of heart;and the *middle myocardium* composed of cardiac muscles and forms the main bulk of heart. The cardiac muscles are voluntary muscles in structure but involuntary in function.

Two auricles are separated from one another by a septum known as *inter-auricular septum.* The right auricle is bigger than the left and possesses a large oval opening known as *sinu-atrial aperture* through which sinus venosus opens into it. The opening is guarded by two lip-like valves, the *sinu-atrial valves.* These valves check the back flow of blood into sinus venosus. The left auricle also possesses a small aperture, the *opening of pulmonary veins*, near the septum. It has no valves. It brings blood from the lungs by two pulmonary veins but open by a single aperture.

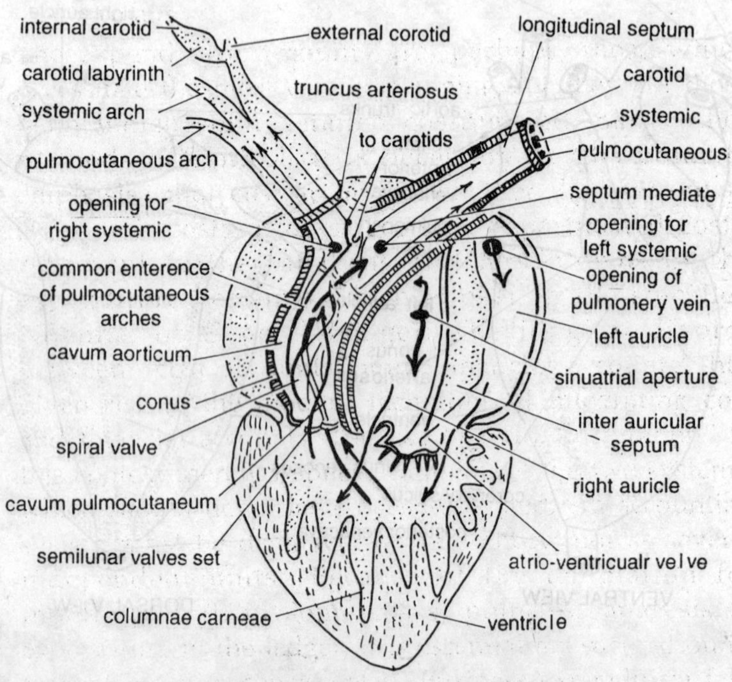

Fig. 8.2. *Rana.* Internal structure of heart.

Both the atria open into the ventricle by a common aperture, the *auriculo-ventricular aperture* located just beneath the inter-auricular septum. This aperture is guarded by four valves. These are flap-like known as *auriculo-ventricular valves.* Two valves are larger and two are very small. The large valves arise from dorsal and ventral borders of the aperture. Several slender, but strong and elastic cords of fibres called *chordae tendineae* connect the larger valves with the muscular wall of ventricle. The smaller valves arise from the lateral walls of the auriculo-ventricular aperture. They lack chordae tendineae. These valves open towards the ventricle only and prevents back flow of blood from ventricle to the auricles. The chordae tendineae check the valves from being pushed into the auricle by too much pressure in the ventricle.

The ventricle is triangular in form. Externally it is separated from auricles by a faint transverse groove, the *auriculo-ventricular groove*. Its inner surface is very uneven due to presence of ridges and depressions. The ridges are known as *columnae carneae* and the depressions as the *fissures*.

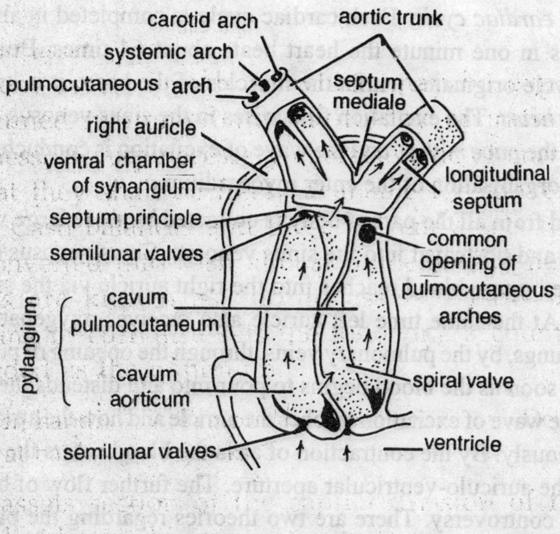

Fig. 8.3. *Rana*. Detailed structure of truncus arteriosus in ventral view.

Truncus arteriosus runs obliquely across the right auricle. The ventricle opens into the truncus and this opening is guarded by three *semilunar valves* whose edges point towards the truncus. The truncus has a small cavity which is divided into two unequal regions-a large proximal region known as *conus arteriosus* or *pylangium* and a short distal *bulbus arteriosus* or *synangium*. The junction of the conus arteriosus and the bulbus arteriosus is also guarded by four semilunar valves which are in two pairs; one pair guards the *systemo-carotid* and other pair to *pulmo-cutaneous*. The pylangium has a spirally-twisted longitudinal fold known as the *spiral valve*. It remains attached to the pylangium wall dorsally but its ventral edge is free. Thus the *spiral valve* divides the cavity of pylangium incompletely into two halves, a right *cavum aorticum* and left *pulmocutaneum*. Cavum aorticum curves round to the left to become dorsal and pulmocutaneum curves round to the right to become ventral. The synangium is also divided by a horizontal septum into a *dorsal* and a *ventral* chamber. Cavum aorticum opens into the ventral chamber which communicates anteriorly with the systemic and carotid arteries. The pulmocutaneum opens into the dorsal chamber and communicate anteriorly with pulmocutaneous arteries. The latter is guarded by *pulmocutaneous valve.*

Working of the heart

The contraction or *systole* and relaxation or *diastole* of the heart is known as *cardiac cycle.* Each cardiac cycle is completed in about 0.94 secs. Thus in one minute the heart beats about 64 times. Because the cardiac cycle originates within the muscles of the heart, it is known the *myogenic heart.* The excitation first arises in the sinus venosus, thus it is known as the *pace maker,* and the wave of excitation is conducted via the syncytial organisation of the enter myocardium.

Blood from all the part of body is collected by three large veins, the precavals and postcaval into the sinus venosus. Sinus venosus contracts so that the impure blood reaches into the right auricle via the sinu-atrial aperture. At the same time left auricle also receives oxygenated blood from the lungs, by the pulmonary veins, through the opening of pulmonary veins. As soon as the blood begins to pour into and distends the walls of auricle, the wave of excitation reaches the auricle and now the atria contract simultaneously. By the contraction of atria the blood enters the ventricle through the auriculo-ventricular aperture. The further flow of blood is a matter of controversy. There are two theories regarding the passage of blood through the ventricle and turncus arteriosus—old theory and new theory.

1. The old theory

It was proposed by *Brucke,* according to him a little mixing of blood takes place in the ventricle. Due to spongy nature of ventricle, the deoxygenated blood remains to the right side of ventricle and the oxygenated blood to the left side. The mixing occurs only in the blood of middle region. Now the right side of ventricle contracts first so that the blood is pumped into the truncus arteriosus to fill into the cavum pulmocutaneum. Then the left side of the ventricle contracts, the blood is now pumped into the truncus arteriosus to fill in cavum aorticum. Finally, the pylangium of truncus contracts and ventricle relaxes. By this contraction the impure or deoxygenated blood of cavum pulmocutaneum passes into two pulmocutaneous arches through the dorsal chamber of synangium.

Simultaneously the mixed blood of cavum aorticum passes into the systemic arch and pure blood to common carotid arches through the ventral chamber of synangium.

This sequence is maintained by the (i) spiral valve (ii) high pressure in pulmocutaneous arch and (iii) by *carotid labyrinth* present in the carotid arch.

This theory is now completely discarded.

2. New theory

The new theory is put-forward by *Van der Vael* (1923) and *Foxon* (1953). According to them the complete mixing of blood takes place in the ventricle and this mixed blood is forced into the truncus arteriosus from ventricle. The truncus arteriosus distributes this blood by the three aortic arches into various parts of body. This view is supported by the following facts—that :

(i) The blood flows into the three pairs of arches simultaneously and not one after the other as suggested in old theroy.

(ii) The pressure of blood in the three pairs of aortic arches is same as recorded by manometer.

(iii) Mixing of blood does not affect the supply of oxygen to the various parts of the body because due to aquatic respiration (cutaneous and bucco-pharyngeal respiration) the veins are containing more oxygenated blood than the one which comes from the lungs into the left auricle during pulmonary respiration. Thus sinus venosus contains more oxygenated blood.

According to this theory the spiral valve in the *truncus arteriosus* and the interauricular septum have become functionless in frogs. However, the finding of *Foxon* does not seem to apply equally well to all kinds of frogs. Studies of *DeLong* (1962) indicate that the corotid arches receive oxygenated blood, pulmocutaneous arch with impure and systemic arch with mixed blood. *Nigam* (1975) has the same opinion, according to him due to contraction of truncus arteriosus the blood is forced with same pressure into the three parts of aortic arches simultaneously. Now there is slight separation of pure, impure and mixed blood in truncus.

Actually how the selective distribution of blood takes place is still of a point of controversy. According to some workers, it is the spiral valve that helps in selective distribution but other workers believe that it is not responsible for selective distribution. It is only to prevent the collapsing of truncus arteriosus.

Blood Vessels

The vessels that carries blood from heart to various parts of body are known as *arteries* forming the *arterial system.* Other vessels that bring blood from various parts of body towards the heart are known as *veins* and they form *venous system.* The arteries and veins give rise fine branches known as *arterioles* and *venules* which are united by *capillaries.*

Arterial system

The arterial system starts from the truncus arteriosus. It divides into two large-*right* and *left trunks.* Each trunk further divides and gives rise to three *aortic arches* known as 1. *Common carotid arch,* 2. *Systemic arch* and 3. *Pulmocutaneous arch.*

1. Common carotid arch

It is short vessel running forward and bifurcates to form an *external carotid* and an *internal carotid.* It supplies blood to the head.

(i) *External Carotid.* It is smaller inner branch supplies blood to the tongue, hyoid and adjacent parts. It is also known as lingual artery.

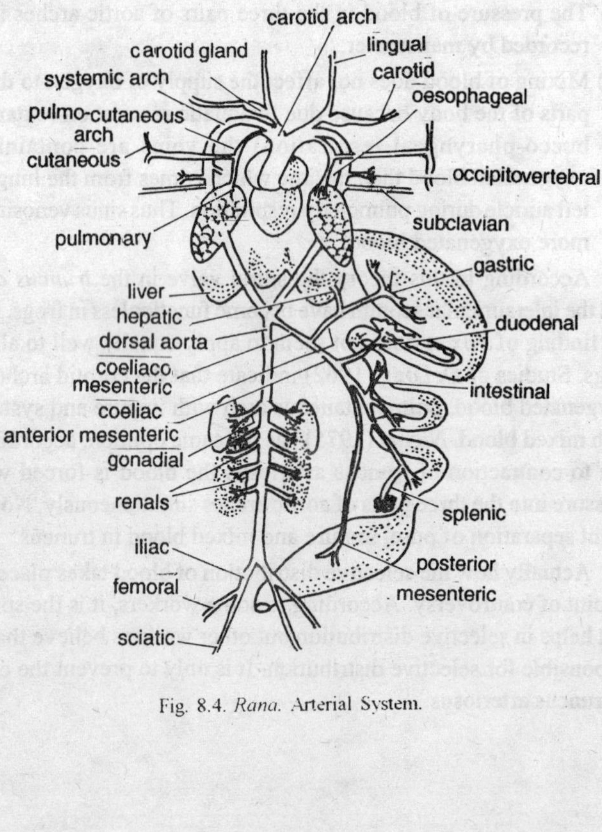

Fig. 8.4. *Rana.* Arterial System.

(ii) *Internal Carotid.* It is larger outer vessel. It bears a knob-like structure, the *carotid labyrinth,* which is probably as sense organ controlling blood pressure in the internal carotid. It is divided into three branches. a *palatine* which supplies blood to the roof of buccal cavity; an *opthalmic* to the eye and a *cerebral* to the brain.

2. Systemic Arch

Immediately after its origin, it runs outwards and backwards and meets with the fellow of the other side in mid-dorsal line to form a *dorsal aorta.* In its course each systemic gives off three arteries :

(i) *Oesophageal.* It is a small artery supplies blood to the oesophagus.

(ii) *Occipitovertebral.* It sends one branch to posterior part of head and other branch to the vertebral column and spinal cord.

(iii) *Sub-clavian.* It is a large vessel supplying blood to the shoulder region and extends into the fore limbs as *branchial artery.*

Dorsal aorta

It is formed by the union of two systemic arches. It runs posteriorly lying mid-dorsal just beneath the vertebral column. Following branches arise from it :

(i) *Coeliaco-mesentric.* It is an unpaired vessel and divided into an *anterior mesenteric* and a *coeliac* arteries. The anterior mesenteric supplies blood to duodenum by *duodenal* artery, to spleen by *splenic* artery and to intestine by *intestinal* artery.

The *coeliac* supplies blood to stomach by *gastric artery* and to liver by *hepatic artery.*

(ii) *Gonadial.* These are a pair of arteries to gonads, called *spermatic* in male and *ovarian* in female.

(iii) *Renal.* These are 4 or 5 pairs of short arteries that leave the dorsal aorta while it passing between two kidneys. They supply blood to kidneys.

(iv) *Posterior mesenteric.* It arises from the posterior end of dorsal aorta behind the last pair of renal arteries. It goes to rectum. Sometimes it arises from anterior mesenteric artery.

(v) *Iliac.* The dorsal aorta finally bifurcated posteriorly into two iliacs. Each iliac artery gives off following branches.

(a) *Epigastric* to the ventral body wall.

(b) *Recto-vesicular* to the rectum and urinary bladder.

(c) *Femoral.* It extends along the outer side of the leg and supplies blood to the hip and upper thigh.

(d) *Sciatic.* It runs along the inner side of the leg and supplies blood to the shank and foot.

3. Pulmocutaneous arch

It is a quite stout vessel and divides into two branches :

(i) *Pulmonary.* It is stout but short vessel and supplies blood to lung of its side.

(ii) *Cutaneous.* It is long, slender artery. It extends towards the shoulder and supplies blood to the dorsal and lateral body wall of trunk region.

Venous System

The venous system is divided into four parts :

(1) Venae cavae, (2) Renal portal system, (3) Hepatic portal system and (4) Pulmonary veins.

1. Venae cavae

Deoxygenated blood from all the parts of the body is brought to the sinus venosus by three large vessels, known as venae cavae, two *anterior venae cavae* and a single *posterior vena cava.*

(i) *Anterior Venae Cavae.* These are short, thick vessels. Each is formed by the union of three veins.

(a) *External Jugular vein.* It is formed by the union of *lingual vein* from the floor of bucco-pharyngeal cavity and a *mandibular vein* from the lower jaw.

(b) *Innominate.* It is also formed by the union of an *internal jugular* vein from the brain, eye etc. and a *scapular* vein from the shoulder and back of the arm.

(c) *Sub-clavian.* It is formed by the *brachial* vein from fore-limbs and a *musculo-cutaneous* vein from the skin and muscles of lateral, and dorsal sides of the abdomen, mucous membrane of the buccopharyngeal cavity and muscles of the head.

(ii) *Postcaval.* It is long and thick vessel. Its posterior end is formed between the kidneys. Anteriorly it opens into the sinus venosus. It receives following veins.

(a) *Renal Veins.* There are five or six pairs of veins carrying blood from kidneys into the postcaval.

(b) *Gonadial Veins.* There are a pair of veins arise from the gonads and open into postcaval infront of first pair of renal veins.

(c) *Hepatic Veins.* The postcaval then runs forwards dorsally to the liver and receives a pair of short hepatic veins from liver.

2. Renal portal system

The venous blood returns from hind-limbs and certain other posterior parts of body emptied in the kidneys. The nitrogenous wastes are excreted here before the blood returned to the heart.

From each hind-limb the blood is collected by two veins :

(i) *Femoral vein* from outer side of the limb.

(ii) *Sciatic vein* from inner side of the limbs.

The femoral vein as it enters the abdominal cavity is divided into two branches, a *renal portal vein* on outer side and a *pelvic vein* on inner side. The renal portal vein unites with the sciatic vein and while running along the outer surface of kidney of its side it receives a *drosal-lumbar vein.* The dorso-lumbar receives blood from lumbar region. The renal portal vein enters the kidney.

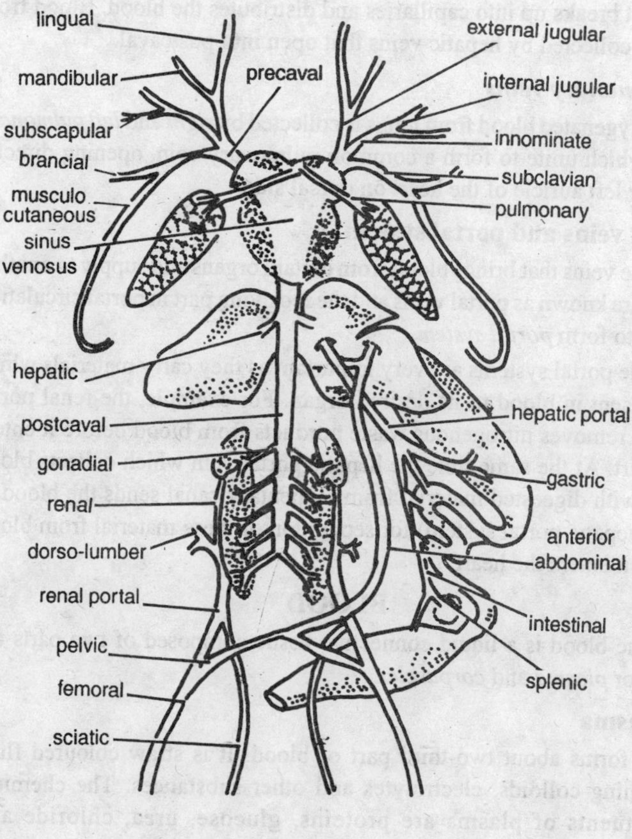

Fig. 8.5. *Frog.* Venous System.

The pelvic veins unite to form a median ventral vein known as *anterior abdominal vein* which terminates in the liver. On its way forwards, it receives a *vesicular vein* from the urinary bladder and several veins from abdominal muscles. The anterior abdominal vein joins the hepatic portal vein before it opens into the liver.

3. Hepatic portal system

A large hepatic portal vein is formed by the fusion of several branches from alimentary canal-*oesophageal* vein from oesophagus, *gastric* vein from stomach, *duodeno-pancreatic* vein from duodenum and pancreas, *intestinal* vein from the ileum, *splenic* from spleen and *rectal* from rectum.

The hepatic portal vein runs in the mesentery and enters the liver, where it breaks up into capillaries and distributes the blood. Blood from liver is collected by hepatic veins that open into postcaval.

4. Pulmonary veins

Oxygenated blood from lungs is collected by *right* and *left pulmonary veins* which unite to form a common pulmonary vein, opening directly into the left auricle of the heart on dorsal side.

Portal veins and portal system

The veins that brings blood from certain organs and supply to another organ are known as portal veins and the receiving part in portal circulation is said to form *portal system.*

The portal systems are very important as they carry materials which are present in blood to its desired organ. For example, the renal portal system removes nitrogenous waste porducts from blood before it enters the heart. At the same time the hepatic portal vein which collects blood along with digeested material from alimentary canal sends the blood to liver (hepatic portal system) for separation of these material from blood before it enters the heart.

BLOOD

The blood is a liquid connective tissue composed of two parts the liquid or *plasma* and *corpuscles.*

A. Plasma

It forms about two-third part of blood. It is straw coloured fluid containing colloids, electrolytes and other substances. The chemical constituents of plasma are proteins, glucose, urea, chloride and bicarbonates of sodium, potassium etc. The inorganic constituents are sodium, potassium, calcium, magnesium etc. The water constitutes about

90% of plasma. The blood pressure of aorta-systolic is 22mm-30mm/Hg and diastotic pressure is 11mm/Hg.

B. Blood Corpuscles

There are three types of corpuscles :

1. Erythrocytes or red blood corpuscles
2. Leucocytes or white blood corpuscles and
3. Thrombocytes

1. Erythrocytes

These are oval, flattened, biconvex and nucleated., The average size is about 22μ in length and 16μ in width. The number of erythrocytes varies from 250,000-450,000 per cubic millimeter of blood. The life-span of erythrocytes is probably 100 days. They bear the respiratory pigment *haemoglobin*. They are removed from blood by the liver and spleen. The new cells are formed in the spleen in adults but in tadpole they are formed in kidneys. The liver does not take any part in their formation (in frogs).

2. Leucocytes

These are colourless, nucleated and mostly amoeboid cells. Their average number is 5000-7500 per cubic millimeter in blood. They are of two types on the basis of presence or absence of granules:

(i) Granulocytes and (ii) Agranulocytes

(i) *Granulocytes.* These cells possess granules in the cytoplasm. The nucleus is made up of several lobes and they form about 70% of total leucocyte counts. They are formed in bone marrow. They are of three types:

(a) *Basophils.* Their nuclei are bilobed and cytoplasm contians large granules. They form only 0.5% of differential counts. They can be stained with basic dyes.

(b) *Eosinophils.* The nucleus is also bilobed and they form about 3% of differential counts. They can be stained with acidic dyes.

(c) *Neutrophils.* The nucleus is multilobed. They form about 67% of differential counts. They are phagocytic in nature.

(ii) *Agranular Leucocytes.* Each cell has a large nucleus and clear cytoplasm. They are of two types:

(a) *Lymphocytes.* They form about 28% and are produced in spleen.

(b) *Monocytes.* They form about 1-3% and each possesses bean shaped nucleus.

3. Thrombocytes

They are known as *spindle cells*. They are nucleated and possess granules in the cytoplasm. They release an enzyme ***thrombin*** when a blood vessel is injured. Thrombin changes soluble protein of blood, ***fibrinogen***, into an unsoluble *fibrin*. Fibrin forms clotting of blood and prevents further loss of blood. Bonc marrow, spleen, liver, kidneys etc. give rise to spindle cells. Their life-span is 2-3 days.

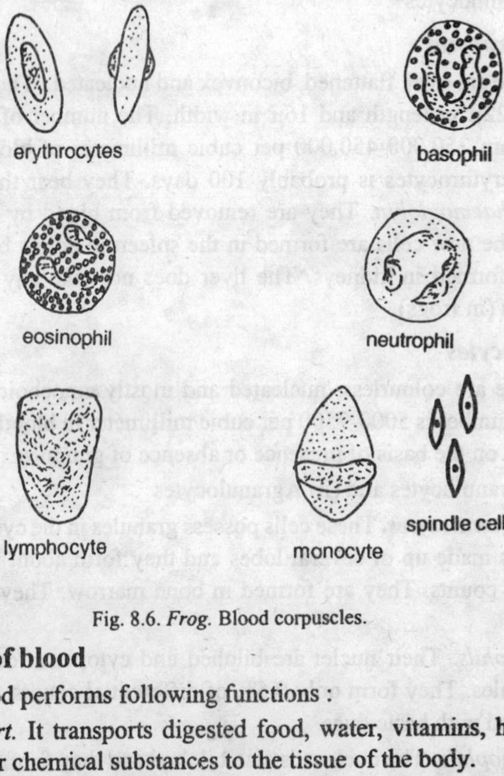

Fig. 8.6. *Frog*. Blood corpuscles.

Functions of blood

The blood performs following functions :

1. *Transport.* It transports digested food, water, vitamins, hormones and other chemical substances to the tissue of the body.
2. *Respiration.* Blood carries oxygen from the lungs to the tissues and carbon dioxide from the tissues to the lungs.
3. *Excretion.* Excretory products like urea and other nitrogenous waste products are carried to kidneys from where they are discharged outside of body.
4. *Regulation of body temperature.* Blood serves to regulate the body temperature as it carries heat from one place to another where heat is lost.

5. As the blood is provided with leucocytes and the circulating antibodies, the leucocytes help in destroying the harmful micro-organisms and the antibodies neuterlizes their effects. Blood also produces antitoxins to neuterlize the effects of toxins produced by the parasites present in the body.
6. Blood aids in the healing of wounds. By clotting it helps in preventing excessive loss of blood.
7. The blood helps in the maintenance of normal acid-base balance of the body through its proteins, electrolytes and colloids.
8. The macrophages of tadpole helps in metamorphosis which phagocytose tissues of tail, gills etc.

LYMPHATIC SYSTEM

During exchange of material between tissue and blood, comes out from capillaries into the extracellular space surrounding the tissue cells. The fluid that is filtered out is called the *lymph.* About 90-99% of this fluid is returned back from the space into their venous region. The remaining 1-10% of the filtered out fluid, better to say lymph, is returned by an additional system of vessels, forming a system the *lymphatic system.*

The lymphatic system is very primitive in frogs and it is composed of :

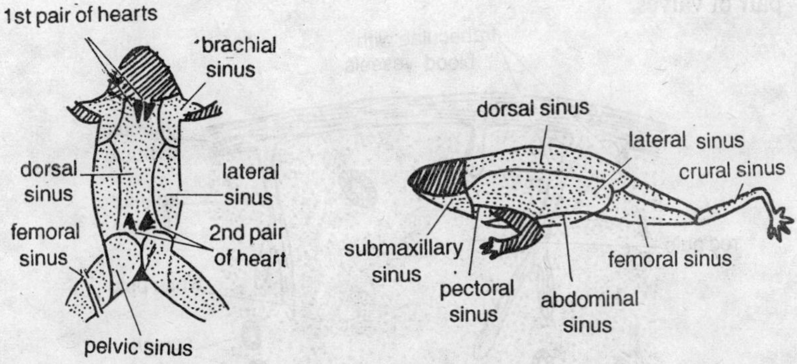

Fig. 8.7. *Rana.* Lymphatic System.

1. Lymph vessels

In frog, there are no regular lymphatic vessels like mammals. These are very thin-walled vessels of various sizes. The lymphatic vessels open into the venous system thus returns lymph back to the blood. The lymph capillaries are thin walled and delicate and are composed of a very thin layer of endothelial cells held together by an intercellular substance. They lack power of contractility. The flow of lymph depends upon contraction of muscles of that region and the pressure generated by filteration of fluid from capillaries.

2. Lymph sinuses

In frog some large vessels become dilated to form huge lymph sinuses. The major lymph sinuses are:

(a) *Sub-cutaneous sinuses.* There are several sinuses present under the skin. These are separated from each other by septa of connective tissue. The main sinuses are brachial lymph sinus, dorsal and lateral trunk lymph sinuses, pelvic lymph sinuses, femoral lymph sinuses.

(b) *Sub-vertebral lymph sinus.* One of the moist important sinus located beneath vertebral column and above kidneys.

3. Lymph hearts

The lymph hearts are two pairs composed of thin walled, transparent, contractile and muscular sac-like structures. Internally they are lined with endothelium and invested with skeletal muscle fibres and connective tissue. The first pair is located behind the transverse process of third vertebra and empty into sub-scapular vein of their side. The other pair lie in the region of urostyle and open into femoral vein. Each heart possesses one pair of valves.

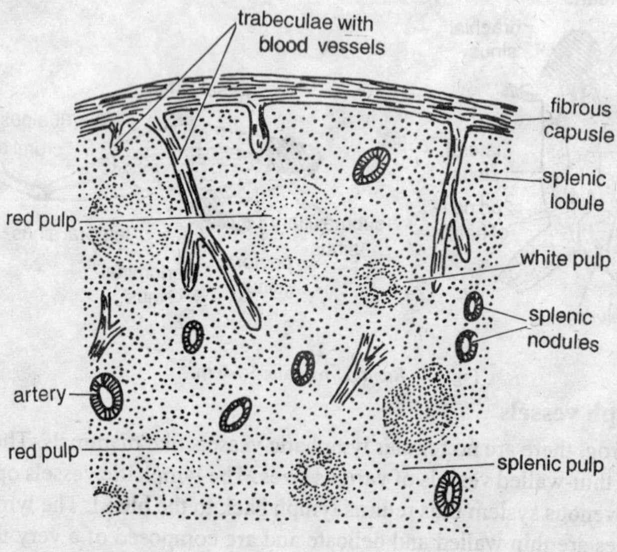

Fig. 8.8. *Rana.* T.S. of Spleen.

4. Lymph

The lymph is a filtered out fluid from blood capillaries. It differs from blood in that it lacks the red blood corpuscles and contains fewer proteins. It contains a number of enzymes derived both from blood and tissues. It functions as a middle man passing over food and oxygen to the tissues and waste products and carbon dioxide to blood.

5. Spleen

It is a dark red, small, rounded body lies near rectum in the mesentery. It is a solid mass of the reticulo-endothelial tissue in the body, covered with fibrous capsule.

It destroys the worn out R.B.Cs. and produce new R.B.Cs. and W.B.Cs. by active cell divisions.

9

Nervous System

The cells of living organisms are excitable i.e. they possess the ability to respond to stimuli. This excitability is expressed in a variety of ways such as muscle contracts, nerve cells conduct impulse, gland cells secrete their products etc. A positive response to a stimulus is known as *excitation* and a negative response as *inhibition.* The nerve cells or *neurons* of nervous system and the gland cells of the endocrine system are the basic structural and functional units of the two integrating systems of the body. These cells are adapted to receive and to process stimuli and then to respond to the stimuli by releasing chemical secretions that can influence each other and other cells of the body. Thus in this way the two systems interact. The nervous system is the high speed co-ordinator and can be divided into three categories :

I. The Central Nervous System.

II. The Peripheral Nervous System.

III. The Autonomic Nervous System.

I. CENTRAL NERVOUS SYSTEM

The central nervous system comprises of the *brain* and *Spinal cord* surrounded by connective tissue membranes called *meninges.*

Brain

The brain is an elongated, somewhat flattened whitish structure lies in the cranical cavity of the skull. It is surrounded by two meninges.

Meninges. The inner meninx is known as *pia-arachnoid membrane.* It is highly vascular and very thin, and lies in close contact with the brain. The outer membrane is known as *duramater.* It is very thick, tough but less vascular. It lies towards the lining of cranial cavity. Between pia-arachnoid and duramater there is a very narrow space known as *sub-dural space.* Likewise an other space is present between durameter and the lining of cranial cavity. It is known as *epidural space.* Both the spaces are filled with *cerebrospinal fluid,* which protects brain from external shocks.

Pia-arachnoid membrane form *tela choroidea.* Folds from tela choroidea project into the third and fourth ventricles of brain to form *anterior* and *posterior choroid plexuses.*

Structure of brain

The brain or encephelon is divisible into three parts:

1. Fore-brain or *Prosencephalon.*
2. Mid-brain or *Mesencephalon*
3. Hind-brain or *Rhòmbencephalon*

1. Fore-brain or Prosencephalon

It is divided into two regions, the *telencephalon* or *end-brain* and *thalamencephalon* or *diencephalon.* The end-brain is composed of two parts *rhinencephalon* or *olfactory lobes* and *cerebral hemispheres.* Thus the fore brain is sub-divided into three parts- The olfactory lobes, cerebral hemispheres and diencephalon.

(i) *Olfactory lobes.* They form the anterior most part of the brain. Both the lobes are united with each other except for a small anterior part, extended upto the lateral border of nasal organs. Anteriorly a pair of olfactory nerves arise from them. These are the first cranial nerve. Each lobe contains a cavity or ventricle known as *rhinocoel* or *olfactory ventricle.*

(ii) *Cerebral hemispheres.* They form the middle region of forebrain, and lie behind the olfactory lobes. Each cerebral hemisphere is large, smooth, ovoid body slightly broader at the posterior end then the anterior end. Both the lobes are separated from each other by a deep median dorsal longitudinal groove. The cavity of each hemisphere is known as *lateral ventricle* or *paracoel.* Anteriorly, the paracoel are continuous with the rhinocoel. The lateral ventricles are connected posteriorly with each other as well as with ventricle of diencephalon or diocoel through a small aperture called *foramen* of *Monro* or *interventricular foramen.* The roof of paracoel is known as *pallium* which is thicker than the pallium of fishes. More cells from the grey matter have moved to the peripheral positions. The ventro-lateral walls and floor of paracoel are known as *corpora striata.* These are very thick. The two corpora striata are interconnected by a tract of transverse fibres known as *anterior commissure.*

(iii) *Diencephalon.* It is an unpaired, small rectangular structure lies between cerebral hemispheres and mid-brain. The cavity of diencephalon is known as *diacoel* or *third ventricle* which is connected with paracoel

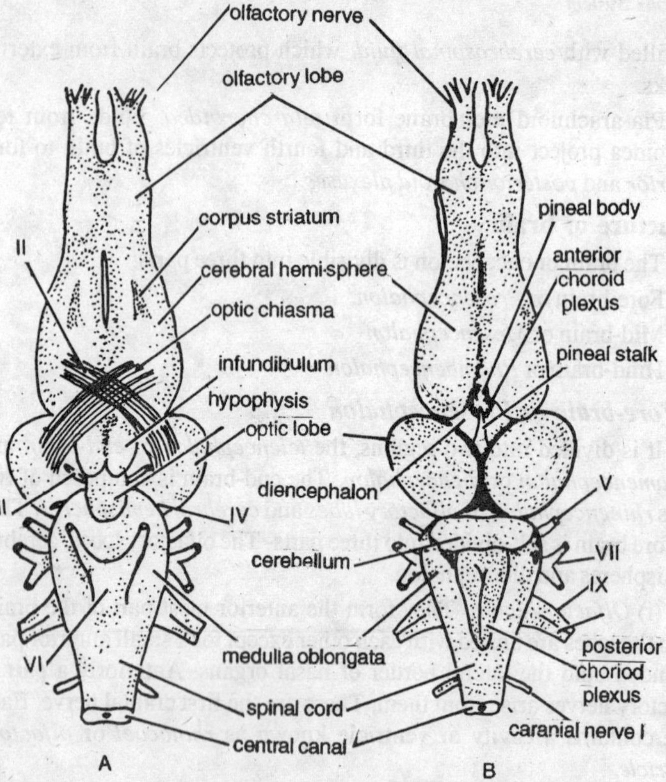

Fig. 9.1. Brain of the *Rana*. A—Dorsal view. B—Ventral view.

by foramen of Monro. The roof of diacoel is known as *epithalamus.* The epithalamus is thin and along with pia-arachnoid membrane constitutes *anterior choroid plexus* which are irregular, branched and highly vascular structures in the diacoel. It forms cerebrospinal fluid. The side walls of diacoel are called *optic thalami.* These are very thick. The floor of the third ventricle is called as *hypothalamus.* On the ventral surface of the hypothalamus is the crosssing of two optic nerves coming from the eyes. It is known as *optic chiasma.* Just behind the hypothalamus gives out a median bilobed structure known as *infundibulum.* Another smaller and oval outgrowth, the *hypophysis* occurs just behind the infundibulum. The infundibulum and hypophysis together form the *pituitary gland* and functions as an endocrine gland.

The dorsal wall of diencephalon is projected upwards in the form of a hollow ridge known as *pineal stalk.* It bears a knob-like structure known as *pineal body*. The pineal body is present in tadpole larva but during metamorphosis it separates from the pineal stalk and shift to lie outside the skull beneath the dorsal skin of head as *brow spot*. It is apparently a vestige of what may at one time have been a third eye.

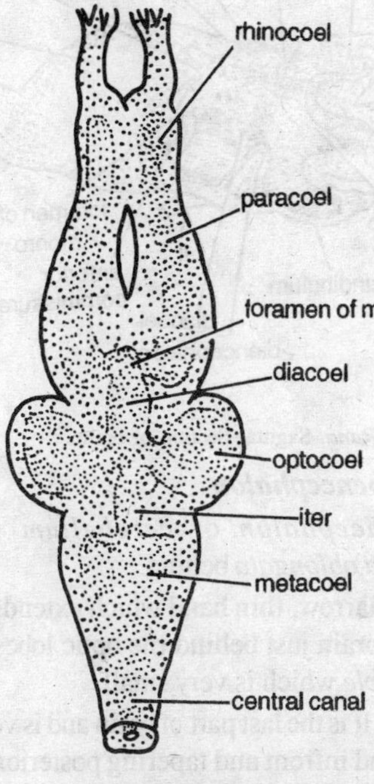

Fig. 9.2. *Rana*. Ventricles of brain.

Two transverse fibrous bands connect the two optic thalami together. These are a *dorsal commissure* infront and a *posterior commissure* behind.

2. Mid-brain or Mesencephalon

Two large prominent oval sac-like structures are situated on the dorsal side of brain. These are known as *optic lobes* or *corpora bigemina*. They are partly visible from the ventral side. Each lobe contains a cavity or ventricle known as *optocoel*. Both the optic ventricles open into a narrow median passage known as *iter* or *aqueduct of Sylvius*. The iter also connects the diocoel with fourth ventricle. Fibres of optic nerves, forming the optic thalami of diencephalon, terminate in the wall of optic lobes. The ventral and ventro-lateral walls are thickened due to presence of two fibrous bands known as *crura cerebri*. They serve to connect the fore-brain to hind-brain.

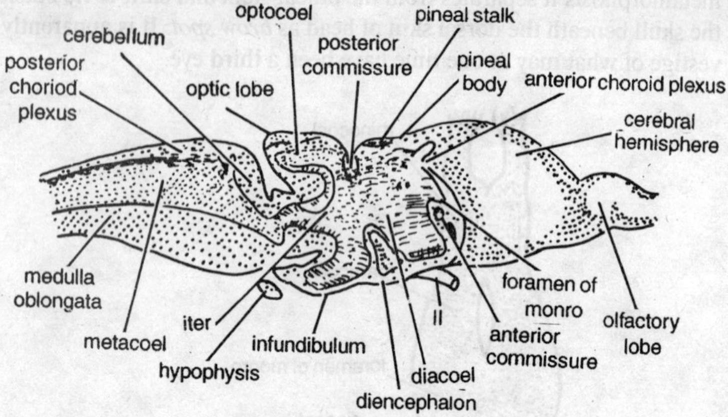

Fig. 9.3. *Rana*. Sagittal Section of brain.

3. Hind-brain or Rhombencephalon

It consist of *Metencephalon* or *cerebellum* infront and *Myelencephalon* or *medulla oblongata* behind.

(i) *Cerebellum*. It is a narrow, thin band which extends transversely upon the dorsal surface of brain just behind the optic lobes. Its cavity is known as *cerebellar ventricle* which is very small.

(ii) *Medulla oblongata*. It is the last part of brain and is very important. It is somewhat conical, broad infront and tapering posteriorly and passes into the spinal cord without any external line of demarcation. Its cavity or ventricle is known as *fourth ventricle* or *metacoel*. The metacoel communicates with the cavity of diocoel by iter anteriorly and with the central canal of spinal cord behind. The roof of metacoel is thin and with pia-arachnoid membrane it forms the *posterior choroid plexus*. The floor of metacoel is very thick.

Histology of brain

The brain is composed of two kinds of materials : the *grey matter* and *white matter*. The grey matter is greyish and compossed of cytons or cell bodies of nerve cells. supporting neuralgia cells and non-medullated basal and terminal parts of their axons. The white matter is composed of whitish and glistening medullated nerve fibres. The grey matter lies on the outer side and white towards the ventricles.

Functions. Various parts of brain are responsible for specific functions :

1. ***Olfactory lobes.*** They are the centre of olfection or smell. These are relatively small and help in detecting their food with the help of smell. If they are removed the power of smell is lost.

2. ***Cerebral hemispheres.*** These are the centres of voluntary actions of the body. They are also the centre of memory, though, and intelligence. Corpora striata regulates the body temperature in the cold-blooded animals.

3. ***Diencephalon.*** The optic thalami are the relay centre for sensory and motor impulses passing to and fro between cerebellum and other parts of brain. The hypothalamus is the centre of autonomic nervous system. It contains the centres which control hunger, sleep, temperature, sex etc. It also controls metabolism of fats, carbohydrates and proteins. The pineal and pituitary bodies are also present in diencephalon act as endocrine glands.

4. ***Mid-brain.*** It is the centre of sight as optic lobes are present. Besides it also maintain the body posture; crura cerebri of mid-brain serve to transmit motor impulses to limb muscles from cerebral hemispheres.

Mid-brain probably controls the muscles which help in breathing, croaking sound and grasping of female by male during breeding season probably also take place under the control of mid-brain.

5. ***Cerebellum.*** It works under the direction of cerebral hemispheres. Its primary function is to maintain body posture, orientation and equilibrium. It regulates the activities of voluntary muscles.

6. ***Medulla oblongata.*** It is the controlling centre of action of involuntary muscles like heart beat, breathing, gut peristalsis, swallowing of food, secretion of glands, blood pressure etc.

Spinal Cord

The portion of the neural tube which forms the spinal cord undergoes considerably less modifications than that forming the brain. It generally assumes the shape of more or less cylindrical, but slightly flattened, tube. Its anterior end is wider and continuous with the medulla oblongata through the foramen magnum of skull. The posterior end usually tapers down to a fine thread, the *filum terminale.* The entire spinal cord is safely enclosed in the continuous passage formed by the neural canals of successive vertebrae.

Like the brain, spinal cord is also surrounded by meninges. These meninges are similar as present over the brain. The outer is duramater and inner is pia-arachnoid membrane with epidural and sub-dural spaces, and filled with cerebro-spinal fluid.

The spinal cord is uniform except that two swellings which are seen in the regions of limbs. The swelling in the region of fore- limbs is known as *cervical enlargement* or *swelling* and other is *lumbar enlargement* in the region of hind-limbs. Since with the development of limbs, the nerve supply to these structures is increased, these enlargements are actually places in which greater numbers of neuron bodies are situated than are present at other levels of the spinal cord.

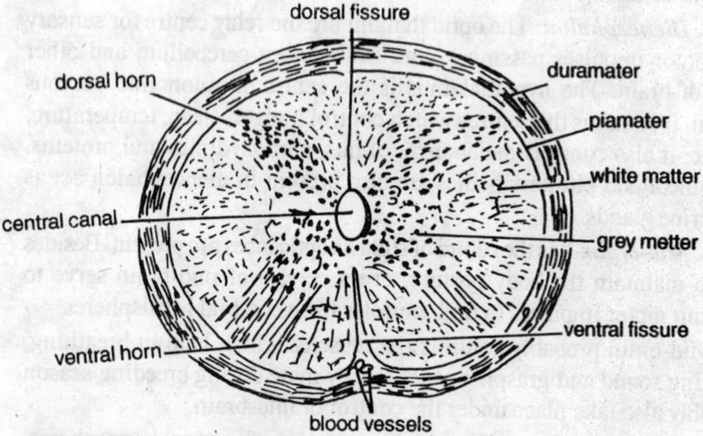

Fig. 9.4. *Rana*. T.S. of Spinal cord.

Internal structure

In the centre of spinal cord there is a canal known as *central canal* which is in communication with the metacoel. The central canal is lined with columnar ciliated epithelium and contains cerebro-spinal fluid. Around the central canal there are two matters, the *grey matter* and *white matter*. The grey matter being almost completely surounded by the white matter. The grey matter is in the form of a rectangular mass with projecting corners. These are known as *dorso-lateral* and *ventro-lateral horns*. These horns incompletely divide the white matter into dorsal, ventral and lateral zones called *funiculi*.

The grey matter contains neurons or nerve cells and their processes and supporting cells. the *neurogleal cells*. Besides. some non-medullated nerve fibres are also present. These fibres pass through dorsal and ventral horns into dorsal and ventral roots of spinal nerves. The white matter is chiefly composed of meduallated nerve fibres whcih are white in colour

The inner meninx i.e. pia-arachnoid membrane invaginates in the middle of dorsal and ventral surfaces of spinal cord to form *dorsal* and *ventral fissures.* Due to presence of these fissures the spinal cord is divided into lateral halves.

Functions of Spinal Cord. The spinal cord has two main functions :

1. It forms the connection between the brain and the spinal nerves as the stimuli received from the spinal nerves are conveyed to the brain.
2. It is the centre of different reflex actions taking place in the body.

II. PERIPHERAL NERVOUS SYSTEM

The nerves and ganglia which form connections with the central nervous system, and which are distributed to all parts of the body, comprise the peripheral nervous system. Connection with the central nervous system is mediated via *cranial* and *spinal nerves.* Thus the peripheral nervous system comprises :

1. Cranial nerves arising from the brain and
2. Spinal nerves arising from the spinal cord.

1. Cranial Nerves

In frogs there are 10 pairs of cranial nerves. In 1894 a new cranial nerve was discovered connecting the anterior end of cerebral hemispheres. This cranial nerve is designated as nerve O or the *terminal* nerve to avoid the confusion with other cranial nerves.

O. Terminal nerves

Each originates from the mucous membrane of the olfactory capsule and enters the cerebral hemisphere. It is a *sensory* nerve and bears one or more ganglia. The function of this nerve is not clear. It has been suggested that it may represent the remains of an anterior branchial nerve which long ago lost its significance.

I. Olfactory nerves

The first cranial nerve is composed of non-medullated fibres. These are purely *sensory* nerves. Their cyton lie in the olfactory epithelium and axons joins the olfactory lobes of brain. They carry the stimuli of smell to the brain.

II. Optic nerves

Each optic nerve consists of a bundle of *sensory* nerve fibres, the *cytons* of which are located in the retina of eye. The fibres grow down through the walls of the optic stalk, reaching the brain at the level of the diencephalon. The fibres of each nerve then cross and pass to the lateral geniculate bodies or to the optic tectum in the roof of the optic lobes. The point at which the nerves cross is called *optic chiasma.* The optic nerves convey impulses of the sight to brain.

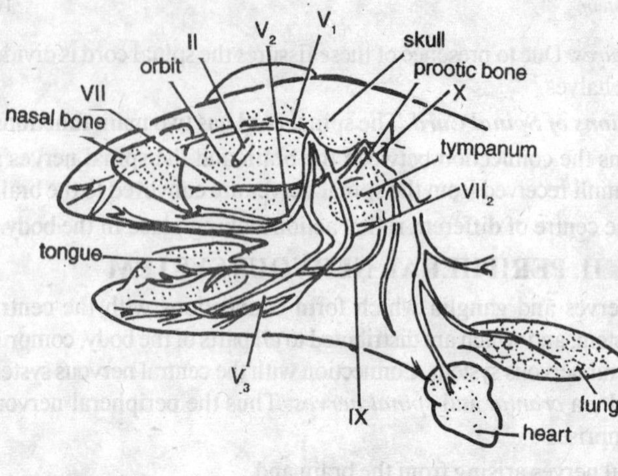

Fig. 9.5. *Rana*. Cranial nerves.

III. Occulomotor nerves

As its name indicates it is a *motor* nerve. They arise from the *crura cerebri* and are distributed to the inferior oblique, superior rectus, inferior rectus and internal rectus eye muscles. Some fibres also pass to the muscle (*levator palpebrae*) elevating the upper eye-lid.

IV. Trochlear or Pathetic nerves

The somatic *motor* trochlear nerve is the smallest of all the cranial nerves. They arise from the dorsal surface of the brain between the optic-lobes and cerebellum. Each then enters the orbit to supply the superior oblique muscles of the eye.

V. Trigeminal nerves

They are large nerve arising from the lateral sides of the anterior end of medulla oblongata. Near its point of origin it bears a large *Gasserian* or *semilunar ganglion*. Trigeminal is divided into three main branches as

V_1. *Opthalamic nerves*. It is a *sensory* nerve and smallest of the three branches. It supplies sensory fibres to the conjunctiva, cornea, iris, ciliary body, lacrymal glands, part of mucous membrane of the nose and the skin of the forehead, nose and eye lids.

V_2. *Maxillary nerves*. It is the main branch to the upper jaw and is *sensory* in nature. It supplies to the upper lip, side of the nose, lower eye-lid, teeth of upper jaw etc.

V_3. *Mandibular nerves*. It is a *mixed* nerve. Its somatic sensory portion is distributed to the lower lip and the teeth of lower jaw. The visceral motor fibres of the mandibular branch go directly to the muscles of lower jaws.

VI. Abducens nerves

There are purely *motor* nerves. They arise from the ventral side of medulla oblongata. Each supplies to the *external rectus* eye muscle. A branch of the abducens goes to the nictitating membrane.

VII. Facial nerves

These are *mixed* nerves arise from the lateral sides of medulla oblongata. Each facial nerve joins the *Gasserian ganglion* of its side and than gives rises two branches:

VII_1 Palatinus nerves. It is a *sensory* nerve from the olfactory chamber and buccopharyngeal cavity.

VII_2 Hyomandibularis nerves. It is a *motor* nerve to the muscles of lower jaw and tongue.

VIII. Auditory nerves

It is a *somatic* nerve. The auditory nerve comes from the lateral side of the medulla oblongata and supply the internal ear. Its ganglion is often inseparably fused with those of the trigeminal and facial nerves. These bring sensory impulses from internal ears.

IX Glossopharyngeal nerves

They are *mixed* nerves which arise from the sides of *medulla oblongata*. Each glossopharyngeal soon enters a *jugular ganglion* and then gives rise two branches : a sensory branch arises from the mucous membrane of tongue and pharynx which brings sensory impulses to brain; and a motor branch which soon joins the hyomandibular branch of fascial nerve of its side supplies hyoid apparatus and lower jaw muscles.

X. Vagus nerves

They are one of the most important cranial nerve perhaps of all the cranial nerves, because the preganglionic fibres of the parasympathetic portion of autonomic nervous system which they contain. Through these fibres, it controls vital activities as heart-beat, peristalsis of gut and respiratory movements. These are *mixed* nerves arises from the lateral sides of medulla oblongata. After its emergence it enters the *jugular* ganglion of its side along with glossopharyngeal. Then it gives rise a number of branches to various parts - The *laryngeal* branch goes to laryngo. tracheal chamber; *cardiac* branch to the heart; the *gastric* branch to the stomach and *pulmonary* branch to the lung.

2. Spinal Nerves

There are nine pairs or sometimes ten pairs of spinal nerves in the frog. Each nerve is a *mixed* and arises from the horns of grey matter of spinal cord by two roots - a *dorsal* and a *ventral.* The dorsal root starts from the dorsal horn and bears a swelling on it known as *dorsal root ganglion.* It is purely *sensory* and conveys the impulses towards the spinal cord. It is, therefore, called the *sensory root* or *afferent root.* A ventral root starts from the ventral horn of grey matter. There is no ganglion on it. It carries the impulses towards the muscles or effector organ and causes movement due to contraction. Thus it is a *motor* nerve in function and known as *motor root* or *efferent root.* Beyond the dorsal root ganglion, each dorsal root bends ventral side and joins the ventral root to form a *spinal nerve.* The spinal nerves emerge out from the neural canal through apertures, the *intervertebral foramina,* present between the successive vertebrae. *Glands of Swammerdam* are located at the points of emergence of spinal nerves. These are soft, white and calcareous masses.

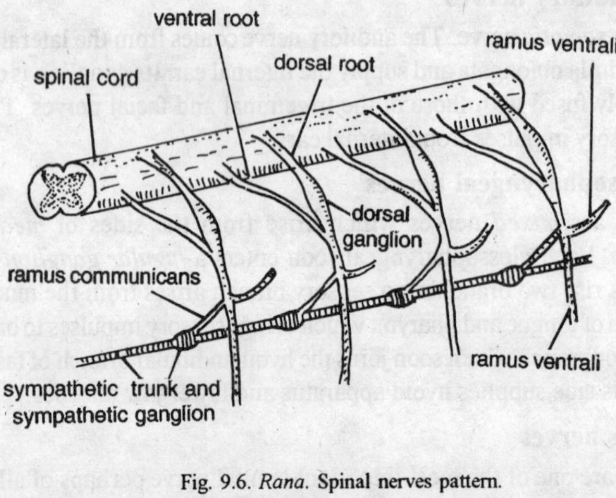

Fig. 9.6. *Rana.* Spinal nerves pattern.

Each nerve immediately divides into three branches a *dorsal branch* or *ramus dorsails, a ventral branch* or *ramus ventralis* and a *ramus communicans.* The dorsal branch is short and innervates the skin and muscles of the dorsal side of the trunk. The ventral branch is long and prominent and supplies to the skin and muscles of the lateral and ventral sides of trunk. Ramus communicans is very short and joins the sympathetic cord of its side. All the three branches receive fibres from both the roots i.e., dorsal and ventral roots. Thus these are all mixed nerves.

The distrubution of dorsal rami and rami communicans is similar in all the nerves but ventral rami differ in their course of distribution. Thus on the basis of distribution of their ventral rami, the spinal nerves of frog are divisible into four groups.

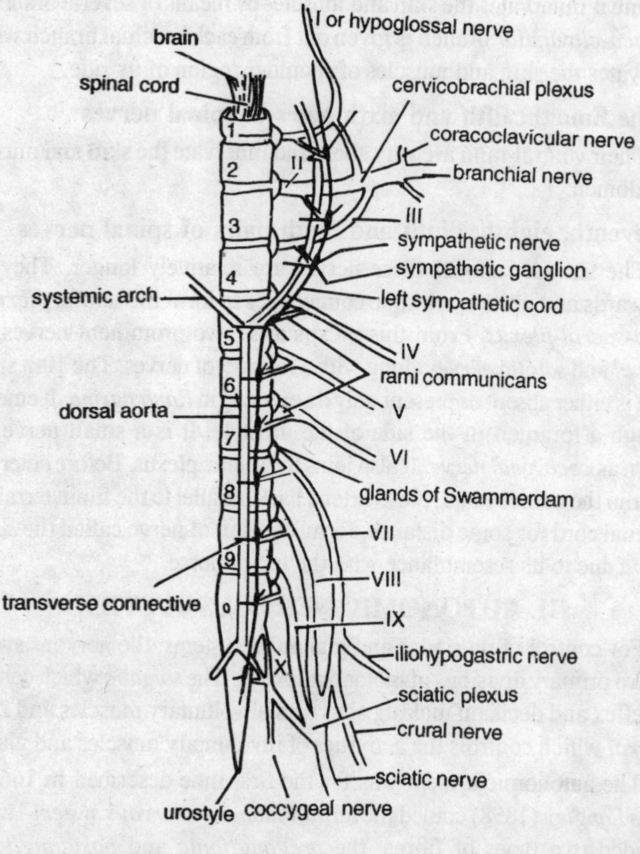

Fig. 9.7. *Rana*. Spinal nerves and sympathetic chain.

1. First pair of spinal nerves

They leave the neural canal between the first and the second vertebrae through the inter-vertebral foramen. The ventral ramus of each of these nerves runs forwards and supplies the tongue muscles, and is known as *hypoglossal nerve*. It is motor in nature.

2. The second and third spinal nerves

The ventral rami of second pair of spinal nerves are thick and short. Eacn ventral ramus, joins with the ventral ramus of third spinal nerve and first spinal nerve of its side, forming a *brachial plexus*. A *brachial nerve* emerges out from the plexus and extends into the forelimb of its side. In the limb it innervates the skin and muscles by means of several branches. A *coaco-clavicular* branch is given out from each brachial branch which innervates the skin and muscles of shoulder region of its side.

3. The Fourth, fifth and sixth pairs of spinal nerves

Their ventral rami are very short and innervate the skin and muscles of abdomen.

4. Seventh, eighth, ninth and tenth pairs of spinal nerves

The ventral rami of these nerves are relatively longer. They run backwards and unite by oblique connectives to form the *sciatic plexus* or *limbo-sacral plexus.* From this plexus arise two prominent nerves, the *femoral* and *sciatic nerves* along with a number of nerves. The 10th spinal nerve is either absent or present only on one side in *Rana tigrina.* It emerges through a foramen in the side of the urostyle. It is a small nerve and known as *coccygeal nerve*. It also joins the sciatic plexus. Before emerging out from the neural canal, these extend back parallel to the filum terminale of spinal cord for some distance, forming a tuft of nerve called the *cauda equina* due to its resemblance with the tail of horse.

III. AUTONOMIC NERVOUS SYSTEM

For control of muscular and glandular systems, the nervous system has two primary divisions of motor outflow - 1. The *somatic* which controls the reflex and decision making activities of voluntary muscles and 2. the *visceral* which controls the activities of involuntary muscles and glands.

The autonomic system was for the first time described in 1664 by *Willis Langley* (1898) coined the term "*autonomic nervous system*" which included two types of fibres, the *preganglionic* and *postganglionic. Langley et al.* grouped autonomic system into *cervical, thoracolumbar* and *scaral* divisions. *Oliver* and *Schafer* showed that the thoracolumbar was stimulated by adrenaline while the sacral and cervical were stimulated by another drug. On this basis the cranial and sacral divisions were called the *parasympathetic nervous system* and the thoracolumbar region as *sympathetic nervous system*. Thus the autonomic nervous system has two sections :

1. The Sympathetic Nervous System.
2. The Parasympathetic Nervous System.

Sympathetic Nervous System

It includes a chain of 9 or 10 small ganglia known as *sympathetic ganglia*. They are located in a longitudinal series on either side of dorsal aorta. All the ganglia of one side are interconnected by a *sympathetic chain*. The anterior end of chain extends along the systemic arch of its side and enters the cranium along with vagus nerve and finally ends into Gasserian ganglion. The posterior end of the sympathetic chain joins with 10th spinal nerve of its side and terminates. Each sympathetic ganglion is connected with the ramus communicans of corresponding spinal nerve. Moreover, the corresponding ganglia of two sympathetic chain are also inter connected by slender *transverse connectives*.

The sympathetic ganglia possess a number of motor neurons. The fibres which are coming out along the ventral root and leave the spinal nerve are called *preganglionic fibres*. The preganglionic fibres enter the sympathetic ganglia and establish connection with the *post ganglionic fibres* coming out of the ganglia. These fibres are extended into the skin to innervate cutaneous glands and blood vessels, heart, smooth muscles and blood vessels and other glands.

The fibres which are coming from the first pair of sympathetic ganglia anastomose with one another forming a *cardinal plexus* and from this plexus the fibres are supplied to heart and muscles of that part. Similarly, the fibres emerging from 3rd, 4th, 5th and 6th pairs of ganglia of each side anastomoses to form the *solar plexus* and the fibres of this plexus supply to the gut wall, liver and pancreas, the post- ganglionic fibres which are coming out of 2nd, 7th, 8th, 9th and 10th do not form plexuses.

Parasympathetic Nervous System

The parasympathetic nervous system consists of the small and microscopic group of neurons which are present in the wall of visceral organs. These groups of neurons are known as *parasympathetic ganglia*. The pre-ganglionic fibres of this system are contained in the 10th cranial nerve or vagus and the last pair of spinal nerve, the *sacral nerve*. The term *cranosacral outflow* is frequently used to designate the complex of preganglionic fibres of the parasympathetic nervous system. Thus, the preganglionic fibres are very long and the post-ganglionic fibres (arising from parasympathetic ganglia) are very short as compared to the pre-and post-ganglionic fibres of sympathetic nervous system.

Both the system of autonomic nervous system are antagonistic to each other. The functions of both the systems are :

Sympathetic nervous system	*Para sympathetic nervous system*
1. Constriction of cutaneous blood vessels causing pallor.	1. Dilation of blood vessels.
2. Dilation of the pupil, permitting more light to enter the eye ball.	2. Constriction of pupil.
3. Reduction in the amount of saliva secreted so that small quantaties of a thick, mucinous secretions are given off.	3. Increase in the salivary and gastric secretion.
4. Acceleration of heart beat.	4. Decreases heart beat.
5. Dilation of the bronchi.	5. Constriction of bronchi.
6. Relaxation or inhibition of walls of digetive tract, causing temporary cessation of peristalsis.	6. Contraction of walls of the digestive system, bringing about peristalsis.
7. Relaxation of bladder musculature	7. Contraction of bladder musculature
8. Increase in blood sugar.	8. Not known.
9. Rise in blood pressure.	9. Not known.
10. Decrease in clotting time of blood.	10. Not known.
11. Contraction of sphincter of urinary bladder.	11. Relaxes

10

Sense organs

Sense organs or receptors are the transducers of energy. They change mechanical, thermal, chemical or radiant energy into nerve impulses in an afferent nerve fibre. The energy constitute a stimulus which is send to the central nervous system. Therefore, the presence of nerve is neccessary for obtaining informations about the internal and external changes in the environment of an organism. The sense organs are grouped under two categories- *general receptors* are sense organs of wide distribution upon or within the body; and *special receptors* are those that are concentrated in small areas particularly on the cephalic end.

Receptors that respond to environmental stimuli are known as *exteroreceptors.* They inform the organism changes taking place outside the body. There are five such types of receptors.

1. Organs of touch or tangoreceptors.
2. Organs of taste or gustatoreceptors.
3. Organs of smell or olfactoreceptors.
4. Organs of sight or photoreceptors.
5. Organs of hearing or phonoreceptors.

Receptors that respond to stimuli arising in the muscles, joints and tendons and within the semicircular canals and utriculus of ear are *proprioreceptors.*

1. Organs of Touch or Tangoreceptors

The skin of frog is sensitive to mechanical stimulation. The skin possesses two types of tangoreceptors - (i) *nerve endings* and (ii) *corpuscles.*

(i) Nerve endings

Free nerve endings are numerous between the cells of epidermis. Through these nerve endings the sense of touch is carried to the brain.

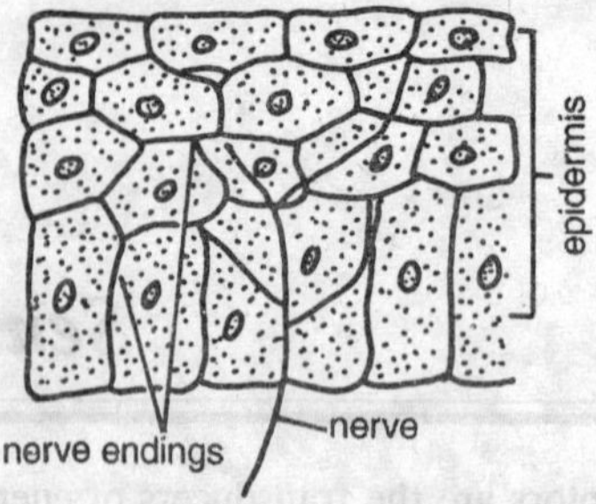

Fig. 10.1. *Rana*. Free nerve endings.

(ii) Corpuscles

The corpuscles consists of nerve endings associated with epithelial cells and surrounded by a sheath of connective tisssue. They are generally found in the dermis, projecting into papillae of epidermis. Sense papillae are seen on the head and feet of some species of frogs. They are sensitive to various type of stimuli such as touch, temperature, humidity, chemicals etc.

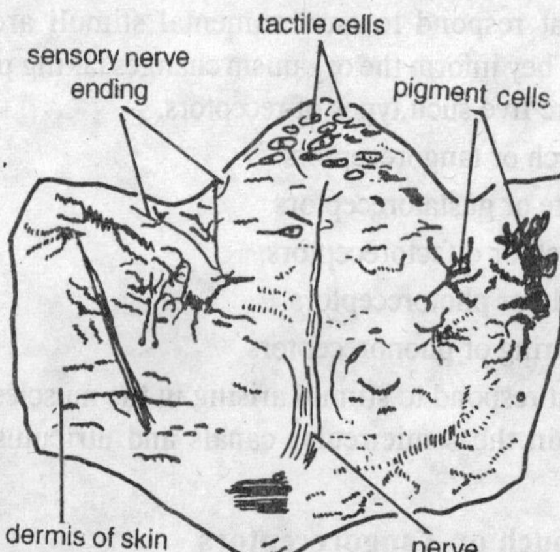

Fig. 10.2. *Rana*. Touch corpuscles.

2. Organs of taste or Gustatoreceptors

The organs of taste are called *tastebuds.* Frogs have taste buds on the tongue situated on the rounded knob-like papillae called *fungiform papillae* of the mucous membrane of the tongue. They are also found on floor and roof of buccal cavity near the vomerine teeth.

Each taste bud is composed of two types of cells:

(i) The sensory epithelial cells.

(ii) Supporting cells.

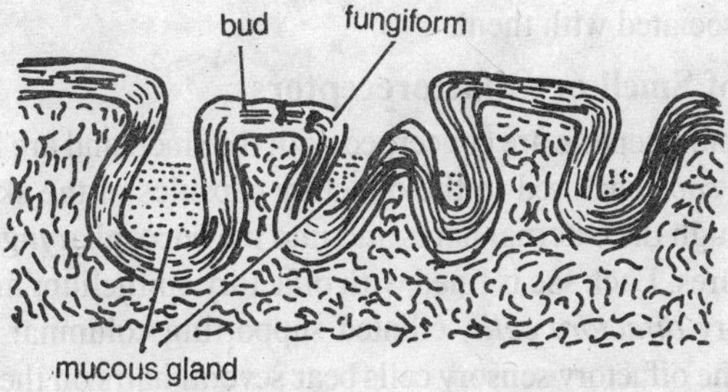

Fig. 10.3. *Rana.* T.S. of Tongue.

The sensory epithelial cells are narrow, elongated and pointed at the upper end bearing a fine process known as the *taste hair*. The inner end is attached to the sensory nerve fibres of VII and IX cranial nerves. The sensory cells are sensitive to the chemicals present in the food. The solid substances are first dissolved in mucous and then tasted. In soluble state, the particles of the substances strike the sensory hair which conveys the stimuli of taste to the sensory nerves and the nerves send the information to the brain.

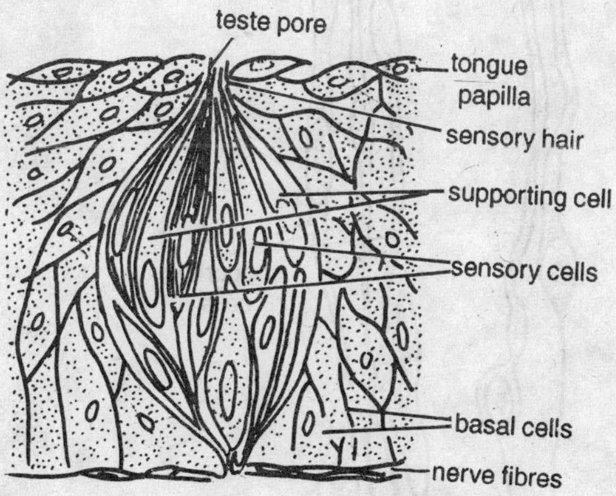

Fig. 10.4. *Rana.* V.S. of teste bud.

The supporting cells are larger than the sensory cells. The supporting cells are devoid of sensory hair. The supporting and sensory cells are arranged in such a way that the taste bud is narrow at the anterior and posterior sides but swollen in the middle.

Besides fungiform papillae, filiform papillae are also present on tongue. These are conical in appearance. They practically never have taste buds associated with them.

3. Organs of Smell or Olfactoreceptors

The olfactoreceptors are concerned with the smell and are located in the *olfactory sacs* enclosed in the olfactory capsules of the skull. They open out through the external nares and into the buccopharyngeal cavity by internal nares. Each sac is lined with olfactory epithelium made up of special sensory *olfactory cells,* ciliated supporting columnar cells and basal cells. The olfactory sensory cells bear several hairs on the free end. The sense cells vary greatly in length and according to *Hopkins,* the hairs may be longer than the thickness of the epithelium. Its other end is continued as a fine fibre. The Ist cranial nerve supplies the olfactory capsules.

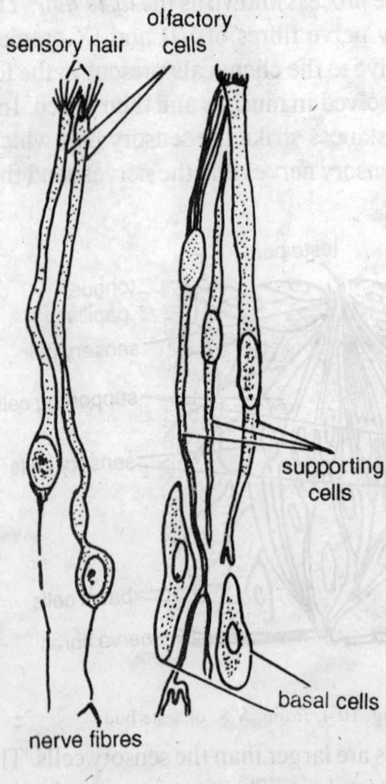

Fig. 10.5. *Rana.* Cells of olfactory epithelium.

Two glandular masses develop in association with the nasal passages. They serve to keep the olfactory epithelium moist. The secretion of gland is of mucous nature and covers the sensory epithelium. Olfactory hairs pass through the mucous layer, so that their free ends are exposed.

A new structure first makes its appearance in amphibians known as *Jacobson's organ* or *vomeronasal organ*. It arises as an anterior, ventromedial evagination of the nasal passage to which it ultimately connects by means of a short duct. Jacobson's organ is believed to be used in testing food substances held in the mouth.

4. Organs of Sight or Photoreceptors

Eyes are the complicated photoreceptors in frog. The eye balls are spherical structures, situated in the orbital fossae on either side of the head. Only 1/3 part is visbile from outside but remaining part lies hidden in the orbit. Its wall is made up of as usual three coats: the outer fibrous coat known as *sclerotic,* the middle highly vascular *choroid* and inner most sensitive *retina.*

1. Sclerotic

It is the outermost thick, protective coat made up of white fibrous connective tissue and cartilage. It is opaque and about 2/3 part remains within the orbit while1/3 exposed and raised circular part is modified into the transparent *cornea* to permit light rays entry into the eye. Cornea is externally covered by a thin transparent membrane known as *conjunctiva.* Conjunctiva is the continuation of skin which has become transparent. It is continued with the inner lining of the eye-lids. The conjunctiva is kept moist by the secretion of *Harderian gland* along with nictitating membrane the gland generally lies behind the eye ball.

2. Choroid

It is the middle layer which lies closely applied inside to sclera. It is composed of loose connective tissue and is richly supplied with blood vessels and pigment cells. It is mainly nutritive in function. In front, at the junction of sclerotic and cornea, the vascular coat forms a thick ring known as *ciliary body.* The ciliary body has some processes but no ciliary muscles. Just in front of the ciliary body the choroid separates from sclerotic coat and continues inward as a circular membrane, the *iris.* It is highly yellow in colour. The iris has a horizontal central aperture known as *pupil.* The iris contains muscle fibres arranged in two sets-circular *sphincter muscles* and radial *dilator muscles.* These muscles regulate the amount of light entering the eye ball by varying the size of pupil with contraction and expansion.

Behind the pupil is present an almost spherical and perfectly transparent crystalline *lens*. It is enclosed in a thin transparent membrane, the *lens capsule*. It is held in place by a membranous ligament , the *suspensory ligament*, attached to the margin of lens capsule and ciliary body. Two muscles arise from cornea and are attached to the dorsal and ventral surfaces of ciliary body. These muscles are known as *protractor lentis muscles*. By the contraction of these muscles the lens is moved a little towards the cornea. Similarly two other muscles arise from cornea and attached to the ciliary body. These are known as *retractor lentis muscles*. By the contraction of these muscles the lens is moved towards the retina.

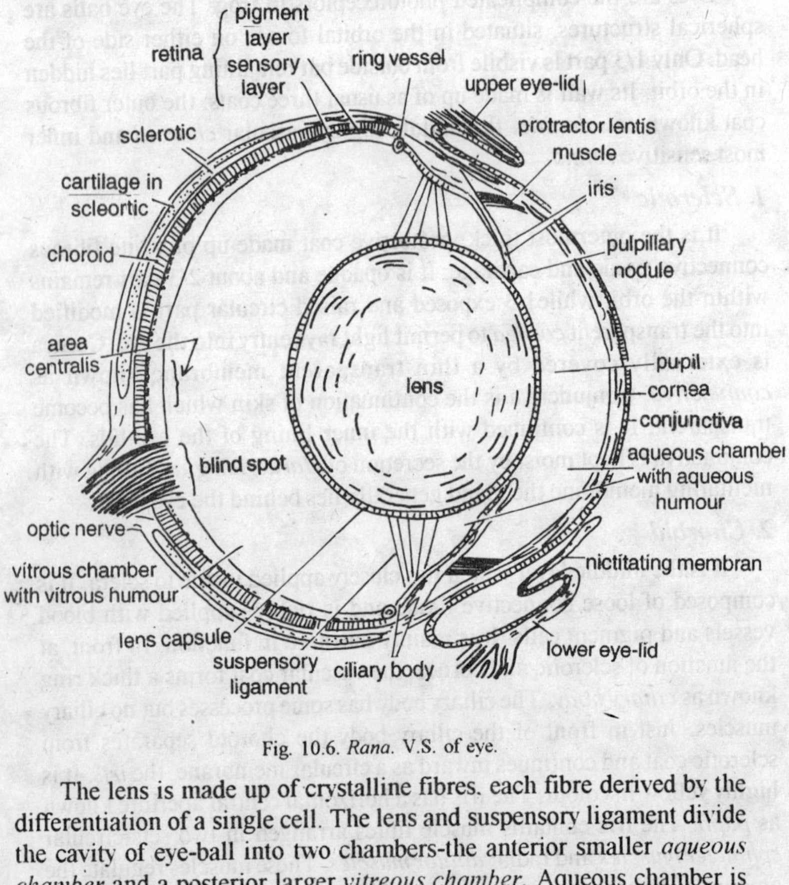

Fig. 10.6. *Rana*. V.S. of eye.

The lens is made up of crystalline fibres, each fibre derived by the differentiation of a single cell. The lens and suspensory ligament divide the cavity of eye-ball into two chambers-the anterior smaller *aqueous chamber* and a posterior larger *vitreous chamber*. Aqueous chamber is filled with a watery *aqueous humour* and the vitreous chamber contains a thick jelly-like *viterous humour*. Both the humours serve to maintain the form of eye ball.

3. Retina

It is the innermost layers of the eye. It is made up of two layers :

i. The pigmented layer—It remains attached to the choroid and contains flat pigmented cells.

ii. The sensory layer—It is the inner layer, thinnest and softest. It consists of three layers :

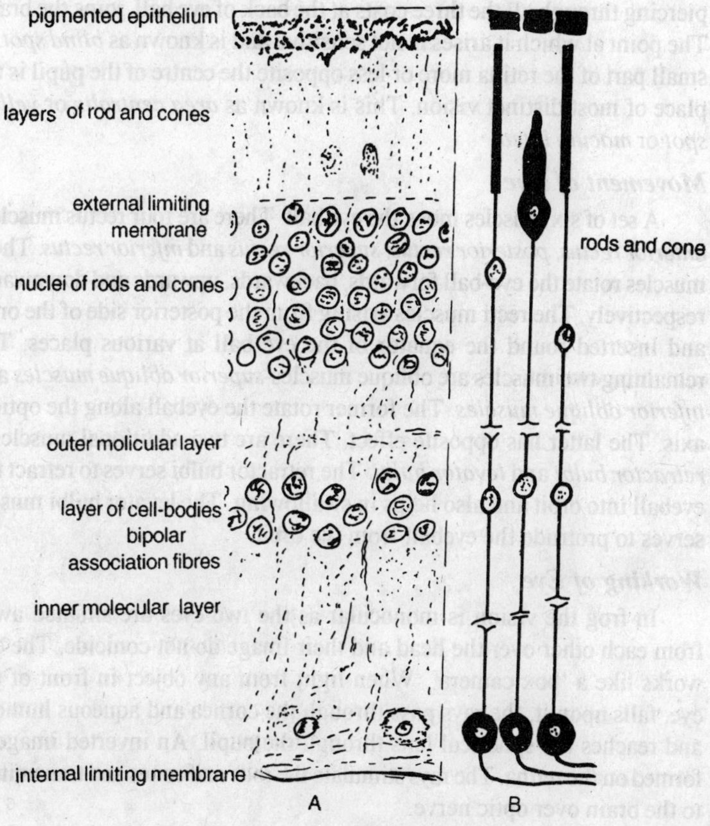

Fig. 10.7. *Rana*. Retina.

(a) *Layers of Rods and Cones.* The rods are very thin thread like structures containing a special type of pigment. They function in dim light.

The cones are smaller than rods and are conical. They function in bright light.

(b) *Layer of bipolar neurons.* The dendrites of neurons form synapses with rods and cones and their axons form synapses with the cells of ganglionic layer.

(c) *Ganglionic layer.* It contains ganglion cells the dendrite of which forms the synapses with axons of bipolar neuron layer. The axons are very large and join the optic nerve.

The optic nerve originates from the inner surface of the retina and piercing through all the three coats at the back of eye ball, joins the brain. The point at which it arises is not sensitive and is known as *blind spot.* A small part of the retina more or less opposite the centre of the pupil is the place of most distinct vision. This is known as *area centralis* or *yellow spot* or *macula lutea.*

Movement of Eye

A set of six muscles move the eye ball. There are four rectus muscles-*anterior rectus, posterior rectus, superior rectus* and *inferior rectus.* These muscles rotate the eye-ball forwards, backwards, upwards and downwards respectively. The recti muscles arising from the posterior side of the orbit and inserted round the equator of the eye ball at various places. The remaining two muscles are oblique muscles-*superior oblique muscles* and *inferior oblique muscles.* The former rotate the eyeball along the optical axis. The latter has opposite effect. There are two additional muscles-a *retractor bulbi* and *levator bulbi.* The retractor bulbi serves to retract the eyeball into orbit and also helps in swallowing. The levator bulbi muscle serves to protrude the eyeball from the orbit.

Working of Eye

In frog the vision is monocular as the two eyes are situated away from each other over the head and their image do not conicide. The eye works like a 'box camera'. When light from any object in front of the eye, falls upon it, the rays pass through the cornea and aqueous humour and reaches the spherical lens through the pupil. An inverted image is formed on the retina. The rays stimulate the rods and cones and transmitted to the brain over optic nerve.

During image formation the iris acts as a diaphragm. Pupil can be dilated or contracted to admit more light in darkness or less light in brightness.

There is no power of accomodation in frog i.e. they can not be adjusted to see near or far objects. They have a fixed focus and can see objects distinctly at a certain distance from them. Frog is short sighted on land and far sighted in water.

5. Organs of Hearing or Phonoreceptors

The ear is the phonoreceptors. But it usually functions in a dual capacity, serving, both as an organ of hearing and of equilibrium. The equilbratory function of the ear is more fundamental.

The ears of frog are attached to the skull posterio-laterally and consist of two parts-*middle* and *internal ears.* The *external ear* or pinna is absent which is found only in mammals.

Middle Ear

The cavity of middle ear is known as *tympanic cavity.* It is filled with air. It is enclosed by a thin but stout circular membrane known as *tympanic membrane* or *ear drum* which is stratched over a cartilaginous ring called *annulus tympanicus.* The tympanic cavity is connected with pharynx ventrally through a narrow *Eustachian tube.* Similarly the cavity is connected with the auditory capsule, whcih contains internal ear, through an oval aperture known as *fenestra ovalis.* Fenestra ovalis remains closed by a membrane and a cartilaginous nodule, the *stapedial plate.*

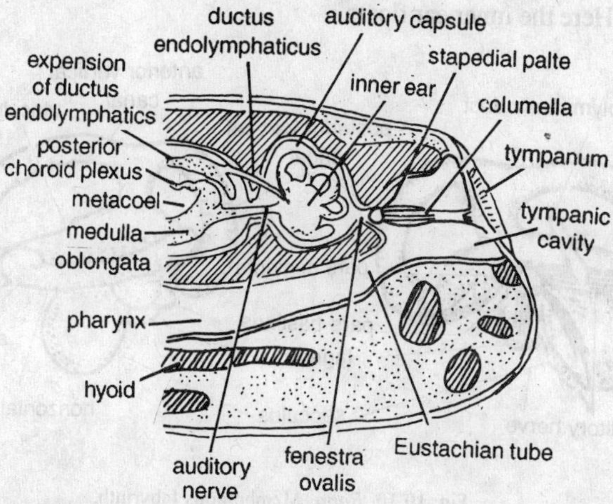

Fig. 10.8. *Rana.* T.S. through the head showing the region of ear.

A slender rod-shaped bone. *columella auris* is present in the tympanic cavity. Its one end is attached to the tympanum and other to the stapedial plate.

The tympanic cavity and Eustachian tube are lined by endodermal epithelium. The Eustachian tube serve to keep the pressure of the air inside the tympanic membrane equal to that outside it.

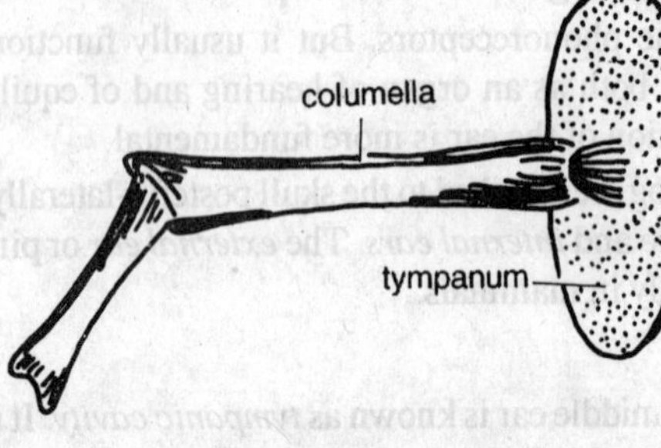

Fig. 10.9. *Rana.* Columella auris.

Internal Ear

The inner ear or *membranous labyrinth* lies entirely within a closed, bony, *auditory* or *otic capsule.* The capsule is formed by the *prootic* and *exoccipital* bones. Its cavity is filled with a clear, protective watery fluid known as *perilymph* which is derived from cerebrospinal fluid of the brain. Here the inner ear floats.

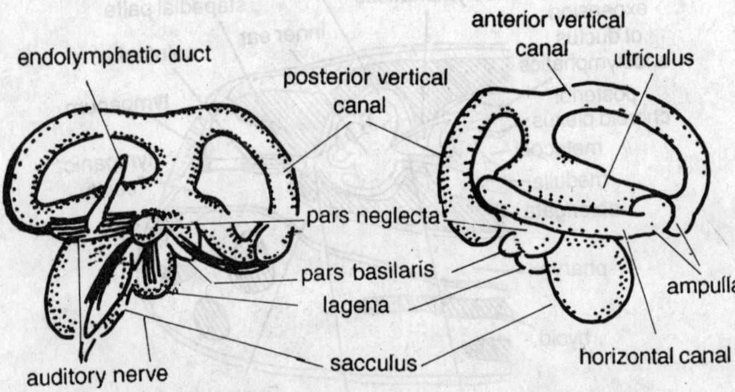

Fig. 10.10. *Rana.* Membranous labyrinth.

The internal ear has two sac-like bodies, upper is called *utriculus* and the lower is known as *sacculus.* Both the sacs are united by a small *sacculo-utriculus duct.* A small *endolymphatic duct* extends dorsally from the sacculus and terminates in an expanded thin-walled endoly-mphatic sac over hind-brain inside the skull. Posterior portion of sacculus forms two small rounded diverticulae *lagena* and *pars basilaris.* Both the diverticulae have auditory cells. A similar small diverticulum arises from utriculus which is known as *pars neglecta.* It is found close to lagena and pars basilaris.

Three long and narrow *semicircular ducts* arise from the utriculus. They curve to open back into it. These are arranged in different plans which are approximately at right angle to each other. Two canals are vertical in position hence called *anterior vertical semicircular canal* and *posterior vertical semicircular canal.* The third is known as *horizontal canal.* The ends of each canal are swollen to form a structure called *ampulla.*

The internal ear or membranous labyrinth is a hollow structure filled with *endolymph.* Endolymph is a viscous milky fluid contains numerous white crystals of calcium carbonate and a protein whcih from *otolith* or *otoconia.*

Histology of Internal Ear

It is lined with an epithelium which is made up of cubical epithelium and the connective tissue form outer layer. In the ampulla its wall is thickened and raised inwards into its cavity at one or more places. These are called the *acoustic ridges.* At the ridge cubical epithelium is several layer thick and the upper most layer becomes columnar. Some of the columnar cells are sensory, they bear a long, pointed and mobile sensory hair at their free ends and several immovable microvilli projecting into the endolymph. Basally they are connected to fibres of VIII cranial nerve. These acoustic ridges are called *cristae.* Similar ridges are found in utriculus and sacculus. In utriculus two ridges and in sacculus one acoustic ridge occur. These ridges are called *maculae.*

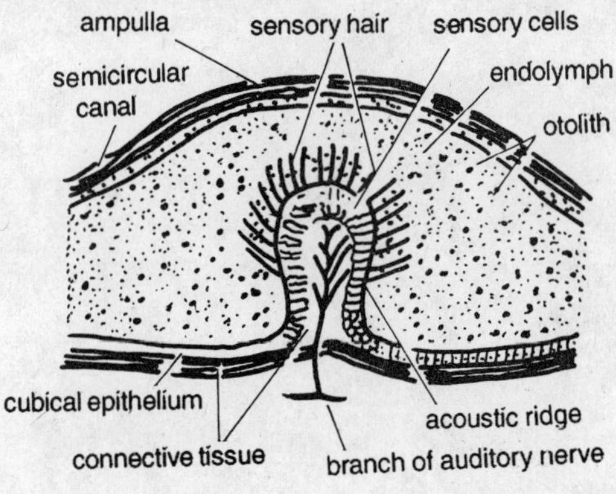

Fig. 10.11. *Rana.* Section of ampulla of semicircular canal.

Working of Ear

The ear performs two functions :

1. Hearing and (2) Equilibrium

1. Hearing

The sound waves strike at tympanic membrane produce vibrations which are transmitted through columella and stapedial plate of middle ear to the perilymph. From perilymph the vibrations are transmitted to the endolymph of internal ear and stimulate the sensory hair cells of sacculus and lagena. From the auditory nerve they are conveyed to the brain in the form of impulses. Thus the outside sound in heared.

2. Equilibrium

Utriculus and three semicircular canals are concerned with the equilibrium. The endolymph of membranous labyrinth contains otoconia. Any change in the position of body disturbes the suspended otoconia of endolymph which stimulate the sensory hair cells of utriculus and three semicircular canals. Impulses are carried to the brain by auditory nerve. The brain then sends impulse to the muscles to correct the position. Since the semicircular canal are arranged in three different planes, disturbance of equilibrium in any direction is detected by one of the cirstae.

11

Urinogenital System

Although the function of the kidney is different from that of the gonads, the ducts of two organs are so closely related that neither the urinary nor the genital system can be discussed without constant reference to the other. For this reason both the systems i.e. excretory and reproductive systems are discussed in a single heading.

EXCRETORY SYSTEM

The excretory system consists of a pair of *kidneys, ureters, urinary bladder* and *cloaca.*

Kidneys

These are a pair of compact, dark-red elliptical structures located, a little behind the middle of the trunk above the coelom, in a subvertebral lymph sinus, one on each side of the dorsal aorta. Each kidney is covered ventrally with peritoneum. The inner border is straight and intented but the outer border is convex and smooth. An elongated, irregular and yellowish *adrenal* or *suprarenal gland* is present on the ventral surface of each kidney.

On the ventral side at the anterior end the gonads are attached to the kidneys by means of a fold of peritoneum.

Each kidney is composed of a large number of coiled tubules, the *uriniferous tubules* or *nephrons* which are held together by highly vascular connective tissue. These are richly supplied with blood capillaries. Each nephron is a much-coiled structure which is lined by a cubical, glandular and ciliated epithelium.

The proximal end is dilated and terminally invaginated, forming a double walled cup called *Bowman's capsule.* It encloses a bunch of capillaries known as *glomerulus.* A Bowman's capsule and glomerulus together form the *Malpighian body* or *renal corpuscle.* The glomerulus is attached on one side with afferent arteriole and on other side by efferent arteriole. The efferent arteriole ramifies into a network of peritubular

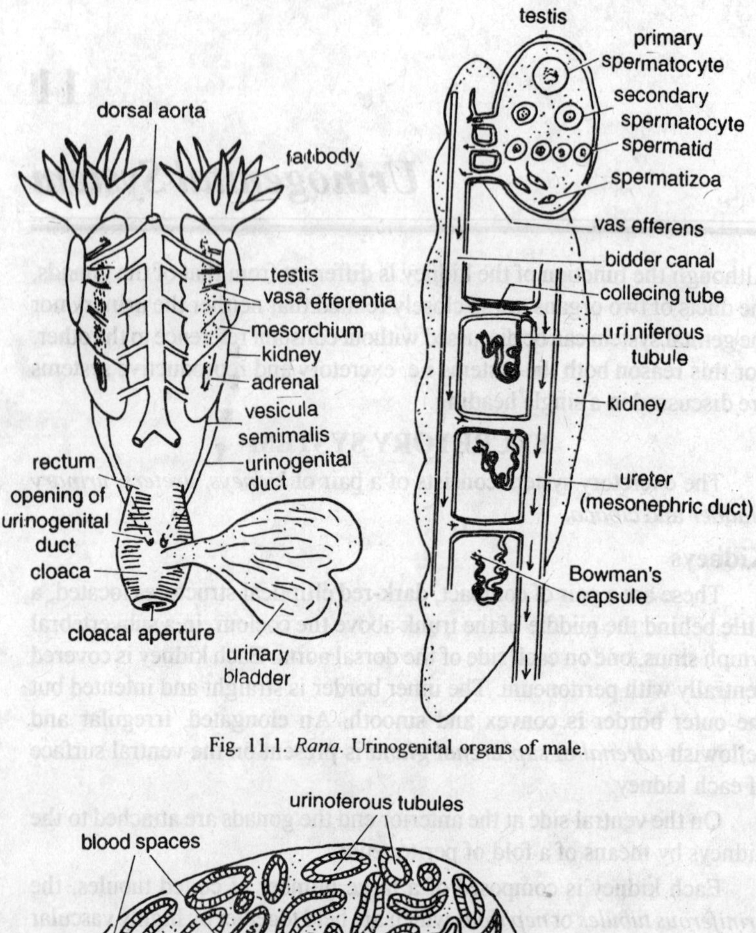

Fig. 11.1. *Rana*. Urinogenital organs of male.

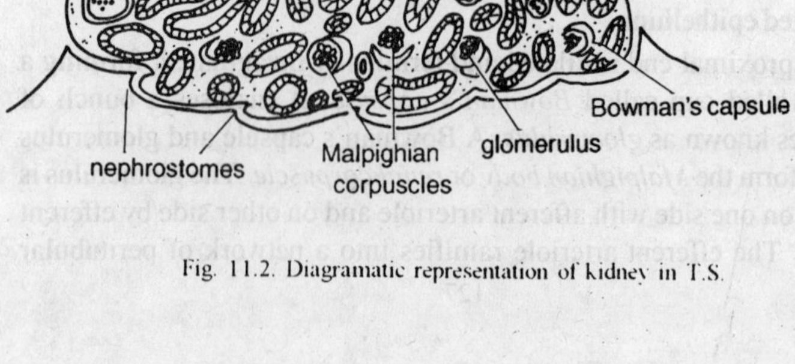

Fig. 11.2. Diagramatic representation of kidney in T.S.

capillaries around the convoluted tubules of the nephron. The *neck* of the nephron is small region next to Bowman's capsule. It is lined with ciliated cuboidal epithilium. Behind the neck, the tubule runs dorsally and becomes coiled on the ventral surface and again goes to dorsal surface and opens into the *transverse collecting tubules.* Transverse collecting tubules extend transversly across the width of kidney near its dorsal surface, all open medially into a *Bidder's canal* and laterally into *longitudinal collecting duct* or *ureter.* The ureter emerges out the kidney is known as *urinogenital duct* in male. In female the genital and excretory ducts open separately hence called ureters.

Nephrostomes

On the ventral surface of the kidney a number of small ciliated funnels are present known as nephrostomes. These open through the peritoneum into the coelom. Internally, each funnel opens into a branch of renal vein. These funnels connect the coelomic fluid and blood vascular system. According to *Marshall,* in tadpole, these funnels open into the uriniferous tubules instead of blood vessel.

Ureters

In female frog from each kidney a slender transparent duct arise on the posterior side and runs backwards to open into the cloaca through its dorsal wall. In male these are called *urinogenital ducts.*

Urinary bladder

It is a thin walled, transparent, bilobed structure. It is situated in the posterior part of coelom, ventral to the rectum and cloaca and opens into cloaca through its ventral wall. Its opening is guarded by a sphincter.

Cloaca

The cloaca is a small median chamber where urinogenital ducts and rectum opens. It opens out by a cloacal aperture situated at the end of the trunk between the hind-limbs. This opening is also guarded by sphincter.

The kidneys are mainly responsible for removal of nitrogenous waste products from body. The nitrogenous waste product is mainly the *urea.* Thus frog is a *ureotelic.* The urea is formed in the liver from ammonia and carbon dioxide. Ammonia is liberated by deamination of amino acids (proteins). The urea is brought to the kidney by renal arteries which form the afferent arteriole in the kidney. The afferent arteriole and efferent arterioles are joined by fine capillary mass, the *glomerulus.* In Bowman's capsule the ultrafilteration takes place. With the filterate useful as well as waste products are passed out from the glomerulus. The useful substances are reabsorbed from the uriniferous tubules and the urea, salts, water remain in the filterate known as *urine.* Urine from uriniferous tubules passes into the transverse collecting tubules, it is brought to the cloaca via ureters or urinogenital ducts. The urine is stored in urinary bladder. When the bladder is full to its capacity the muscles of the bladder contract and cause the urine to go out of cloaca.

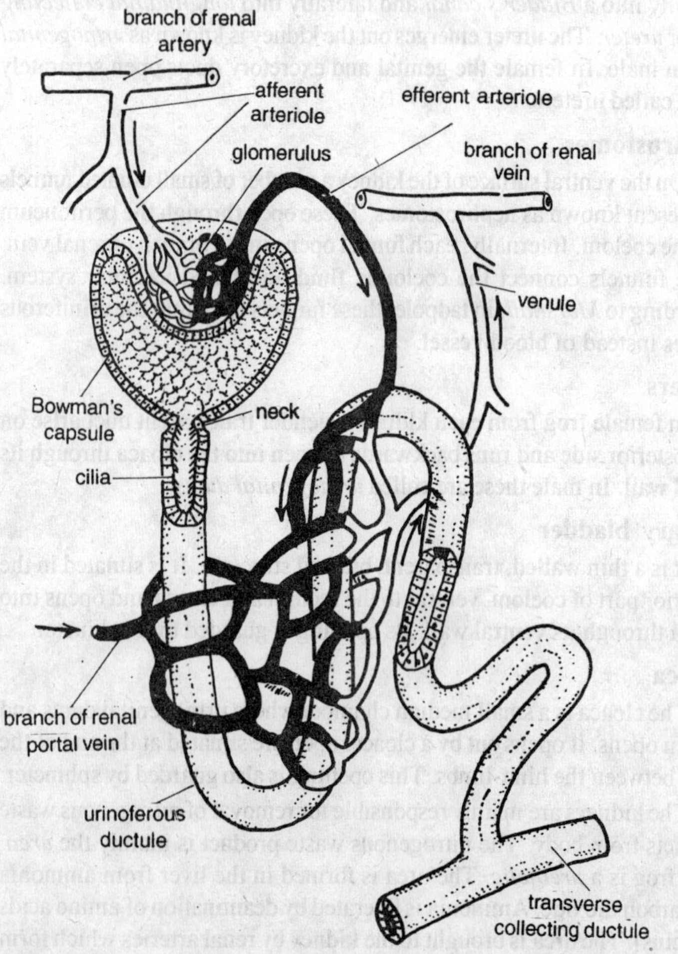

Fig. 11.3. An uriniferous tubule.

Kidneys also regulate water contents of blood. Besides kidneys, the skin, liver, large intestine are also excretory organs.

REPRODUCTIVE SYSTEM

The sexual dimorphism is seen in frogs. The gametes are involved in the sexual reproduction. These are formed in gonads which are a pair of mesodermal structures. Certain other structures called accessory organs help in reproduction. The gonads and the accessory structures form the reproductive system.

1. Male Reproductive system

The male reproductive system is composed of *testes* (gonads), *vasa-efferentia, urinogenital duct* and *cloaca*.

Testes

These are a pair of yellowish, ovoid bodies measuring about 1.25 cm in length. Each testis is attached to the outer part of kidney by a double fold of peritoneum known as *mesorchium*. Beneath mesorchium is a thin connective tissue membrane called *tunica albuginea* which envelops the entire mass of testes. Each testis is composed of a number of *seminiferous tubules* in which spermatozoa are formed. Each seminiferous tubule is formed of a layer of actively dividing cells known as *germinal epithelium*. The *germinal epithelium* rests on a thin basal membrane called *membrane properia* on outside. The germinal epithelial cells are called *primordial germ cells,* proliferate and by the spermatogenesis give rise to the sperms or spermatozoa present in the lumen of tubule. Each seminiferous tubule is connected with a small *collecting tubule.* These tubules unite to form about one dozen of the fine ducts called *vasa-efferentia.* Here and there

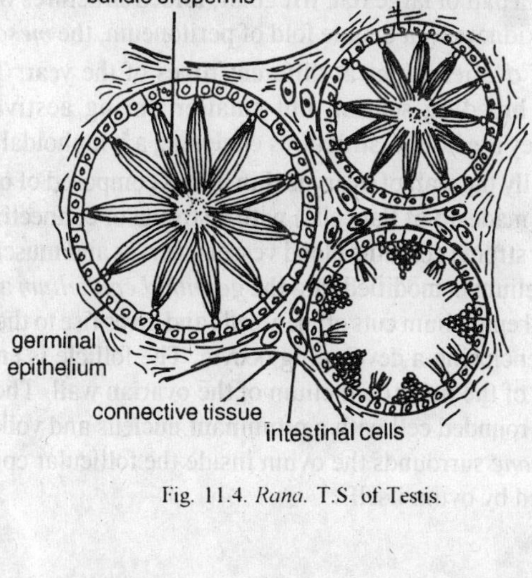

Fig. 11.4. *Rana*. T.S. of Testis.

groups of special cells are present between the seminiferous tubules in the connective tissue known as *interstitial cells* whch secrete hormones. Blood vessels and nerve fibres are also present in connective tissue.

Vasa efferentia

These are about 10-12 in number arising from the inner border of each testis and run inward the mesorchium and enter the kidney of their side. In the kidney they open into the *Bidder's canal* which is longitudinal tube situated along the median edge of the kidney, communicates with the ureter by transverse collecting tubules. The ureters in male are called *urinogenital ducts* which come out from posterior ends of kidneys. Each urinogenital duct possesses an enlargement known as *seminal vesicle.* The urinogenital ducts run backward and downward finally open into cloaca.

Cloaca

The cloaca is a small median chamber opens out through cloacal aperture.

In front of testes, there are paired yellow branched structures known as *fat bodies* or *corpora adiposa.* The fat bodies store food materials here which are utilized during hibernation or aestivation.

2. Female Reproductive system

The female reproductive system is composed of a pair of *ovaries* (gonads), *oviducts* and *cloaca.*

Ovaries

Ovaries are a pair of large flat, irregular, folded structures which are attached to the kidneys by a double fold of peritoneum, the *mesovarium.*

The size of ovaries varies at different times of the year. They are largest during breeding season, but smaller during aestivation or hibernation. They are hollow structures enclosing a lymphoidal space.

Histologically the wall of ovary is thin and is composed of outer and inner epithelia (made up of flat cells) with a stroma of connective tissue in between. The stroma contains blood vessels, nerves and muscle fibres. The outer epithelium is modified into the *germinal epithelium* at certain places. Germinal epithelium cuts off new cells and gives rise to the ovarian follicles. Each enclosing a developing oocyte. The follicle is enveloped by an extension of the inner epithelium of the ovarian wall. The mature ovum is a large rounded cell with a prominant nucleus and yolk. A thin *vitelline membrane* surrounds the ovum inside the follicular epithelium which is secreted by ovum itself.

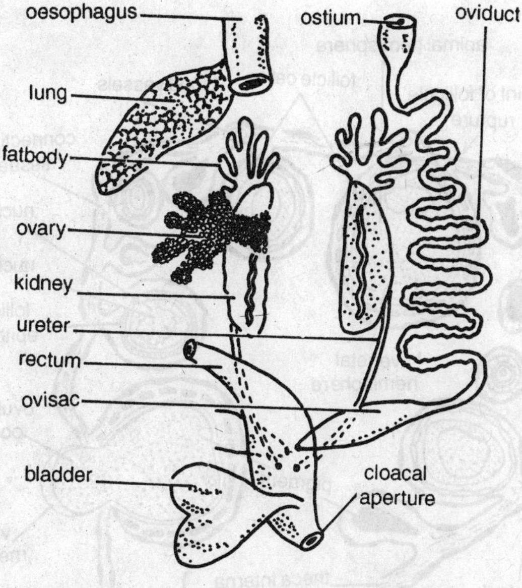

Fig. 11.5. *Rana*. Urinogenital organs of female.

Oviducts

These are long white, highly convoluted tubes situated in the coelom above the ovaries. The anterior end of each oviduct lies on the dorsal aspect of the base of lung of its side and opens into the coelom by a ciliated, funnel like aperture, the *ostium* or *infundibulum*. Posteriorly, each oviduct widens so as to form a large thin walled chamber, called the *ovisac* or *uterus*. It again becomes narrow behind ovisac and opens into the cloaca through its dorsal wall a little in front of the openings of ureters. The oviduct is lined with ciliated cells and glandular cells are present here and there.

Cloaca

It is a median sac opens outside through cloacal aperture.

A pair of yellowish organs attached to the anterior end of the ovaries are known as *fat bodies*.

Eggs

The egg in ovary is separated from the body cavity by the thin non-vascular theca externa, which is ruptured and the egg slowly emerges out of the small opening. The ovulation is under the control of some pituitary hormone. The first maturation division occurs at the time of ovulation

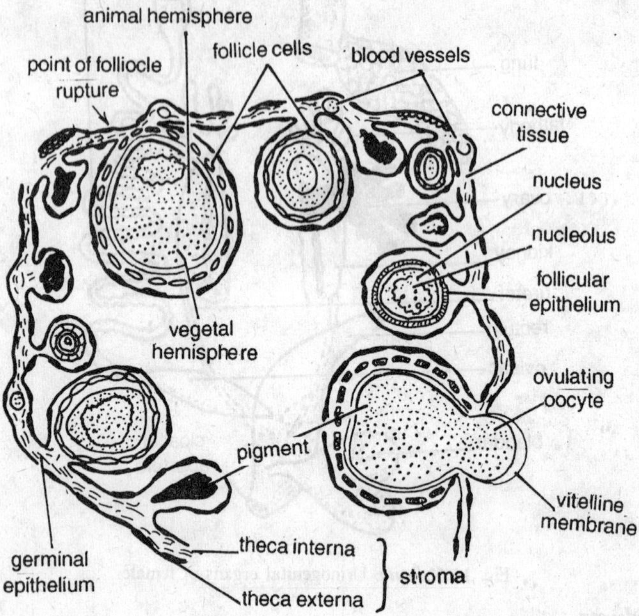

Fig. 11.6. *Rana*. T.S. of ovary.

and the first *polar body* is extruded. Now, the egg is known as *primary oocyte*. It is released in the body cavity. About half of its surface is furnished with a layer of pigment and, therefore, appears blackish brown in colour. This area is called *animal hemisphere* and contains a large egg nucleus or germinal vesicle. The other half is lighter in colour and it is filled with yolk. This area is known as *vegetal hemisphere*. The II maturation division begins soon after. The first is over after the extrusion of I polar body, but it is not completed till the egg is activated by the sperm, as such the egg is laid in metaphasic stage of the II maturation division. The egg measures about 2 mm. in size. As the egg moves down the oviduct it receives a thick coat of albumen which is secreted by the walls of oviduct. The albumen swells to form a jelly when it comes in contact with water in which the eggs are laid. The albumen sticks together forming the characteristic frog-spawn.

Sperm

The sperm of frog is microscopic measuring about 0.03 mm in length. The sperm is made up of *head, middle piece* and *tail*. The head is cylindrical and long. It is made up of *acrosome* and *nucleus.* The middle piece is short and contains mitochondria and two centrioles. The tail is long and vibratile.

Copulation

During breeding season i.e. from July to September, the frogs return to fresh water. In copulation the male clasps the female just behind her fore legs where it hangs tightly and maintains its hold persistently against all efforts to dislodge him. The amplexusory pads, present on the palms of male, enable it to clasp female firmly. The pair remains in this sexual embrace called *amplexus,* for several days. As there is no copulatory organs in male frog, therefore, this process is called amplexus.

12

Development of Forg

FERTILIZATION

The process of fertilization involves two important activities i.e. activation of egg accomplished by the sperm and fusion of gametic nuclei so as to form zygote. It is external i.e. takes place in water. During amplexus, the male frog sheds sperms over the eggs laid by the female. Fertilization takes place immediately and before the albumen round the egg swells up by absorption of water. The sperm pierces through the egg-membranes with the aid of acrosome and meets the egg is animal pole just above the equator. At this point there is a small papilla on egg. It is called *cone of reception*. The sperm tail degenerates soon after the enterence of sperm. Pigment granules from the surface of egg follow the sperm head into the cytoplasm, forming a dark streak, the *penetration path*. Soon the sperm head bends towards the egg nucleus. The path followed by the sperm head to reach the egg nucleus is called *copulation path*. The copulation path is in the line with penetration path, but inclined

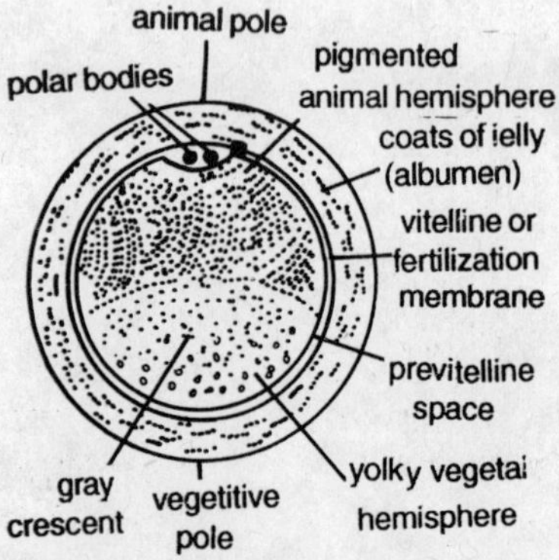

Fig. 12.1. Fertilized ovum.

when the egg nucleus is eccentrally placed. Immediately after the entry of the sperm, the egg undergoes II maturation division results in the formation of second polar body and the ovum. The second polar body extruded through a small pit that appears close to the first polar body. At the completion of II maturation division the jelly swells up to its maximum. Ultimately the jelly becomes arranged in three layers, the thickness of which is severed times the diameter of egg. Soon, after the penetration of the sperm there is an almost immediate loss of water from the egg, so that a space, the *perivitelline space*, between the plasma membrane and the vitelline membrane appears. This space is filled with a fluid, within which the egg is free to rotate. The vitelline membrane is now known as *fertilization membrane*.

Symmetry

When the egg is in the ovary the arrangement of its parts is *radial symmetrical* about an axis extending from the animal pole to the vegetative pole. After fertilization, appearance of the grey crescent establishes a bilateral symmetry of the future embryo. Following the invasion by the sperm the egg substance undergoes many changes, there is a streaming of protoplasm towards the animal pole and yolk towards, vegetal pole. The brown-black pigments which were motionless before fertilization now show violent activity, results in the appearance of grey crescent between animal pole and vegetal pole. This area is crescentic in shape and light in colour. Orientation of the future embryo can also be determined now, for the grey crescent marks the future dorsal surface, the animal pole-anterior end, and the vegetal pole as the posterior end.

CLEAVAGE

An egg contains two different poles called as animal pole and vegetal pole. The yolk which is a non-living inert substance is accumulated in the vegetal pole. In amphibians the eggs are of *telolecithal type*. The yolk cells undergo slow divisions whereas cells of animal pole divide rapidly during cleavage. Just after the fertilization, the vitelline membrane is lifted up from egg surface so that the egg is free in jelly. But due to the heavier vegetal half and the lighter animal half, the egg rotates in such a way that animal half is placed uppermost. If, however, the mass of fertilized egg is inverted the egg will rotate to attain original position. And if the egg is maintained in its inverted position for some time during cleavage, then abnormality will be produced. Double monsters may be produced by inverting the egg during cleavage.

The jelly around the egg imbibes water and swells to greater volume and thus separating the eggs from each other. This separation also provides favourable environment for eggs. All the cleavage divisions and further development upto early larva, takes place within the jelly and fertilization membrane. At hatching, an enzyme is produced within the egg which dissolves some of jelly and membrane forming an exit for the embryo which after coming out, starts free-swimming life.

The first cleavage is said to be *holoblastic*, *equal* and *meridional*. Or we can say that during the first cleavage, the egg is completely divided into two halves resulting in two equal sized cells and this is what is holoblastic and equal. The third term, meridional, means the cleavage furrow forms along a meridian of the egg. The terms holoblastic, equal and meridional are in contrast to meroblastic, unequal and horizontal respectively.

The divisions start rapidly at the animal pole where the nucleus and most of the active cytoplasm are accumulated. The nucleus divides by typical mitotic division. In the cytoplasm the divisions are quite rapid but in yolk mass this process is much restricted. Due to this slow process, the succeeding cell divisions in the animal pole start earlier than the first cleavage is completed in the vegetal pole. The cells of vegetal hemisphere are much larger than that of animal pole.

The rate at which the cleavage starts with respect to time is directly proportional to absolute temperature. But in frog the temperature is not constant so rate of development is dependent on the temperature of the environment. For example, it is seen that egg attains any given stage almost three times faster at 20°C that at O°C.

Water provides another environmental condition that can check the development of frog. Here the volume of water concerned is of importance. As a result of vital activities in egg, there is usage of oxygen and release of CO_2, NH_3 and urea. If the egg is surrounded in small volume of water it will be soon accumulated with CO_2, NH_3 and urea and there will be deficiency of oxygen and therefore the eggs will die. It is, therefore, necessary that eggs must be surrounded by large volume of water.

Before hatching, the egg is provided with much yolk as food and other salts necessary for development, so the external supply of food and other salts is not important until the larva hatches.

First Cleavage

The first cleavage starts about 2 hrs. after the fertilization has taken place. It starts with a very short inverted fold, which is a depression, near the center of the animal pole and this, later on, extends in both directions. Thus first cleavage furrow appears from which, a number of lines radiate outwardly. This indicates that some internal forces are pulling the surface of the egg towards its center and as a result, many tension lines appear radiating. But they may not be developing in different types of eggs, when the cleavage furrow is completely formed, these lines are smoothened. In the same way, these tension lines appear with the second and succeeding cleavages but not so conspicuous.

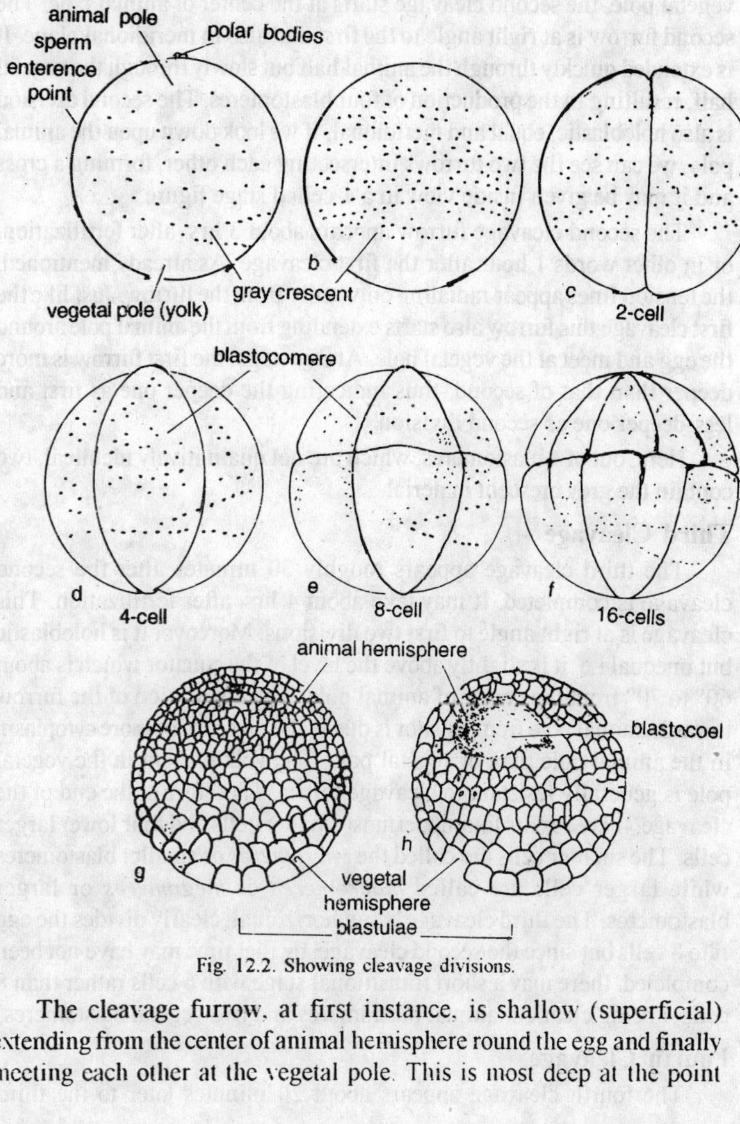

Fig. 12.2. Showing cleavage divisions.

The cleavage furrow, at first instance, is shallow (superficial) extending from the center of animal hemisphere round the egg and finally meeting each other at the vegetal pole. This is most deep at the point where it appears first. About 3 hrs, after fertilization the furrow is completed and egg is bisected into two equal and identical blastomeres. The plane of first cleavage is meridional.

Second Cleavage

Even before the complete extension of first cleavage furrow into the vegetal pole, the second cleavage starts at the center of animal pole. The second furrow is at right angle to the first and also in meridional plane. It is extended quickly through the animal half but slowly through the vegetal half, resulting in the production of four blastomeres. The second division is also holoblastic, equal and meridional. If we look down upon the animal pole, we can see the two furrows intersecting each other, forming a cross and it may be given inside view in a 4-celled stage figure.

The second cleavage furrow appears about 3 hrs. after fertilization, or in other words 1 hour after the first cleavage. As already mentioned, the tension lines appear radiating outwardly from the furrow. Just like the first cleavage this furrow also starts extending from the animal pole around the egg and meet at the vegetal pole. At this stage, the first furrow is more deeper than that of second, thus indicating the deeper one as first and less-deeper one as second division.

Here, out of 4 blastomeres, which are not qualitatively identical, two contain the grey crescent material.

Third Cleavage

The third cleavage appears roughly 30 minutes after the second cleavage is completed. It may take about 4 hrs. after fertilization. This cleavage is at right angle to first two divisions. Moreover it is holoblastic but unequal i.e. it is slightly above the level of the equator which is about 60° to 70° from the center of animal pole. The dislocation of the furrow towards animal pole from equator is due to the presence of more cytoplasm in the animal pole than of vegetal pole. The yolk present in the vegetal pole is generally resistant to cleavage forces. Therefore at the end of the cleavage, there results four uppermost smaller cells and four lower larger cells. The smaller cells are called the *micromeres* or smaller blastomeres while larger cells are called *macromeres* or *megameres* or larger blastomeres. The third cleavage being horizontal, clearly divides the egg into 8 cells but since the second cleavage, by that time may have not been completed, there may a short transitional stage with 6 cells rather than 8 cells-4 being clear cut animal blastomeres and two vegetal blastomeres.

Fourth Cleavage

The fourth cleavage appears about 20 minutes later to the third division. This division is double one in the vertical plane but is seldom meridional. This furrow starts from the center of animal pole and extends toward vegetal pole. It divides each of the four animal blastomeres. The fourth cleavage furrows, in place of intersecting at the center of animal half, may run along the first or the second cleavage furrow. It makes its appearance in regular pattern even before the third cleavage is completed. The cleavage rate is speeded up with each of the early division. Due to unequal size of blastomeres and varying amount of cytoplasm and yolk, the synchronous cleavage is lost which results in the over-lapping of divisions. As the micromeres are more dividing cells, there exist a short transitional stage with 12 cells, out of which 8 being micromeres and 4 megameres. But as a result of fourth cleavage, on completion, 16-celled ball of cells is formed. Although the perfect symmetry in cleavages and blastomeres is rare yet the perfectly normal embryo is developed.

Fifth Cleavage

The fifth cleavage is horizontal resulting in the formation of 32-celled embryo. This cleavage is again double-one dividing the animal blastomeres and other the vegetal blastomeres, forming four tiers of cells. The upper two tiers are of micromeres which are pigmented while lower two tiers are of macromeres without any pigment. However, some movement of cortical pigments is seen in the way towards pole with each division that divides blastomeres. This is what is called epiboly which will be dealt with in details in gastrulation.

The Role of the Nucleus and *Cytoplasm during cleavage* : In amphibians, about one hour after the fertilization the replication of DNA is increased to great extent but the synthesis of rRNA and tRNA is resumed only after the cleavage is completed. During cleavage, the nucleoli are absent and no new ribosomes are produced. The old RNA and ribosomes carried over from oocyte, synthesize the proteins which are used for production of chromosomes and mitotic materials. These are sufficient for the needs of the embryo until early tadpole stage is reached. The new rRNA is synthesized by the embryo only after gastrulation has started. The nucleoli also make their appearance by this time.

Messenger RNA behave in a some what altered manner. Only a little amount of mRNA is said to be produced during cleavage but does not take any part in synthesis of proteins during cleavage. The mRNA starts its activities only after gastrulation has started and new mRNA is produced. It migrates from nucleus to cytoplasm and forms chains of mRNA. These chains unite with the ribosomes forming polyribosomes and new proteins are manufactured. This process. being selective. gives rise to different tissues.

A number of experiments were done by *Gurdon* and *Brown* to regulate the activities of nucleus and cytoplasm during cleavage. They made the undermentioned inferences from their works.

(i) The nucleus undergoes differentiations, if any during early development, which are reversible.

(ii) All genes remain as such within the differentiated cells. But it may be that some of the genes are needed for functioning; and

(iii) The cytoplasm surrounding nucleus regulates its activity in some un-identified manner. The cytoplasm, during cleavage switches on the DNA synthesis and off the RNA synthesis and at the beginning of gastrulation, the processes are reversed.

BLASTULATION

With the completion of third cleavage, there appears a small cavity in the center of blastomeres, which increases in size with further cleavages. Thus the egg is a hollow ball of cells and called as *blastula* with the cavity called *blastocoel*. The blastocoel is roofed with micromeres and the floored with macromeres.

With the further cleavages, the roof of the blastocoel expands and becomes thinner and the floor of yolk- filled cells are pushed up within the cavity from below. So the blastocoel is reduced in space. Moreover some of the cells from the vegetal pole at the center are raised upward in floor of blastocoel, as a result of which the blastocoel acquires a shape of an inverted bowl. Most of the yolky cells retain their contact with the external surface.

Formation of Blastocoel

The segmental cavity or blastocoel is developed from the cells that are resulted by the divisions of the ovum. The cells enclosing the cavity are pressed closely against one another. The inner ends of the cells are somewhat rounded and by the eight to the sixteen cell stage, their inner ends become sufficiently curved due to sudden loss of water from blastomeres and there remain no contact and as a result of which the blastocoel is developed. The blastocoel is located some what at animal pole and this cavity increases in size gradually with cleavages upto the beginning of gastrulation, due partly perhaps of the closure packing of cells and to the secretion of albuminous fluid from them.

Late blastula

In the later stages of blastula following conditions may be recorded.

(i) The blastula so formed is about five times larger than the size of original egg. The increase in size is due to the absorption of water.

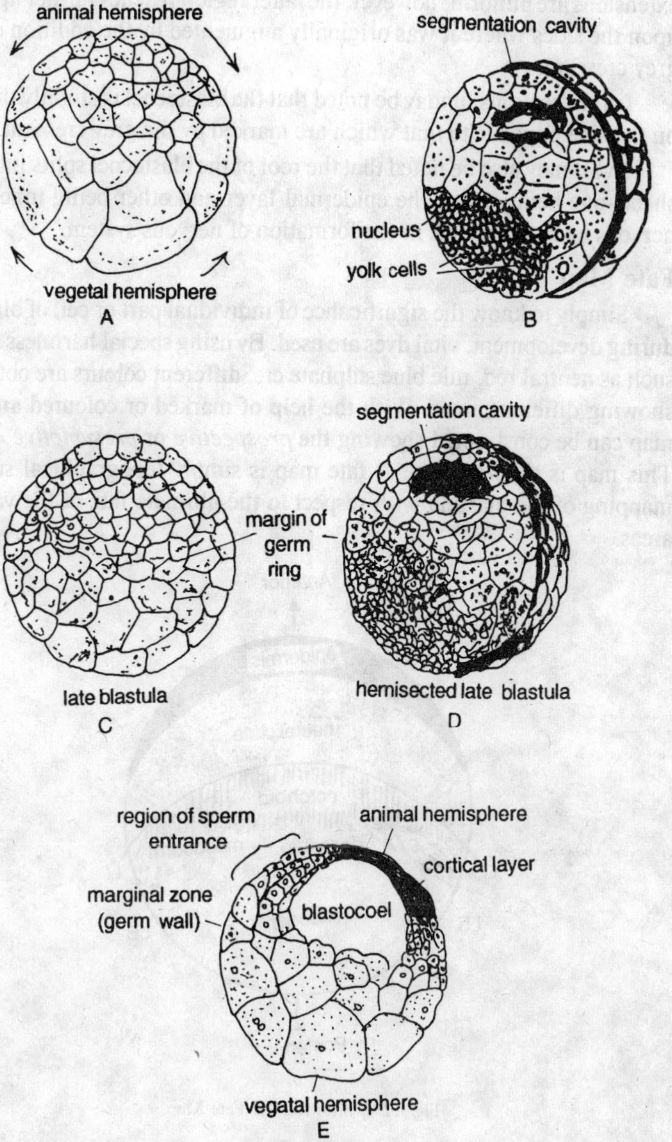

Fig. 12.3. Formation of blastula.

(ii) The non-pigmented or white area is restricted or decreased due to the extension of superficial pigmented cells downward. These extensions are uniform, however, the latter region reaches further upward upon the sides where it was originally augmented by the addition of the grey crescent.

(iii) In sections, it may be noted that the blastocoel is slightly thicker on the side opposite to that which are marked by the grey crescent; and

(iv) It may also be noted that the roof of the blastocoel splits into two sheets-one being outer, the epidermal layer and other being inner, the nervous layer as it helps in the formation of nervous system.

Fate Map

Simply to know the significance of individual part or cell of blastula during development, vital dyes are used. By using special harmless stains such as neutral red, nile blue sulphate etc. different colours are obtained showing different areas. With the help of marked or coloured areas, a map can be constructed showing the *prospective* or *presumptive areas*. This map is the *fate map*. A fate map is simply topographical surface mapping of the blastula with respect to the ultimate fate of the various areas.

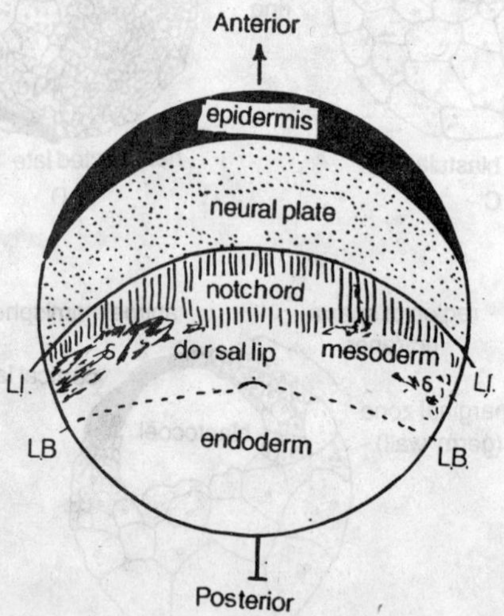

Fig. 12.4. Showing the Fate Map.

This technique of constructing a fate map was used for the first time by *Walther Vogt*. He used certain harmless dyes as nile blue sulphate. neutral red etc. These dyes had little effect on the cause of development.

A fate map of frog shows three primitive zones :

(i) The zone of *prospective ectoderm*, corresponds roughly to the animal hemisphere of the egg. Ectoderm and neural plates are the derivatives of prospective ectoderm. Another term the zone of expansion can also be used for this.

(ii) The zone of *prospective mesoderm* and *notochord* as both mesoderm and notochord are developed from their respective areas. This is also called the marginal zone.

(iii) The zone of *prospective ectoderm* is made up of large yolk rich cells of the vegetal hemisphere. This is also called the zone of invagination.

GASTRULATION

Gastrulation is a process of development in which a single layered blastula is transformed into a didermic or double layered embryo. The two layers to be distinguished are the ectoderm and the endoderm, mesoderm which is third layer is developed by these two. No doubt the prospective areas of ectoderm, mesoderm and endoderm can be seen by applying vital dyes as given in the previous heading. On the basis of prospective areas, the gastrulation can be defined as a process where prospective areas of blastula take their final positions in embryo.

Gastrulation in frog can be explained under the following heads:

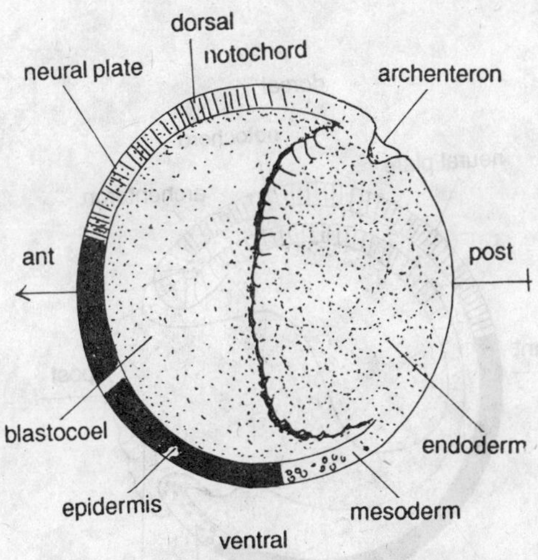

Fig. 12.5. Section of early gastrulation.

(A) Epiboly

This is a progressive extension of the cortical layer of the animal hemisphere toward the vegetal hemisphere. During this process the cells of animal half are micromeres which divide rapidly at the margins touching the vegetal pole. The rate of division of vegetal cells is quite slow so the micromere cells of marginal zone are pushed outwards. This activity shifts

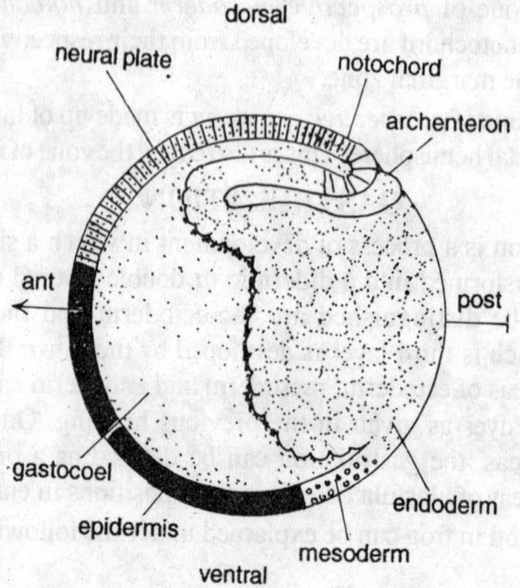

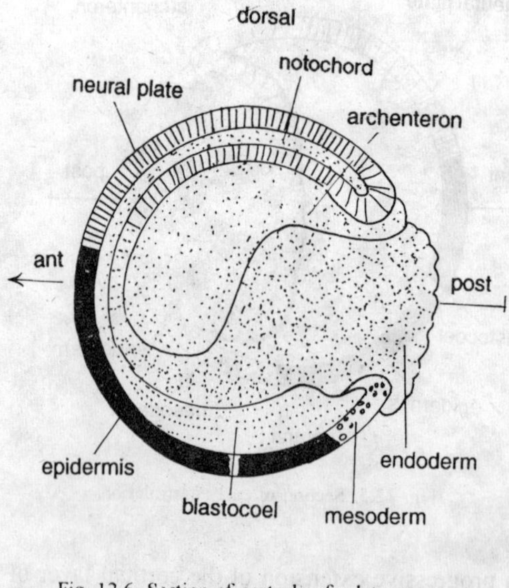

Fig. 12.6. Section of gastrula of a later stage.

the blastopore towards the vegetal pole. Finally the cells of vegetal pole or macromeres are covered by rapidly divide micromeres from all sides leaving only an area encircled off by the lips of blastopore. This is the only region from where we can see the yolky vegetal cells forming the yolk plug. So we see that *epiboly* is a process of cellular migration over the yolk cells, making the roof of blastula thin.

(B) Emboly

Embolic movements are concerned with the inward movement of prospective chorda-mesodermal and endodermal blastomeres from the surface of blastula. Followings are embolic movement :

(i) Invagination

Invagination is the process in which the movements of presumptive areas from outside take place into the interior. During this process a shallow, transverse, and slightly pigmented groove appears on the dorsal surface of the egg. It is located in the region of prospective endoderm, about half way from the equator to the vegetal pole, nearest the lips. The appearance and enlargement of groove depends upon the up pushing of the areas. This up pushing is more central which causes the blastocoel to become crescent shaped. The groove then deepens and the flask shaped cells sink farther inside the blastocoel and finally the blastocoel is completely eliminated except for the narrow slit. This slit separaes the

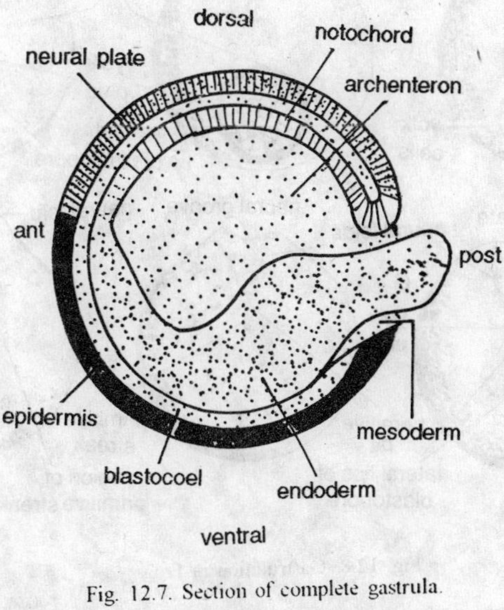

Fig. 12.7. Section of complete gastrula.

outer layer of cells the *epiblast* from the inner yolky cells the *hypoblast.* At this stage the gastrula is having two layers the epiblast, and the hypoblast. Thus the cavity which eliminates the blastocoel by increasing in size, can be named as *archenteron.* Term gastrocoel or future gut can also be applied for the same.

During invagination the movements of other prospective areas like prechordal endoderm, prospective notochord etc. also take place and pass into the interior where they lie out side the archenteron. At the end of this process the archenteron becomes bag like in outline.

(ii) Involution

This term was used by *Vogt.* Involution is a process of turning inward, a rotation of material upon itself so that the movement is directed toward

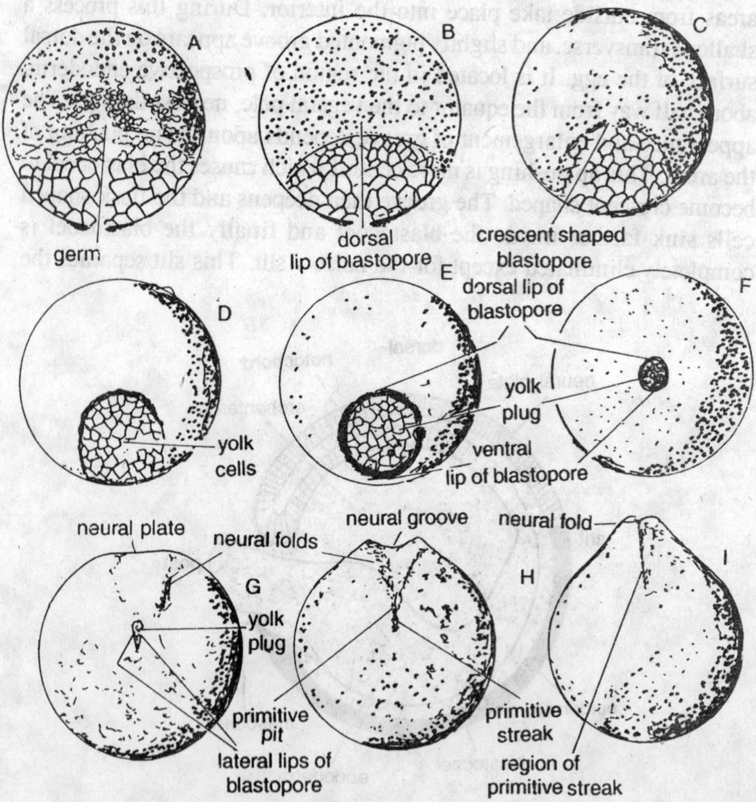

Fig. 12.8. Gastrulation in Frog.

the interior of the egg. During involution the movement of chorda-mesoderm takes place. The cells of chorda mesoderm reach the lip of blastopore by epiboly and invagination but they take their final positions interior of embryo by involution. Toward the close of gastrulation, where the yolk plug is withdrawn into interior, the cells of chorda mesoderm roll around them and then disappear from sight. Inside the egg they migrate upward the animal pole, and form the side wall of the archenteron. In normal development the involution of chorda-mesoderm appears to be the direct successor of endodermal invagination, though both the processes (invagination and involution) are independent.

(iii) Convergence

This term was also applied for the first time by *Vogt*. This is a movement of the marginal or lateral zone cell areas toward the mid-dorsal line during involution and invagination. The first sign of convergence is marked by the closer of blastoporal lip. During convergence neural folds are developed from prospective neurectoderm by shifting of the cells of prospective neurectoderm from lateral to the mid-dorsal side. In the same fashion mesodermal somites are developed from the mesodermal material and notochord is developed from chorda cells.

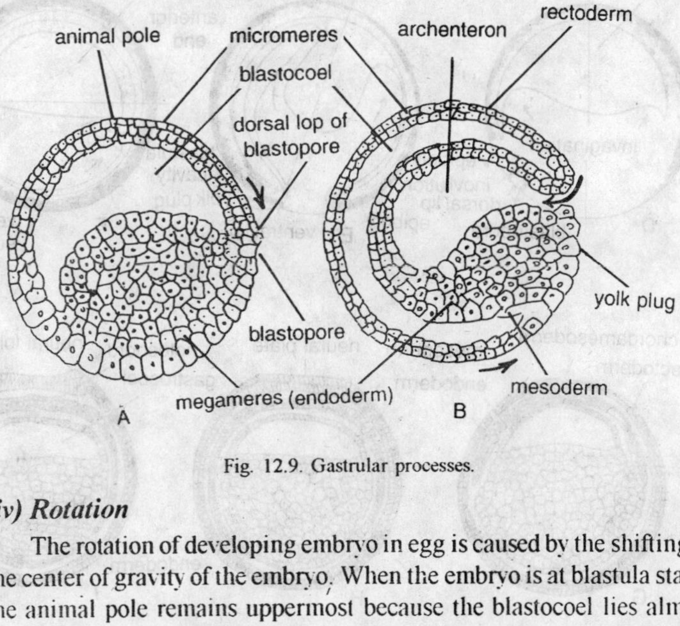

Fig. 12.9. Gastrular processes.

(iv) Rotation

The rotation of developing embryo in egg is caused by the shifting in the center of gravity of the embryo. When the embryo is at blastula stage, the animal pole remains uppermost because the blastocoel lies almost entirely within the animal half and renders it lighter than the vegetal cells full of heavy yolk. But this stability and position of embryo is disturbed by the formation of archenteron. The archenteron lies in the dorsal side of the embryo and occludes the blastocoel. With these changes the ventral side of the embryo in the egg becomes the heaviest. As a result, the egg rotates until its dorsal side (where archenteron lies) is uppermost. The animal pole area is now anterior and the region of the blastopore is posterior.

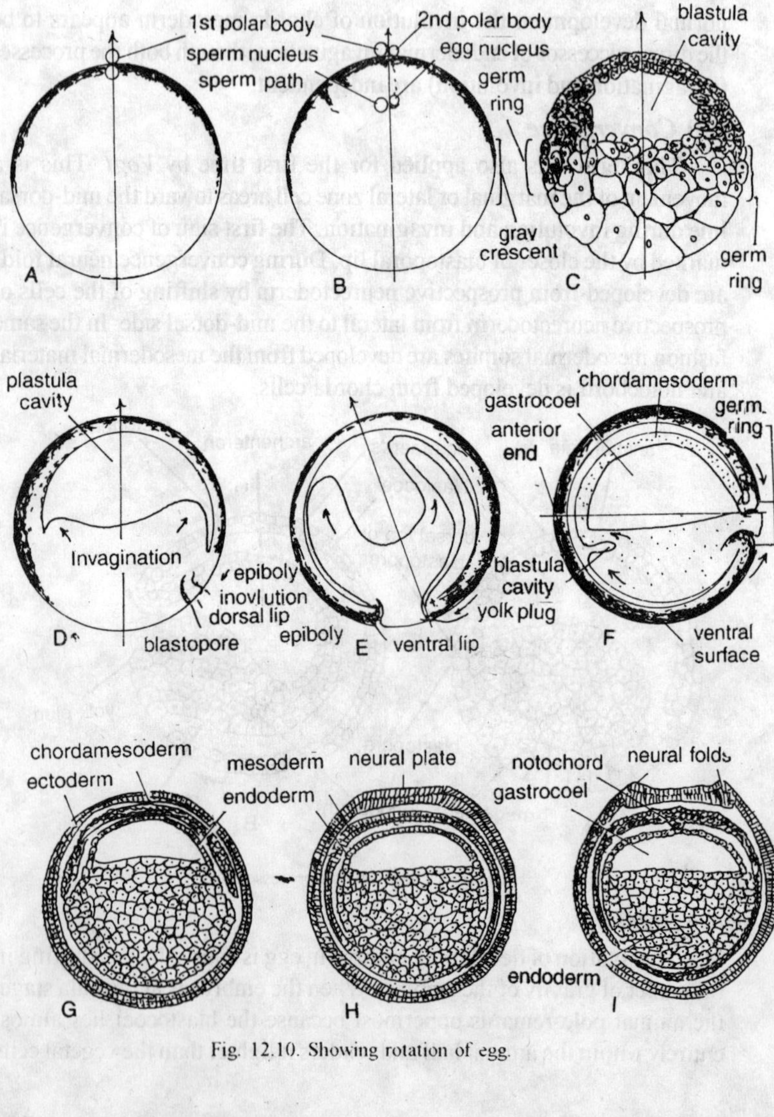

Fig. 12.10. Showing rotation of egg.

(v) Self Stretching of Cells

This term was used by *Schechtman*. This is a process by which an embryo having definite shape is developed from spherical ovum. The stretching ability of cells vary even in the cells produced by one egg

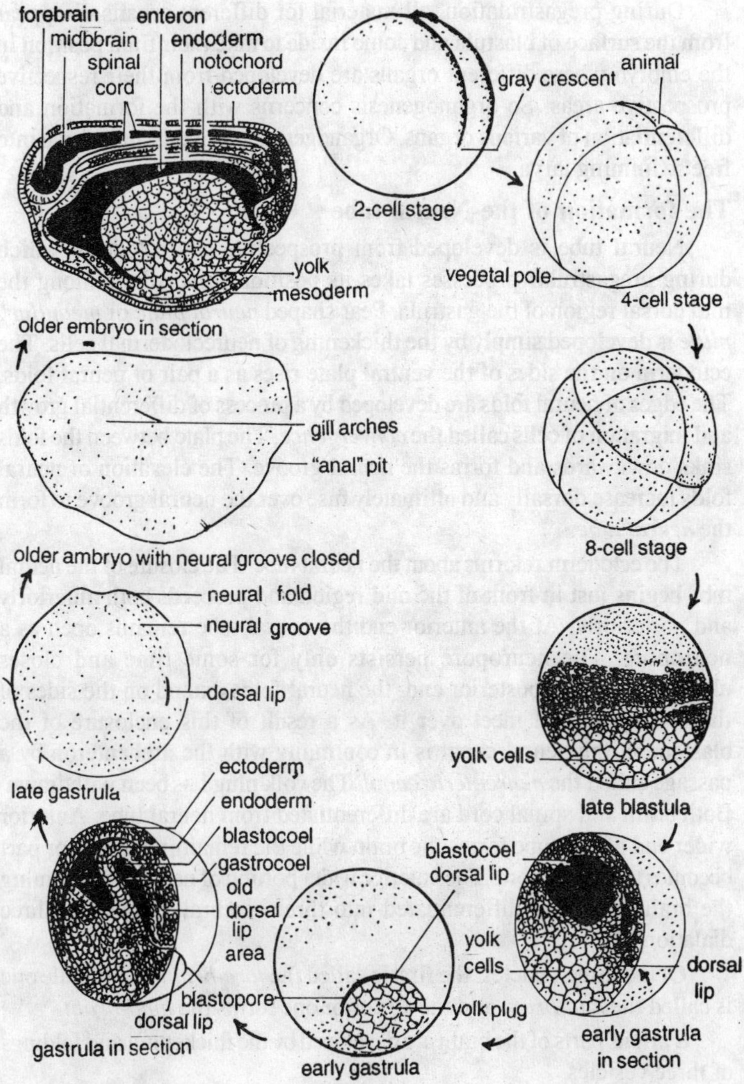

Fig. 12.11. Various stages of development from egg to embryo.

during segmentation. Cells of dorsal side are stretched more than the cells of ventral side. The cell stratch generally in anterioposterior direction. So during this process an elongated embryo is produced.

Post-gastrulation or Organogenesis

During pregastrulation, all material for different organs disappear from the surface of blastula and come inside to take their final position in the embryo where different organs are developed from their respective prospective areas. So organogenesis concerns with the formation and differentiation of various organs. Organogenesis converts an embryo into free swimming larva.

The formation of the Neural tube

Neural tube is developed from prospective neurectoderm which during pregastrular processes takes its position some where along the mid dorsal region of the gastrula. Pear shaped *neural plate* or *medullary plate* is developed simply by the thickening of neurectodermal cells. The ectoderm on the sides of the ventral plate rises as a pair of neural folds. The edges of neural folds are developed by a process of differential growth and migration of cells called the *convergence*. The plate between the folds sinks downwards and forms the neural groove. The elevation of neural folds increase dorsally and ultimately fuse over the neural groove to form the *neural tube*.

The ectoderm reforms about the neural tube. The closure of the neural tube begins just in front of the mid region and proceeds both anteriorly and posteriorly. At the anterior end the neural tube remains open as a neuropore. The neuropore persists only for some time and closes ultimately. At the posterior end, the neural folds extend on the sides of the blastopore and meet over it. As a result of this enclosure of the blastopore, the neural canal is in continuity with the archenteron by a passage called the *neurenteric canal*. The yolk plug has been withdrawn. Both brain and spinal cord are differentiated from neural tube. Anterior wider end of this tube forms the brain while the remaining posterior part becomes the spinal cord. The anterior wider portion of neural tube forming the brain is further differentiated into three cerebral vesicles by three dialations.

Of the three vesicles, the first is called the *fore-brain*, the middle one is called the *mid-brain* and the posterior one forms the *hind-brain*.

Various parts of the brain are developed by the thickening and foldings of three vesicles.

During the differentiation of brain, there develops a liner band of cells forming *neural crest* on the side of the neural tube. This linear band of cells then divides into many small parts forming the *dorsal root ganglia* of cranial and spinal nerves. The arrangement of the ganglia is metameric and their positions correspond with those of the somites. Visceral arch skeleton and symphathetic ganglia are also developed by the proliferated cells of neural crest.

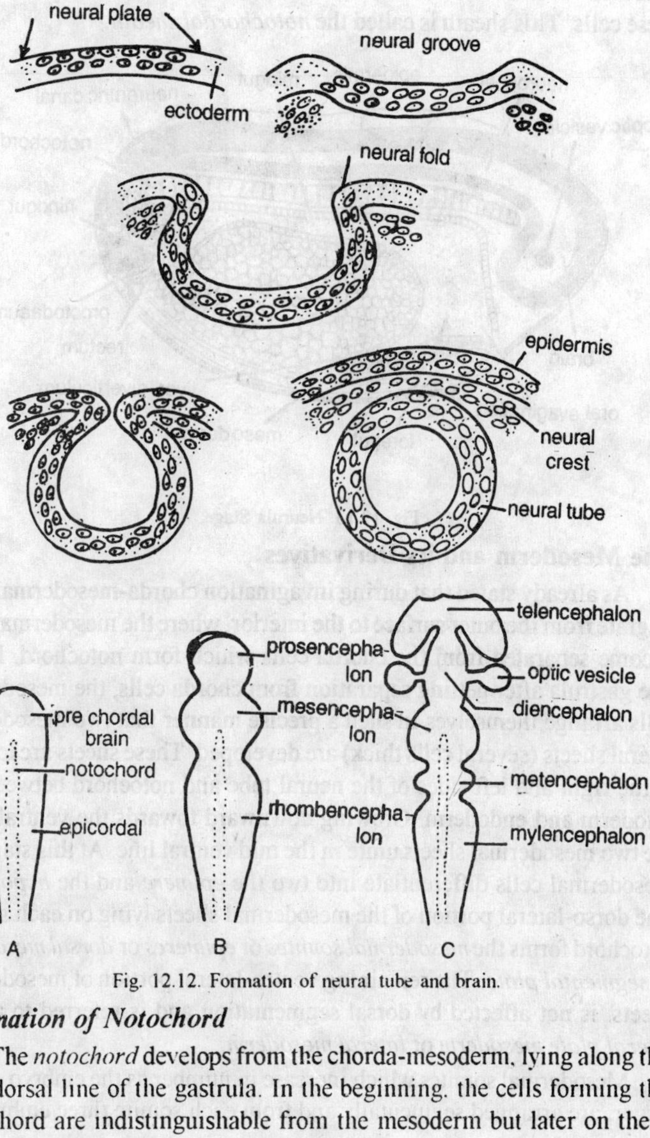

Fig. 12.12. Formation of neural tube and brain.

Formation of Notochord

The *notochord* develops from the chorda-mesoderm, lying along the mid-dorsal line of the gastrula. In the beginning, the cells forming the notochord are indistinguishable from the mesoderm but later on these cells separate from mesoderm by a narrow cleft, by a process of *delamination*. Then these separated chorda cells very quickly expand and arrange themselves in the form of a cylindrical rod and at this stage they become vacuolated. Even the intercellular material of the notochord becomes vacuolated. An elastic and fibrous sheath is developed around these cells. This sheath is called the *notochordal sheath*.

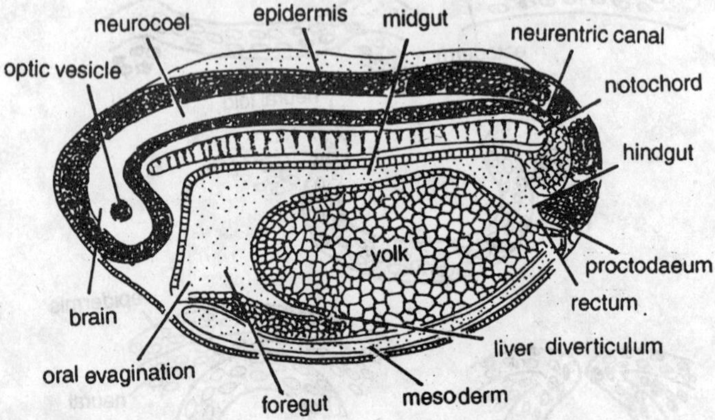

Fig. 12.13. Neurula Stage.

The Mesoderm and its Derivatives

As already stated that during invagination chorda-mesodermal cells migrate from the outer surface to the interior, where the mesodermal cells become separated from the chorda cells which form notochord. In the late gastrula after getting separation from chorda cells, the mesodermal cells arrange themselves in such a precise manner that two mesodermal lateral sheets (several cells thick) are developed. These sheets are located at the right and left sides of the neural tube and notochord between the ectoderm and endoderm. Growing downward towards the ventral side, the two mesodermal sheets unite in the mid ventral line. At this stage the mesodermal cells differentiate into two the *epimere* and the *hypomere*. The dorso-lateral portion of the mesodermal sheets lying on each side of notochord forms the *mesodermal somites* or *epimeres* or *dorsal mesoderm* or *segmental plate*. The remaining ventro-lateral portion of mesodermal sheets. is not affected by dorsal segmentation and is referred to as the *lateral plate mesoderm* or *lateral mesoderm*.

Mesodermal somites which increase in number as the embryo grows larger. are arranged segmentally and from each somite three embryonic structure, the *myotomes*, the *dermatomes*, and the *sclerotomes* are developed in the following way :

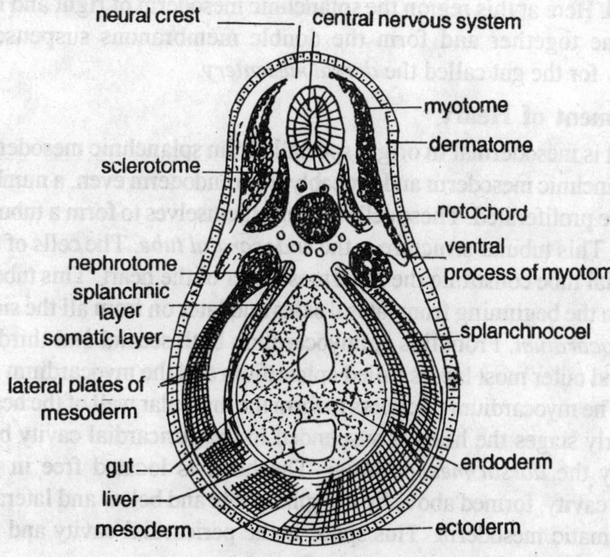

Fig. 12.14. T.S. of Neurula.

After the formation of mesodermal somites from mesodermal sheets, each somite splits in two halves. The portion of this splitted somite laying against the body wall or ectoderm forms the dermatome while the remaining portion of mesodermal somite constitutes the myotome. At the same time a number of cells are proliferated from mesodermal somites that constitute the sclerotome from which the axial skeleton is developed. From dermatomes, the dermis of the skin is formed and from myotomes most of the body muscles are developed.

In the due course of time, the lateral mesoderm is separated into two layers, an outer one of *somatic mesoderm* which lines the ectoderm of the body and an inner of *splanchnic mesoderm* which lines the gut. Both the layers are separated from each other except at their free ends, by a cavity which forms the coelom of the organism. When the two lateral mesodermal plates unite in the *mid-ventral line*, the lateral coelomic cavities also unite to form a single continuous coelom. This coelom is also called the perivisceral cavity or splanchnocoel. From this splanchnocoel, the *pericardial cavity* is developed. Inside the pericardial cavity heart develops. Kidneys are developed from lateral mesodermal plates thus enclosing a part of body coelom. The only region where the coelom does not become continuous is the area dorsal to the gut or ventral to the notochord. Here at this region the splanchnic mesoderm of right and left sides come together and form the double membranous suspensory mesentery for the gut called the *dorsal mesentery*.

Development of Heart

Heart is mesodermal in origin specially from splanchnic mesoderm. From splanchnic mesoderm and probably from endoderm even, a number of cells are proliferated. These cells arrange themselves to form a tubular structure. This tubular structure is the *endocardial tube*. The cells of the endocardial tube constitute the innermost layer of the heart. This tube is covered in the beginning from lateral sides and later on from all the sides by *epimyocardium*. From this epimyocardium both second and third or middle and outer most layers called epicardium and the myocardium are formed. The myocardium thickness to form the muscular wall of the heart. In the early stages the heart is suspended in the pericardial cavity by a mesentery the *dorsal mesocardium*. The heart is located free in the coelomic cavity, formed above by the splanchnic and below and laterally by the somatic mesoderm. This space is the pericardial cavity and the enveloper of this cavity is the *pericardium*.

The heart thus developed, is in the form of a simple tube which in the latter stages of development becomes S-shaped in the pericardial cavity.

The lumen of the heart is divided into chambers by the development of *valves* which are originated by the reduplication of the living membrane. External divisions of heart are due to the formation of some constrictions and valves resulting the formation of different regions of the heart such as *sinus venosus*, *atrium*, *venricle*, and *conus arteriosus*. Out of these four, first two are the receving chambers as they receive the blood from the body organs while the latter two are the distributing chambers and the blood is distributed to every part of the body through them.

Formation of Gut

During post gastrulation, the digestive tract or gut is developed from the archenteron of the pregastrulation. During differentiation, the oesophagus and stomach are developed from the anterior part of the archenteron, while the posterior region differentiates into intestine. Pharynx, oral opening. cloaca and anal opening are formed in the following fashion :

Two process: invagination and evagination. control the formation of pharynx mouth, rectum etc. At the time of hatching of larva an ectodermal

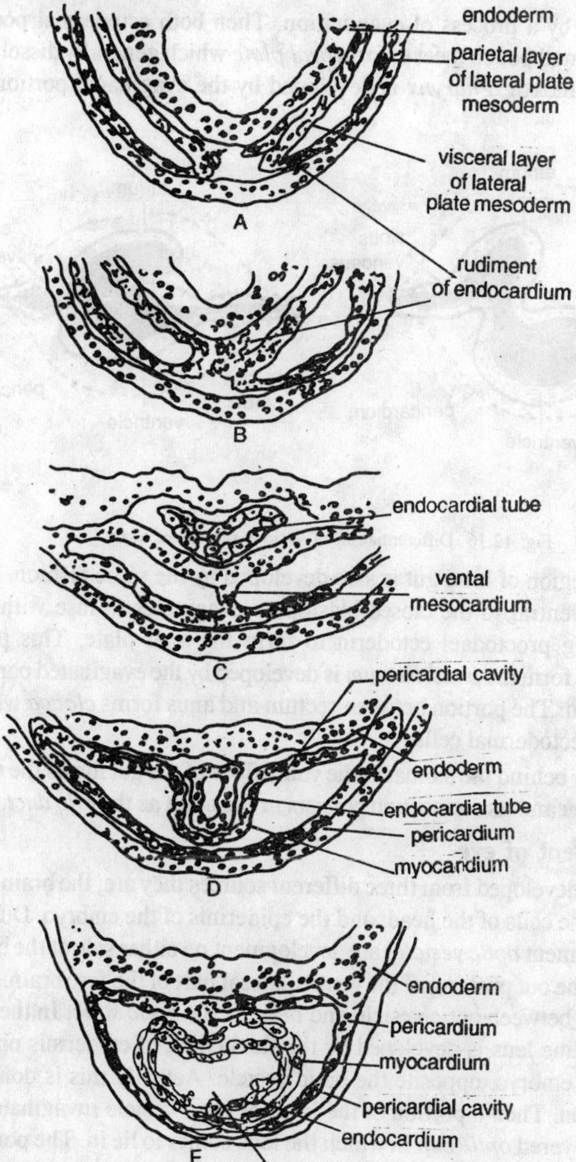

Fig. 12.15. Development of the heart in amphibian embryo.

pocket is developed by a process of invagination and at the same time another pocket or pouch is developed from endoderm lining the archenteron by a process of evagination. Then both ectodermal pouch and endodermal pouch meet to form *oral plate* which generally dissolved to form the mouth. *Pharynx* is developed by the evaginated portion of endoderm.

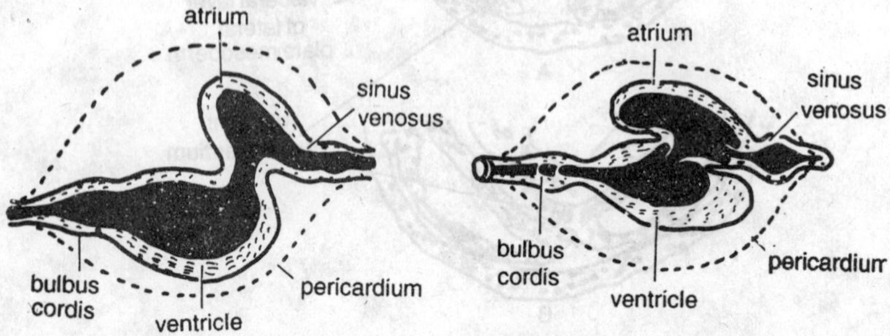

Fig. 12.16. Differentiation of various regions of heart.

Anal region of hind gut is also developed by the same fashion. The endoderm ventral to the closed blastopore evaginates to fuse with the invaginating proctodael ectoderm to form the anal plate. This plate dissolved to form the *anus*. *Rectum* is developed by the evaginated portion of endoderm. The portion between rectum and anus forms *cloaca* which is lined by ectodermal cells.

Shortly behind the stomach, the yolky floor of the gut forms the *liver diverticulum* and its connection persists in the adult as the *bile duct*.

Development of eye

Eye is developed from three different sources they are; the brain; the mesenchyme cells of the head; and the epidermis of the embryo. During the development *optic vesicles* are development on either side of the brain simply by the out pushing of the ventro-lateral part of the fore brain. The connection between optic vesicle and brain is the *optic stalk*. In the due course of time lens is developed by the thickening of epidermis on the side of the embryo, opposite the optic vesicle. Actually this is done by invagination. Then a portion of the layer of optic vesicle invaginates to form two layered *optic cup* in which the lens comes to lie in. The portion of the layer of optic vesicle invaginates. constitutes the *sensory layer* of the retina while the portion of optic vesicle not invaginated constitutes the *pigmented layer* of retina. After some time both nervous layer and pigmented layer of retina come to lie in contact with each other. The retina and lens become enveloped by the mesenchyme cells of the head regions. From these mesenchyme cells *choroid*, *scleroite* and *cornea* are developed. A set of six eye muscles is originated from the mesodermal somites of head.

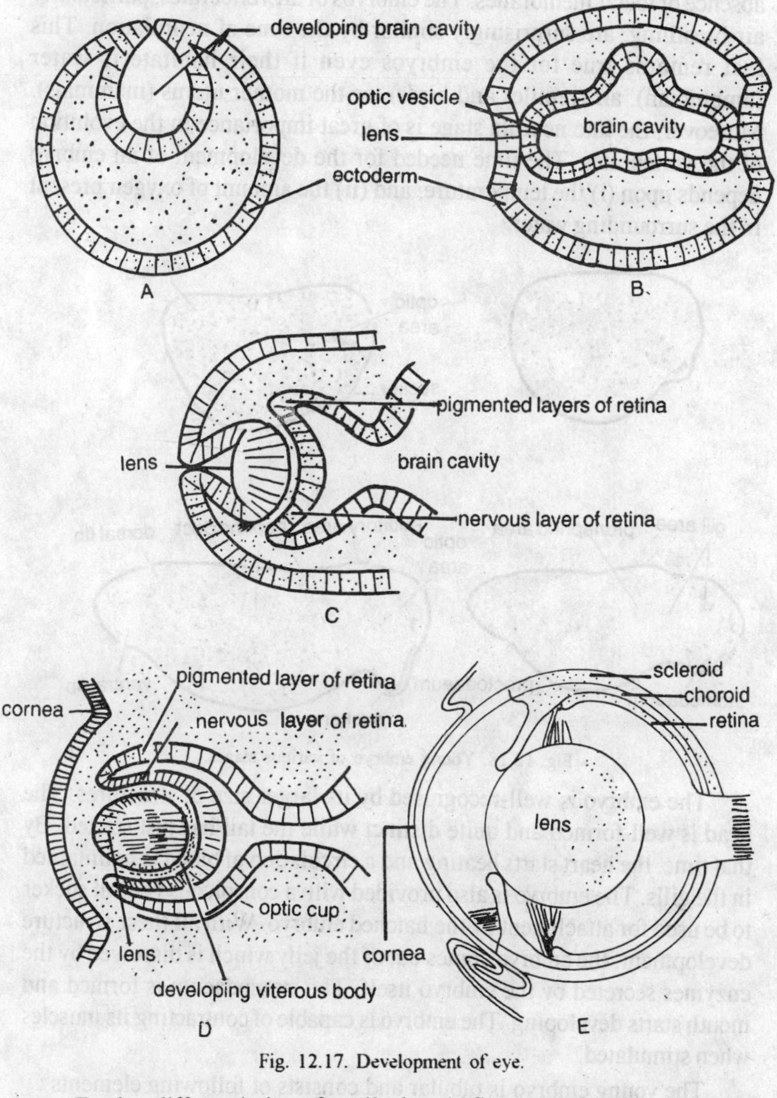

Fig. 12.17. Development of eye.

Further differentiation of pupil. choroid fissure. optic nerve and optic chiasma etc. take place before metamorphosis.

Embryo of Frog

In vertebrates, the earliest stages in development may be modified by the amount of yolk that is present in an egg and also by the presence or absence of foetal membranes. The embryos of all vertebrates, particularly air-breathing, are surprisingly similar by the time of neurulation. This fact remains true for the embryos even if their habitate is water (amphibian), air (reptiles and birds), or the mother uterus (mammals). Moreover, the late neurula stage is of great importance in the evolution of the vertebrates. The time needed for the development of an embryo depends upon (i) the temperature, and (ii) the amount of oxygen present in the surrounding water.

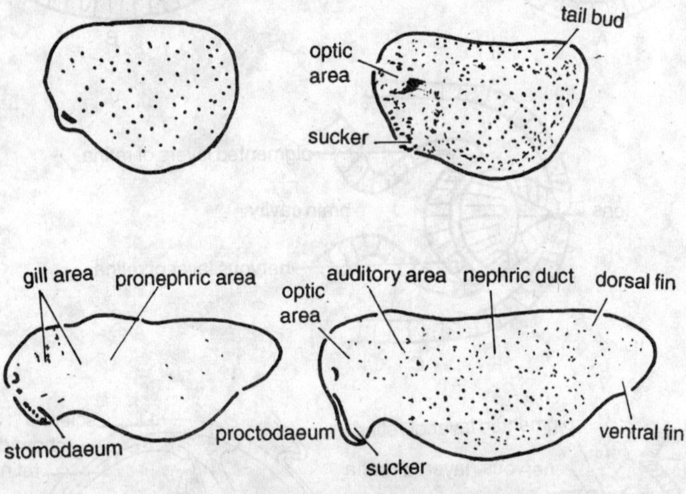

Fig. 12.18. Young embryo of various stages.

The embryo is well-recognised by its larger size of structures. The head is well-formed and quite distinct while the tail has just started. By that time, the heart starts beating and a circulation of blood is maintained in the gills. The embryo is also provided with a conspicous ventral sucker to be used for attachment by the hatched embryo. With all these structure development, the embryo comes out of the jelly which is dissolved by the enzymes secreted by the embryo itself. The stomodaeum is formed and mouth starts developing. The embryo is capable of contracting its muscles when stimulated.

The young embryo is tubular and consists of following elements :

1. Outer epidermal covering.
2. Dorsal neural tube.

3. Notochord.
4. Endodermal canal or gut.
5. Mesodermal plate of right side.
6. Mesodermal plate of left side.

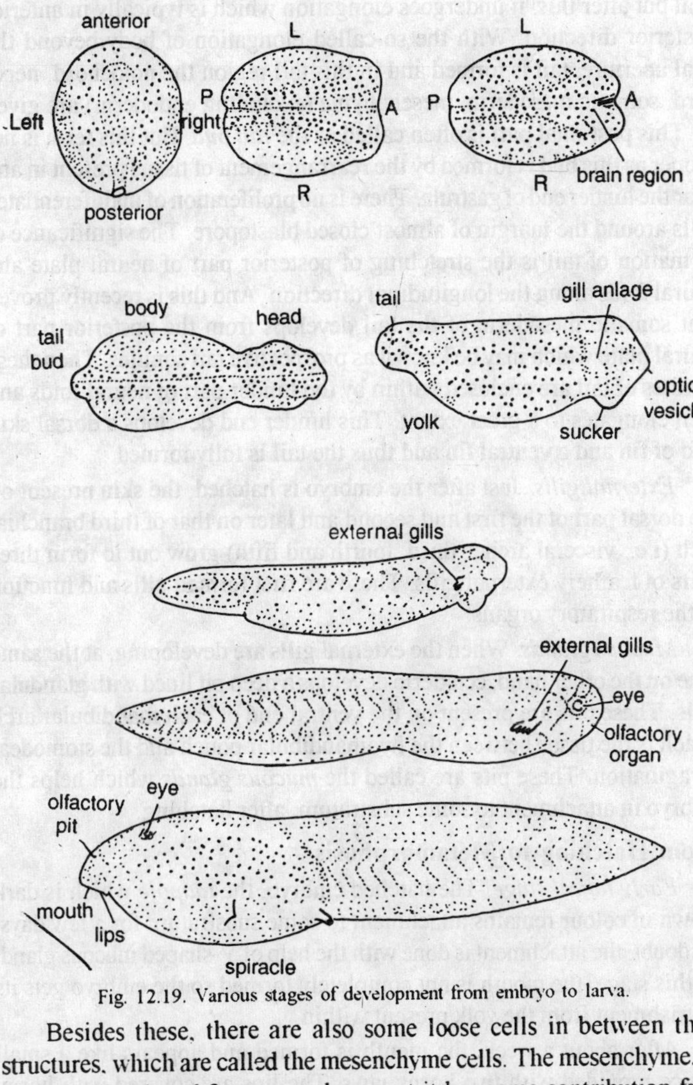

Fig. 12.19. Various stages of development from embryo to larva.

Besides these, there are also some loose cells in between these structures, which are called the mesenchyme cells. The mesenchyme, no doubt, is developed from mesoderm, yet it has some contribution from ectoderm also. These cells form the supporting tissue, or skeletal system.

musculature, blood vessels and the blood. At this stage, the embryo of frog resembles the organisation of a typical vertebrate embryo.

The Elongation of the Embryo

The embryo, till the gastrulation is completed, is almost spherical or oval but after this, it undergoes elongation which is typically in anterio-posterior direction. With the so-called elongation of body beyond the anal aperture, tail is formed and in this tail region the notochord, nerve cord, somatic mesoderm, mesenchyme (excluding endoderm) are given in. This post-anal part is often called as the *tail bud.* But this term is not proper as this bud is formed by the rearrangement of tissue present in and near the hinder end of gastrula. There is no proliferation of undifferentiated cells around the margin of almost closed blastopore. The significance of formation of tail is the stretching of posterior part of neural plate and neural folds along the longitudinal direction. And this is recently proved that somatic mesoderm of the tail develops from the posterior part of neural plate which may be known as prospective tail somites. Then these somites of tail are enclosed within by the hinder part of neural folds and then elongates to a great extent. This hinder end develops a dorsal skin fold of fin and a ventral fin and thus the tail is fully formed.

External gills. Just after the embryo is hatched, the skin present on the dorsal part of the first and second and later on that of third branchial arch (i.e., visceral arches third, fourth and fifth) grow out to form three pairs of feathery external gills. These are first formed gills and function as the respiratory organs.

Mucous glands. When the external gills are developing, at the same time on the other hand, ectoderm develops a deep pit lined with glandular cells. These pits are present on the ventral end of each mandibular arch which is the tissue between the hyomandibular pouch and the stomodeal invagination. These pits are called the *mucous glands* which helps the embryo in attachment to some substratum, after hatching.

From Hatching to Metamorphosis

Early larval stage. The hatched embryo, the *tadpole* which is dark brown in colour remains attachment to some substratum for a few days. No doubt, the attachment is done with the help of V-shaped mucous gland. At this stage, the mouth is not completely formed so the embryo gets its nourishment from the yolk present within.

After about a week, the mouth is formed and appears like a small orifice provided with two horny jaws. The lips are covered with horny rasping papillae and with all these structures, the tadpole is able to feed upon cereal. At the same time, the alimentary canal with its constituents also developed completing the process of feeding and digestion.

Later larval life : In the first two or three weeks, the larva attains above mentioned characters and the changes continue gradually to the time of metamorphosis. This interval is about 2-3 months or some times over the following winter, the larva during this period elongates considerably and loses its brown colour. The tadpole now has more or less green colour on dorsal side and white on ventral side.

LARVA OF FROG

The tadpole readily hatches about 14 days after fertilization if the conditions are normal. The tadpole is a fish-like creature blackish in colour and about 7 m.m. in length. The gut is a straight tube with variable dimensions. There are present four pairs of visceral pouches in the pharyngeal region but they are not in communication with the exterior. The gut of the tadpole, at this state, does not has mouth but a posterior terminal opening-the anus. The neural tube is fully formed but the neurentric canal becomes closed. The rudiments of related structures such as special sense organs are already laid down. The heart, on the other hand, is a S-shaped tube with divisions to form the chambers and the mesoderm starts developing blood vessels. There are also present three tubules of the pronephros but the longitudinal duct run as back as cloacal region.

Larval Life of Tadpole

As already mentioned the young tadpole hatches from the egg membrane within about 14 days and then it adheres to some substratum. This attachment is due to sticky secretion produced by mucous gland. Even after attachment it remains dependent upon the yolk and after a week or so the *mouth* appears and the latter leads into the pharynx. The mouth so formed becomes fringed by a pair of *horny jaws* bearing papillae (*horny teeth*). These teeth are used in rasping the small vegetables which form the food for the tadpole.

The gut, after sometime, elongates greatly and becomes coiled and then starts functioning as a digestive tract. The third branchial (fourth visceral) pouch appears in the pharyngeal region. All the four branchial pouches get in communication with the exterior and thus complete *gill clefts* are formed. But this direct communication does not last for long time but for a short while. A fold of skin from the hinder part of hyoid arch grows back over the gill slits. This fold is called as *opercular fold*. The folds of both lateral sides fuse with each other on the ventral surface and due to their continued growth, the gill slits, on either side open into a common chamber. This chamber is named as the *gill chamber*. The opercular folds fuse with the skin behind the fourth gill slit forming the hinder wall of gill chamber but on the left hand side, at one point there is present a smaller opening called the *spiracle*. The gill chamber opens to the outside world through this aperture or the spiracle. In the meantime, the tissues of branchial arches are differentiated and form the true or *internal gills*. On the other hand, the external gills disappear.

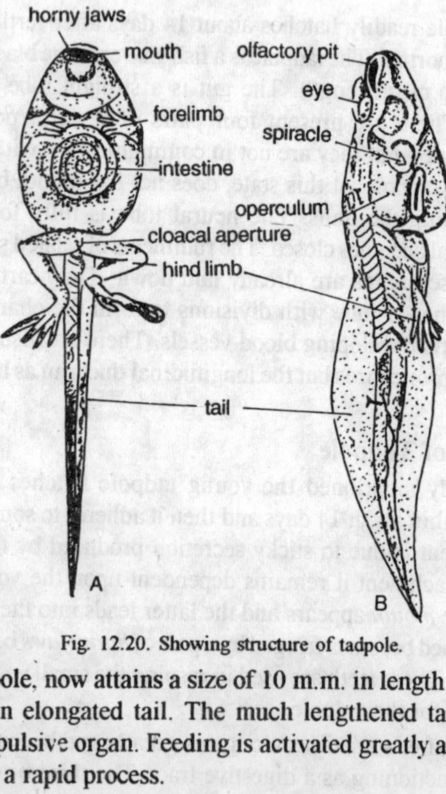

Fig. 12.20. Showing structure of tadpole.

The tadpole, now attains a size of 10 m.m. in length and a globular shape with an elongated tail. The much lengthened tail functions as powerful propulsive organ. Feeding is activated greatly and growth size also becomes a rapid process.

The internal structures are also developing without any interference. The nervous system and special sense organs also make their appearance completely. By the time. the tadpole attains a length of 15 m.m. *lateral line organs* make their existance and are practically completed. The blood vascular system established now is similar to that of fish and remain like this. until the lungs became functional. After about three months. the tadpole is able to come to the surface of pond and takes in air. The larval pronephric kidneys are replaced by opisthonephric kidneys. The opistbonephros starts developing the tubules from the time larva was about 12 m.m. length. The *limbs* make their appearance as buds from the body wall. The hind limbs are visible at first from the outside because the fore limbs remain hidden below the operculum and they come out of it just before metamorphosis. On the left side there is present a small aperture, the "spiracle" and this is the perforation through which left limb emerges but on the right side, at first a small hole is formed in the operculum due to thyroid secretions and from this aperture, right limb comes out.

The skeletal structure in the embryo and early larva, is the notochord but with the formation of limb buds, other parts of skeleton are gradually laid down as cartilagenous. The cartilage deposited by cells from the sclerotomes form the *vertebrae* and *urostyle*. The two pairs of rods viz, trabeculae and parachrodals form the neurocranium and soon the *sense capsules* and *palato-quadrate bar* of *mandibular arch* fuse to it. This segment of mandibular arch forms and upper jaw. The upper jaw, the lower jaw (*Meckel's cartilage*), the hyoid arch and the four *branchial arches* comprise the so called *visceral arch system* and is laid down in the wall of pharynx by neural crest cells. The skeleton of limb or *limb skeleton* and *girdles* make their appearance after the limbs have been differentiated to considerable extent. During most of the larval life, the skeleton is of cartilagenous, but after metamorphosis, this is replaced largely by bones (endochordal or cartilage bones) whereas some other bones or membrane bones are also formed and thus complete skeletal system in adult is formed.

METAMORPHOSIS

In amphibians, further development is of great interest but space permits a short reference to the remarkable phenomenon of metamorphosis and to the role played by hormones.

In 1912, *Gudernatsch* noticed that if the tadpoles were fed dessicated thyroid tissue, they will develop into little frog. The limbs grow rapidly and the tail, as resorbed along with the gills disappear. Due to carnivorous feeding, the intestine is shortened. The skin gets cornified while the lungs enlarge for air breathing. The main nitrogenous waste in the form of urea is produced by the liver.

In 1918, some reverse observations were recorded by *B.M. Allen*, he performed his experiments with the removal of thyroid gland from a frog and he found that the tadpole did not transform into a frog. It certainly fed and grew to many times bigger size but did not become a frog. On the other hand, if it is fed thyroid or is placed in thyroxin solution, it immediately becomes a frog.

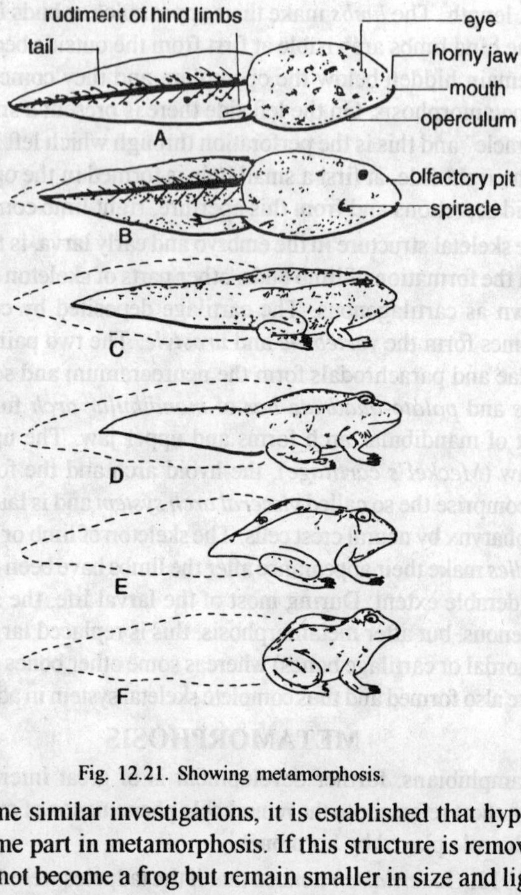

Fig. 12.21. Showing metamorphosis.

With some similar investigations, it is established that hypophysis also plays some part in metamorphosis. If this structure is removed, the tadpole does not become a frog but remain smaller in size and lighter in colouration. In short, we notice that two glands-hypophysis and thyroid-that are necessary for the metamorphosis to take place properly. However, their importance is varying. For example, if we remove both the glands and then feed the tadpole thyroid tissue. there will be metamorphosis and if we remove both glands and graft anterior lobe of hypophysis into a tadpole. there will not be any metamorphosis. however the growth will be there. Therefore the degree of the role of these two glands vary from one to other. Moreover. we can obtain precocious metamorphosis in frog tadpoles. by adding thyroxine to the water in which they live. The metamorphosis is considerably hastened, if even one part of thyroxine is added to 1000,000 parts of water.

Metamorphosis is said to be started with the fact when tadpole starts coming to surface and gulping air for respiration by the lungs. The tadpole soon ceases feeding and *larval skin* is casted off with the *fringed lips* and *horny jaws*. The tail decreases in length while legs increase. The lungs become well established as respiratory organs. The gill slits are closed and the blood vascular system modifies according to air breathing nature. The mouth, now enlarges and *true jaws* are developed. The tongue also enlarges and jaw muscles start functioning. The eyes also increase in size and bulge outwardly as in adult frog. The stomach with the liver is enlarged, while intestine shortens. There occur also changes in their structures in relation to change from a herbivorous diet of carnivorous. The young frog so formed still are provided with a stump of a tail. They at this stage come to land from water. They are preferably seen in damp pastures for their love for moisture. They feed mainly on insects and continue to grow and those which won the natural selection attains the adult stage and start living as common animals-the frogs.

13

Parental Care in Amphibians

The life history of a typical frog shows many of the essential features of the class Amphibia. The main character is the egg laying, and its development which normally takes place in water. The eggs are rather small and without protective membranes or shell. When the embryo hatches out it is still very small and must find its own food in water for its further development. Such development of young ones without any one of the parents in tropical openes to many enemies in water, they are exposed to many dangers of being eaten away by aquatic animals which are mainly inhabiting in such areas. In such circumstances; it becomes necessary for the care of eggs and maintenance of young ones which later develop into adults.

There are various controversies which have been restored to, by which the young ones are protected during the course of their early stages. These controversies fall into the following heads:

ORDER ANURA

1. Protection by means of nests and nurseries or Indirect nurseries

Here the parents prepare or construct nests for the eggs and small developing stages as given under the following heads:

(a) In enclosures in water. The large tree frog, the *Hyla faber* (also known as Ferreiro in Brazil) protects its progeny by building a basin shaped nursery in shallow water and at the border of ponds with the aid or help of webbed feet. The female scoops or digs the mud to a length of 3" to 4" and construcs a circular wall with the material, thus removed from the hole. the wall which emerges above the surface of the water. Thus the eggs and early larvae are protected in these so called constructed nurseries, avoiding the attack of aquatic fishes and other animals.The heavy rains destroy the wall of nursery and the larvae go into the water.

(b) In holes near water. A Japanese tree frog-*Rhacophorus schlegelii* protects its eggs and early stages in a some what better way.The male and female in embrace bury themselves in a damp soil on the edge of pond, ditch or flooded rise field. A hole or chamber is made on the soil but a few inches above water level, on reaching the chamber the passage is blocked and the oviposition begins. Actually after polishing the wall of the chamber the female produces some secretion which is beaten into a froth or foam by the treating of legs. The female deposits the eggs which are latter impregnated by male. The parents make their way out by boring the hole or exit which of course is directed towards the water, so that when the larvae are hatched, they may find their way into water immediately. The eggs are well protected and aerated by means of air bubbles in the frothy mass surrounding them.

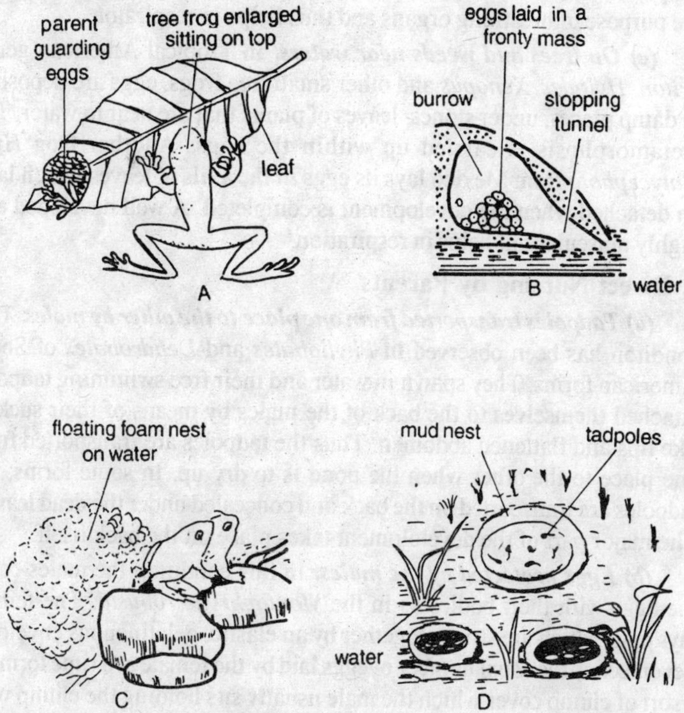

Fig. 13.1. Parental care in some amphibians.

Some species of S. American genera such as *Hypodactylus* and *Plaudicola* have been observed to treat their eggs in the similar fashion, but under stones.

(c) In nests on trees or on rocks over hanging the water. This type of nurseries has been studied in two forms of tree frogs. *Phyllomedusa*

(South American), and *Chiromantis* (Tropical Africa). These forms deposite their spawn on trees and the nests attached to one or many leaves stuck together and overhanging a pool. Then the larvae move with considerable freedom in frothy mass. Within a few days after loosing their external gills, they dropped into water, where they complete their development as an ordinalry way.

(d) In transparent gelatinous bag. The genus *Phrymixalus biroi* from New Guinea lays its eggs in a sausage shaped shallow transparent membranous bag which is secreted by the female. The whole development takes place in the bag. The miniature frogs leave the gelatinuous bag in the perfect condition. The larvae are without gills and the large tails serves the purpose of breathing organs and thus helps in respiraton.

(e) On trees and weeds near waters. In Tropical American genus *Triton*, *Hylodes*, *Xenopus* and other small tree frogs, eggs are deposited in damp places, under stones, leaves of plants that are near to water. The metamorphosis is carried up within the eggs. Another frog *Hyla platycephala* from Mexico lays its eggs in the axils of leaves which later on detached when the development is completed. A well developed and highly muscular tail helps in respiration.

2. Direct Nursing by Parents

(a) Tadpoles transported from one place to the other by males. This conditon has been observed in *Phyllobates* and *Dendrobates* of South American forms. They spawn in water and their free swimming tadpoles attached themselves to the back of the males by means of their sucker-like lips and flattened abdomen. Thus the tadpoles are transported from one place to the other when the pond is to dry up. In some forms, the tadpoles are transported on the back and concealed under the dead leaves. The major part of the develolpment takes place on the back itself.

(b) Eggs protected by the males. In this condition the males cover the eggs with their bodies as in the *Montophryne robusta*. The female lays eggs which are strung together by an elastic, gelatinouous envelope. Seventeen is the usual number of eggs laid by the female at a time forming a sort of clump cover which the male usually sits holding the clump with its hands. The male remains there till the development is completed. The development may occur outside the water. The larvae are devoid of gills. Tail which is well developed helps in respiration and locomotion as well.

(c) Eggs carried by parents. In different species of the group Amphibia, the eggs are carried from one place to the other by the parents as stated under the following heads :

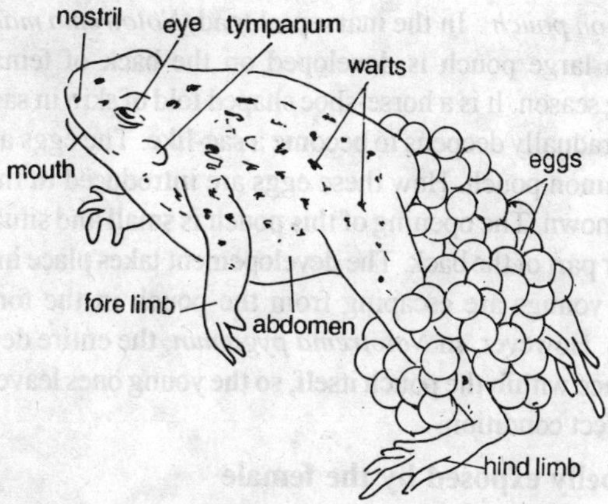

Fig. 13.2. *Alytes.*

1. Round the legs by the male. In the mid wife frog, *Alytes obstetricans*, the males take care of the eggs after they have been deposited by the female and the fertilization is also made. The male carries the eggs with its limbs, specially by hind- limbs, which serve as a recepticle. Here the eggs are held together by an elongated filament continous with gelatinouous capsule thus forming a large mass. The male rests, to usual treat in a hole and keeps up the moisture. It now and then takes eggs into the water by making them attached to the hind-legs. When the eggs are ready to hatch the male enters into the water. It remains until all the young ones are liberated in perfect condition.

2. On the back of the female

(i) *Exposed :* In *Hyla goeldii* (Brazilian tree frog) the females take incharge of the eggs and carry them along their backs. The eggs are placed by the male on the back skin of the female which is extended into narrow folds, which border and support the egg mass on the sides to form pouch. The young leaves the egg and emerges out of pouch in perfect condition.

Hyla evansi (British genera) also behaves in the same way.

(ii) *In cell-like pouch:* In *Pipa americana* the eggs are carried on the back of the female. Here it is interesting because the skin thickens and grows round the eggs until each is completly enclosed in a dermal pouch formed from the secretion of skin glands. The eggs develop in these cell-like pouches and young ones leaves out these pouches in a perfect condition. even without vestigial of tail.

(iii) In common pouch : In the marsupial toad, *Nototrema marsupium*, a common large pouch is developed on the back of female during breeding season. It is a horse-shoe shaped fold of skin in sacral region which gradually deepens to become a sac-like. The eggs are filled in this common pouch. How these eggs are introduced in the pouch is still unknown. The opening of this pouch is small and situated on the posterior part of the back. The developement takes place in the pouch and the youngs are escaping from the pouch in the form of only tadpoles. However, in *Nototrema pygamun*, the entire development takes place within the pouch itself, so the young ones leave the pouch in a perfect condition.

3. On the belly exposed by the female

In the case of *Rhacophorus reticlulatus* (Ceylonese genera), the female carries eggs on its belly, which bears shallow impressions which after the removal eggs are visible.

4. In the mouth and gular pouch by the male

In *Rhinoderma darwini*, the youngs are sheltered and developed in gular pouches, which are simply the modified vocal sacs of the male. These pouches extend over the entire ventral surface at side. In this genera the eggs are taken into the mouth by the male with the help of hands, and then are forced into the sub-gular region. About 10-15 young ones can get shelter in the gular pouch of a male.

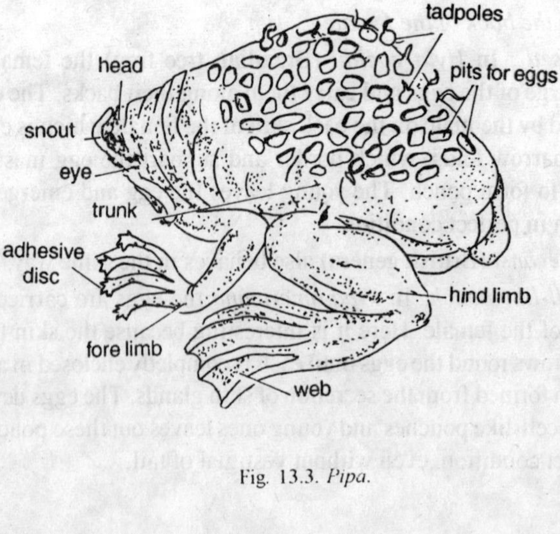

Fig. 13.3. *Pipa*.

5. By Female

In *Hylambates breviceps*, the female carries the eggs in her mouth. The eggs are large and few in number.

ORDER-URODELA

In urodela the ferilization is internal. In such forms a least care of progeny is taken. But in some Newts, the eggs are deposited one by one in a small group attached to the stones. The female folds leaves with her hind limbs so as to afford some protection to eggs. The development is like ordinary frogs and the larvae are very much like the adults. The different modes of protection have been displayed.

(i) In the holes on land or trees

Autodax lays its eggs in a dry hole on the ground or on tree. The parents remain in the hold during the developmental period to provide moisture and suitable temperature.

(ii) In transparent gelatinous bag

In case of *Salamandrella keyserlingii*, the female deposits its eggs in a gelatinous bag on the branch of a plant near water. The larvae when hatched are dropped to the bottom of bag and then into the water. Thenafter metamorphosis takes place.

(iii) Mother coils around the eggs

Plethodon lays its eggs in small packages beneath the stones and the mother remains coiled around them until they are hatched out.

(iv) Father coils around the eggs

In *Megalobatrichus maximum* and *Cryptobrachus allighanianses*, the eggs contained much yolk, are deposited by the females and then after surrounded by the male partner as father. These eggs are connected by a string, and whole mass forms a large clump round which the male coils itself. The larvae on leaving the eggs are with 3 pairs of external gills and show rediments of free limbs.

(v) Mother carries the eggs on its back

Desmognathus lays its eggs in a rosary-like string, female, takes charge of this rosary by winding it several times around the body and nurses it in a comparatively dry spot. Sometimes the eggs formed in a bunch are kept in an underground hole.

(v) Eggs retained in the uterus

Salamanders copulate on land and several months later, the female goes to water and gives birth to the youngs with fore limbs developed. In

S. atra the mode of reproduction is very remarkable. The uterine eggs are large and numerous but as a rule only one develops. The embryo passes through the following three stages :

(i) Still enclosed witin the egg and living on its own lodged yolk.

(ii) Free with the vitelline mass which is product of other generated eggs.

(iii) Vitelline mass disappears and it possesses external gills.

ORDER APODA

In this group fertlization is internal and breeding habits of *Ichthyophis glutinosa* have been observed, which show the remarkable parental care in this group. The female digs a hole close to the surface in a damp ground near the water. The eggs are deposited there. The eggs are strung together by a mass of thread containing many distinct twisted and formed by vitelling membrane round which the mother coils with its snake like body. The larvae appear in a gill like condition.

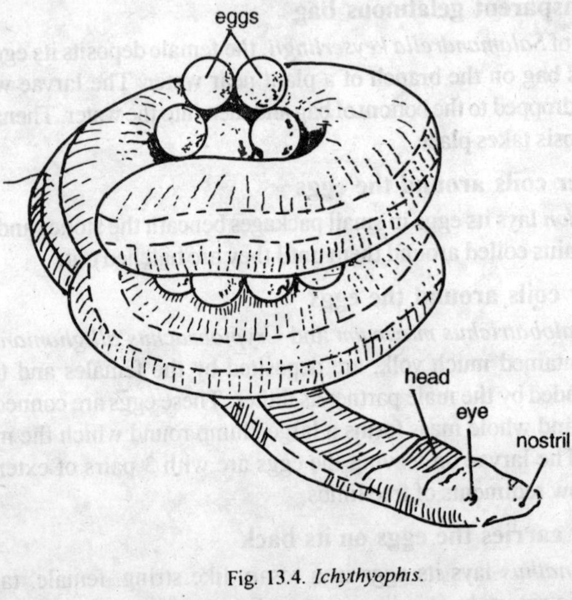

Fig. 13.4. *Ichythyophis.*

In *Hypogvophis* there is no larval life. The young ones leave their respective egg capsules in a perfect condition.

SIGNIFICANCE

So far we do not know the exact signi-ficance but it is generally assumed that it is a device to keep up their progeny by means of protecting them in all stages. Thus offering the life to the young and avoid dangers during their complicated life cycle. It is obvious by the fact that it seems as a device for the future of its race, thus leaving us a scarse played by the nature.

Revision Questions

1. What do you mean by parental care ? Write an essay on parental care in Amphibia.
2. Describe the phenomenon of parental care in Amphibia.

14

Neoteny & Paedogenesis

Neoteny and paedogenesis are the two terms which are often used as synonyms. But both the terms have different meanings. *Neoteny* is a phenomenon that can be described as the prolongation of the larval stage *paedogenesis* refers when these larvae mature sexually, breed and produce young ones. In certain species of Mexican salamanders (*Ambystoma*) the larva known as tadpole, is fairly often incapable of achieving metamorphosis. The larva continues to grow and reaches the stage of sexual maturity when it is still in larval stage. These giant larvae are known as *Axolotls*. Although spontanous metamorphosis is rare among axolotls. Artificial metamorphosis can be induced by providing thyroid extract. In the axolotls it seems that the metamorphogenic hormone is present in thyroid gland. But it is not discharged into the blood stream in sufficient amount. It may be possible that their pituitary glands are deficient as not producing thyroid stimulating hormone. It is also possible that animal's entire organ is less sensitive to the effects of hormone, and demand greater quantities of it in order to achieve metamorphosis.

For the first time axolotls were described by *Hernandez* (1600), in his book *History of the Animals of New Spain*, and named *Atolacalt*. *Johnston* (1767) affirmed that the axolotl was only a water illusion. *Cuvier* was aware that the axolotl must be the larvae of some large unknown salanmander. In January 1865, shortly after laying the eggs, the female axolotl underwent metamorphoses and Cuvier's openion that it was salamander was justified.

Environmental factors affecting neoteny. The significance and cause of neoteny are not properly understood. Environmental factors affect metamorphosis in several ways. Excess of food, cold climate or insufficient iodine may cause failure of metamorphosis and retaintion of larval characters. This is indicated by the fact that drying up of swamps, scarcity of food and higher temperature in surrounding water induce metamorphosis in axolotl.

In United States, the axolotl metamorphoses in the ordinary manner from the larvae to the adult but the case is different in Mexico. In Mexican lakes, the axolotl remains permanently in water, possessing gills throughout the life and lays eggs. When transferred to the eastern states these axolotls lose their gills, develop lungs and become adult air breathing native tiger salamanders (*Ambystoma tigrinum*). Response of larval tissue to thyroid hormones is reduced with the fall of temperature and entirely disappears below 5°C.

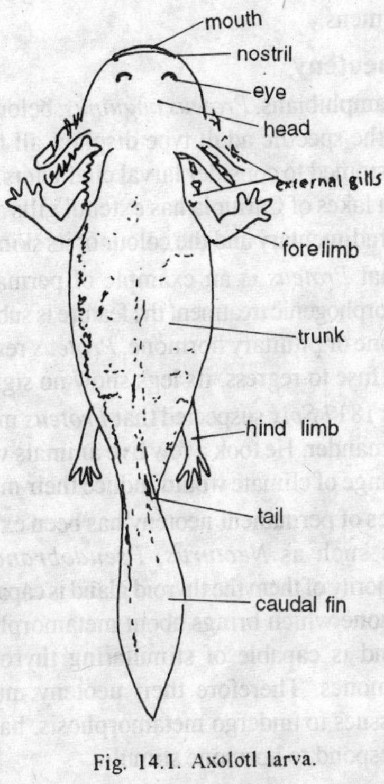

Fig. 14.1. Axolotl larva.

There are other tailed species of amphibians which can exhibit neoteny under the influence of cold and attitude. In the lakes of Lombardy alpine newts or tritons are found which reproduce in the larval stage. In other species of tritons total neoteny is limited to the female sex. In other amphibians neoteny is only partial. One example of this is midwife toad (*Alytes*) and another the edible queen frog whose tadpole can reach as much as 12cm instead of the usual 4cm in length and never acquire the faculty to reproduce.

TYPES OF NEOTENY

1. Artificial neoteny

Attempts have been made to bring about neoteny in amphibians by artificial means. As we know that metamorphosis is brought about by the hormone of thyroid gland, permanent and more or less giant larvae obtained, either by removing thyroid gland or by submitting the animal to chemicals with anti-thyroid or anti-pituitary effects-thiouracil, basolan etc. But total neoteny is not obtained by these means because the gonads do not mature in laboratory specimens.

2. Permanent neoteny

Among some amphibians, *Proteus anguinus*, belonging to the family Perennibrachiats, the specific adult type displays all the characteristics which we are accustomed to consider larval characters. *P. anguinus* lives in the subterranean lakes of Carniola has extenul gills and two little fore-lianbs. Its eyes are rudimentary and the colour of its skin is very pale-pink.

This shows that *Proteus* is an example of permanent neoteny, no matter what metamorphogenic treatment the feature is submitted to, whether it be thyroid hormone or pituitary hormone, *Proteus* remains unshakably *Proteus*. Its gills refuse to regress, its legs show no sign of growth.

As long ago as 1817 *Spix* suspected that *Proteus* might be the larvae of a terrestrial salamander. He took a few live animals with him to Brazil hoping that the change of climate would induce their metamorphosis.

The hypotheses of permanent neoteny has been extanded to include other amphibians such as *Necturus*, *Pseudobranchus, Siren* and *Typhlomolge*. In majority of them the thyroid gland is capable of functioning and produces hormone which brings about metamorphosis. In addition their pituitary gland is capable of stimulating thyroid gland for the production of hormones. Therefore their neoteny must be due to an incapacity of the tissues to undergo metamorphosis, having presumably lost the faculty to respond to hormone stimuli.

SIGNIFICANCE OF NEOTENY

Neoteny may he one of the basic processes which evolution employs to bring about important changes in organic species. *Weismann* (1875) thought neoteny to beacase of retarded evolution or *atavism*, i.e., reversion of ancestral condition. According to *Bolk, de Beer, Cuenot* and others, neoteny has played its part in the genesis of our own species. Man resembles the giant foetus of the great ape for more than the adult ape, and it is thus tempting to imagine that the passage from ape to man involved some process of *foetalization*, connected with variations of hormonal equilibrium and a slowing down in rate of growth. However, the neoteny is now regarded to be of secondary specialization, a physiological adaptation of advantage.

15

Stegocephalia

Stegocephalians are the extinct amphibians appeared in lower *Carboniferous* and extended to the *Permian*, upto the upper *Triassic* where they became extinct and thus disappeared there. They were salamander like amphibians. Due to having a covering of dermal bones to cover the roof of cranium, the term *Stegocephalia* was give to them. They had a typical pentadactyle plan of limbs, two occipital condyles and some times none, and their vertebrae were also pseudo-centrous or notocentrous type. Due to these characters they were not supposed to be the fishes. At present there is, however, no detailed fossil evidences of stegocephalians. The fossils that appear to be closest to the possible tetrapod ancestor.

FEATURES OF STEGOCEPHALIA

Stegocephalians were the tetrapod and had massive endoskeleton with a well developed dermal armour of bony scales or scutes. This dermal armour was also extended to the ventral side of the body and the back and underside of limbs. The scales were of various forms like oval, rhomboid, oblong, fusiform etc. and were made up of free bony tissues. Two pairs of limbs marked their tetrapod affinity. Tail was invariably present. Other important features of stegocephalians are given below:

Vertebral column

The vertebral column of stegocephalia resembles that of ganoid fishes. In some forms the persistence of notochord has been reported as in *Branchiosauridae*. However, in *Phyllospondyli* complete ossified centra have been observed. The neural arch extends downwards and joined a pair of delicate hypocentra to enclose the notochord. In some cases a constricted bony cylinder enclosed the persistent notochord as in Lepospondyli. The ossification begin with the neural arch whose halves remained separate in the beginning. In neck region the only representative of cervical vertebrae is the atlas having concavities on both the sides.

Skull

In stegocephalians, the skull resembles with that of the skull of fish representing the piscian ancestory of Amphibia. The number and arrangement of plates forming the roof of skull were also identical. Lateral line canals were crossed the same bones in both fishes and amphibians. Tympanium replaced. In Labyrinthodont the interpterygoid vacuities were small. Acrodont type of dentition in both fishes and tetrapods present. As far as lower jaw of Embolomeri was concerned it resembled with that of Osteolepidae with some striking difference from that of modern amphibia. It was sheathed outwardly by the dentary and supra-angular mesially three coronoids and a pre-articular ventrally, by two splenials and the angular. The teeth of both upper and lower jaws were arranged alternatively.

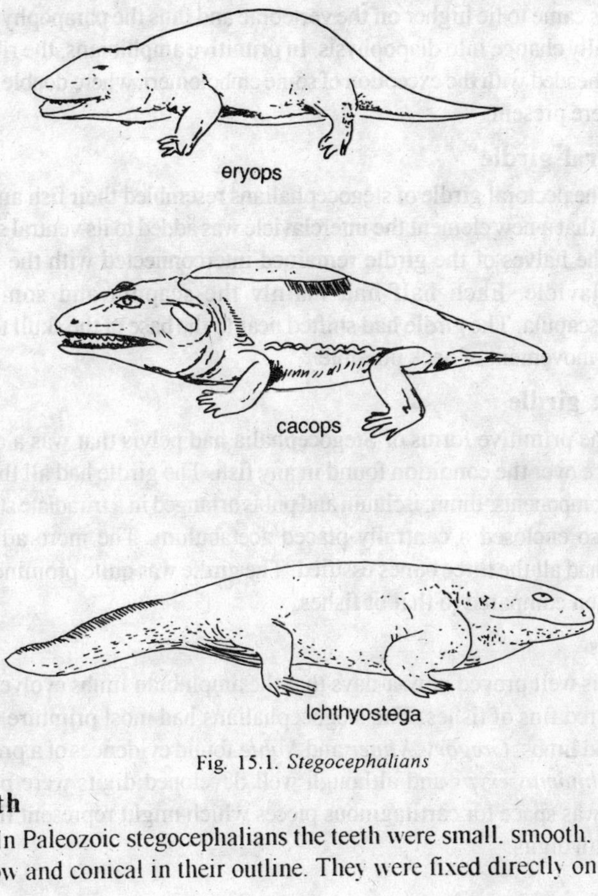

Fig. 15.1. *Stegocephalians*

Teeth

In Paleozoic stegocephalians the teeth were small. smooth. slender. hollow and conical in their outline. They were fixed directly on the jaw bones. This is the acrodont dentition still remained in the modern amphibian. The evolutionary stages, however, showed the occurrence of secondary and tertiary branches of dentine, and at the same time the undulated or folded layers of cement provided the characteristic labyrin-thodont structure as in extinct crossopt-erygean fishes. The vomers and sometimes palatines showed the occurrence of teeth on them.

Ribs

In the primitive amphibians the ribs were long and tended to surround the body like a series of loops. They were articulated with the vertebrae upto the middle of the tail. Genetically the ribs are related to the different processes of the vertebrae viz. diapophysis, usually arise in the septa at a distance from the notochord. With the shifting of horizontal muscle septum the ribs came to lie higher on the vertebrae and thus the parapophysis may gradually change into diapophysis. In primitive amphibians, the ribs were single headed with the exception of some embolomeri, where double headed ribs were present.

Pectoral girdle

The pectoral girdle of stegocephalians resembled their fish ancestors except that a new element the interclavicle was added to its ventral surface. Both the halves of the girdle remained interconnected with the help of interclavicle. Each half had mainly the scapula and sometimes coracoscapula. The girdle had shifted near to the base of the skull to make a little movement of neck possible.

Pelvic girdle

The primitive forms of Stegocephalia had pelvis that was a distinct advance over the condition found in any fish. The girdle had all the three basic components: ilium, ischium and pubis arranged in a triradiate structure and also enclosed a centrally placed acetabulum. The more advanced forms had all the three bones ossified. The girdle was quite prominent and big when compared to that of fishes.

Limbs

It is well proved now-a-days that the amphibian limbs evolved from the paired fins of fishes. The stegocephalians had most primture type of tetrapod limbs. *Gregory*. *Miner* and *Noble* found evidences of a propellar in *Rachitomus eryps* and although well developed digits were present. There was space for cartilaginous pieces which might represent the fifth and sixth digits.

AFFINITIES OF STEGOCEPHALIA

The exact position of stegocephalian is still uncertain. Their position is a very controversial matter. They appear to be fresh water or terrestrial animals. They had both reptilian as well as amphibian characters that is why generally referred to as Amphibia but some times as Reptilia. The affinities of Stegocephalia are as given under the following heads.

Resemblance with Amphibia

(i) Presence of gill arches in some genera.

(ii) The presence of grooves on cephalic scales represent the traces of lateral line sense organs.

(iii) Presence of all the three basic bones like clavicle, coracoid, and scapula in pectoral girdle.

(iv) Dicondylic skull i.e. with two occipital condyles.

(v) Autostylic type of jaw suspensorium in which the upper jaw bones are fused with the cranium.

(vi) Amphicoelous type of vertebrae having concavities anteriorly as well as posteriorly.

(vii) Presence of four digits in fore limbs and five digits in hind limbs.

(viii) Most of them were carnivorous like the modern amphibians.

(ix) Acrodont teeth on jaw bones, vomers and palatines.

(x) Cartilaginous carpalas and tarsals.

Differences with Amphibia

(i) The outer covering of skull in smooth in modern amphibia while it is covered by bony plates in Stegocephalia.

(ii) Ossification reduced in modern Amphibia and the neurocranium is extremally ossified.

(iii) In Stegocephalia the presence of sclerotic plates around the eyes marks another difference.

(iv) The members of Stegocephalia show the presence of bronchial arches.

Resemblances with Reptiles

(i) Presence of bony plates on the skull and body is the strongest affinity between Stegocephalians and reptiles.

(ii) The clavicle which is a bone of pectoral girdle is very long in both the cases.

(iii) The pelvic girdle is arched in both.

(iv) The presence of sclerotic bony plates around the eyes is again a common feature

(v) Tetrapod pentadactyle nature of limbs in both the cases.

Peculiar characters of Stegocephalia

(i) The presence of dermal bony plates on the skull and on the body.
(ii) There is a parietal formen between the parietal bones.
(iii) The persistence of notochord in adults.
(iv) Massive and properly ossified endoskeleton
(v) The skull is well developed and is considerably large.

As stated already that the Stegocephalia is an extinct order of class Amphibia. They resembled the modern salamander or lizard-like in several characters. They appeared in lower *Carboniferous* and persisted upto upper *Triassic*. Generally they refer to amphibia but they are also regarded as reptiles due to having reptilian affinities. Since they show more close resemblance with amphibians than reptiles that is why can be placed along with amphibians, which is still controversial.

16

Origin and Evolution of Amphibia

The origin of Amphibia is a problem of unique interest and a most fascinating problem of phylogeny. The word "Amphibia" in the first time used by *Linnaeus* to designate a class which includes the animals that partly live on land and partly in fresh water. There is no doubt that the amphibian organization has emerged out of the Piscian (fish-like) ancestor. But a great gulf appears between fishes and Amphibia i.e. between the absoulutely aquatic creatures with internal gills, fins and terresterial tetrapod creatures with lungs, fingers and toes. However, there are so many evidences which support the origin of Amphibia from fishes as shown below.

(A) Taxonomic Evidences

Taxonomy forms one of the best evidences in suport of organic evolution. In the classification of chordates Amphibia has been arranged between fished and reptiles i.e. between absolute aquatic animals (fishes) on one side and complete terrestrial animals (reptiles) on the other and being present in between them. Amphibia itself shows the dual nature of life. Since the classification has been arranged in a ladder manners, Amphibia has been arranged short above the fishes must have originated from their pre-existing ancestors, i.e. fishes. Hence the classification is the strong taxonomic evidences showing the origin of Ambhibia from fishes.

(B) Embryological Evidences

There is a striking resemblance in the mode of development of Amphibia with that of the fishes.

(i) There is holoblastic segmentation or cleavage in both.

(ii) The tadpole larva of Amphibia resembles with that of a fish.

Since it is usually accepted that ontogeny repeats the phylogeny, the tadpole larva shows almost exact resemblance with the fish in the possession of a (i) caudal fin. (ii) lateral line sense organs; and (iii) gills and gill slits. Also in aquatic breathing and of common habit of living in water.

(C) Anatomical Evidences

The anatomical resemblances between fishes and amphibians are so close that it led *Huxley* to put both amphibians and fishes under Ichthyopsida.

(D) Evidences from present day habits

The indespensible watery habits of amphibians suggests their origin from aquatic animals i.e. fishes. The need of an aquatic environment reaches its peak when the amphibians go to the water to reproduce and laying their eggs. The whole cycle of development takes place in water, and the adults which come to live on land but these adults live near water.

(E) Evidences from palaeontology

Palaeontology forms the best and direct evidence of organic evolution. Even though there are many lacunae in the palaeontological records of amphibians. The recent researches of *Gregory* (1915). *Watson* (1917, 1926) and *Williston* (1925) proved the origin of Amphibia from fishes.

Fig. 16.1. Labyrinthodontia.

All the above evidences which we have studied now unanimously agree the origin of Amphibia from fishes. Now we will study the Piscine ancestors which have flourished during the lower Carboniferous Period so that we may find the exact group of fishes from which Amphibia have been originated.

PISCINE ANCESTORES

Modern Amphibians have arisen from a group of more or less aquatic tetrapods which flourished from atleast early Carboniferous to Triassic times. At that time there were three distinct orders of Amphibia, as revealed by the fossil history. These includes (i) Labyrinthodontia; (ii) Lepospondyli; and (iii) Phyllospondyli. The first two were present not only in abundance, but presented a variety of flows in the lower Carboniferous which indicate that they must have originated earlier atleast in the Devonian and possibly in the Silurian Periods.

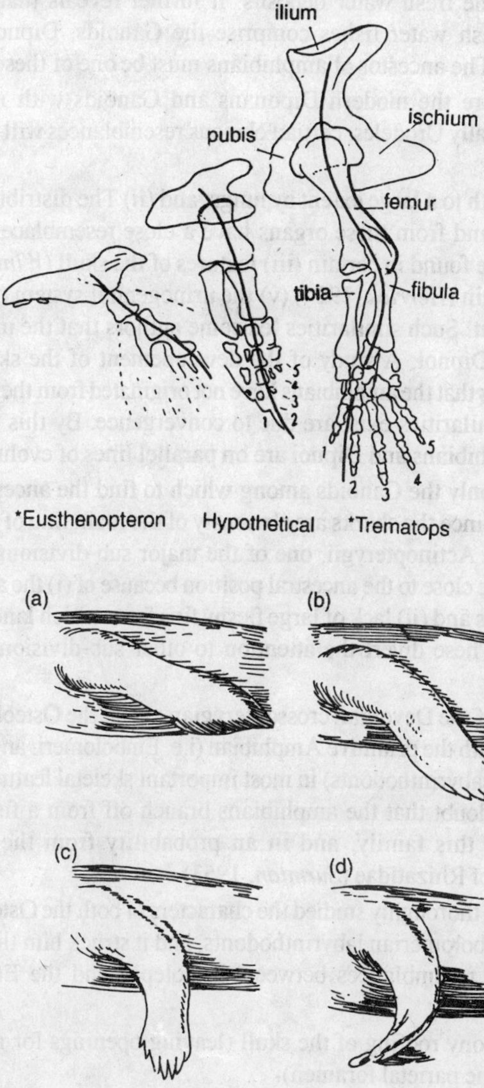

Fig. 16.2. Evolution of limbs from fins.

Another important point that limits our researches for the tetrapod ancestor is the fact that the amphibians arose from ancestors in the fresh water, because all the fossils record that establishes the relataionship is obtaiaued from the fresh water deposits. It further reveals that in the Devonian the fresh water fishes comprise the Ganoids, Dipnoans or aberrant sharks. The ancestor of amphibians must be one of these.

If we compare the modern Diponans and Ganoids with modern Amphibia, especially Urodeles, certian obvious resemblances will at once appear. They are :

(i) Both breath to a large extent by lungs; and (ii) The distribution of blood vessels to and from these organs have a close resemblace. Other similarites may be found in certain (iii) features of the skull (*Wintiebert*, 1922) (iv) the brain (*Herrick*, 1924) (v) the urinogenital system (vi) and early development. Such similarities led some authors that the urodeles originated from Dipnoi. A study of the developement of the skull (*de Beer*, 1937) shows that the amphibians have not originated from the Dipnoi and whatever similarities exist are due to convergence. By this we can say that the Amphibians and Dipnoi are on parallel lines of evolution.

This leaves only the Ganoids among which to find the ancestors of the amphibians, since the sharks are obviously of the main line of ascent. Among these the Actinopterygii, one of the major sub-divisions of the group do not come close to the ancestral position because of (i) the absence of internal nostrils and (ii) lack of large fleshy fins from which land limbs might develop. These divert the attention to other sub-division of the fishes.

One family of the Devonian crossopterygian called the Osteolepidae agree so closely with the primitive Amphibian (i.e. Embolomeri, an extinct sub-order of the Labyrinthodonts) in most important skeletal features that there can be no doubt that the amphibians branch off from a fish very closely allied to this family, and in an probability from the genus *Eusthenopteron* of Rhizatidae (*Surmtan*, 1953).

Prof. *Watson* thoroughly studied the characters of both the Osteolepid fishes and the embolomerian labyrinthodonts, and it struck him that they shared excellent resemblances between Osteolepid and the Embolomerians are as follow :

(i) Complete bony roofing of the skull (leaving openings for nostrils orbits and the parietal foramen).
(ii) Labyrinthodont pattern of teeth.
(iii) Autostylic skull.
(iv) The arrangement of the palatal bones
(v) Presence of internal nostrils for aerial respiration.

(vi) The pectrol girdle is attached to the skull by supraclathrum.

(vii) No connection exists between the pelvic girdle and the vertebral column. So far as the limbs are concerened they are smaller and resembled more the later Amphibia than they do with the fins of Osteolepid fishes. Thus the Embolomeri shows an advancement over the Osteolepid fishes.

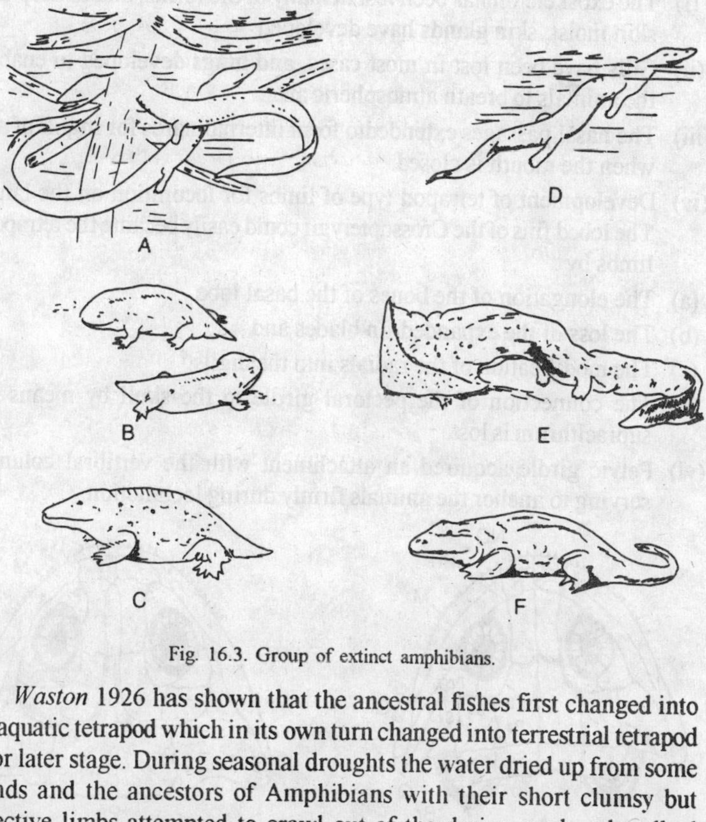

Fig. 16.3. Group of extinct amphibians.

Waston 1926 has shown that the ancestral fishes first changed into an aquatic tetrapod which in its own turn changed into terrestrial tetrapod at or later stage. During seasonal droughts the water dried up from some ponds and the ancestors of Amphibians with their short clumsy but effective limbs attempted to crawl out of the drying pool and walked over the land to reach the next pool where water still remianed. Thus the " land limbs" as held by *Romer*. (1947). were developed to reach water and not to leave it. Apparently they seem to have been aquatic forms in the begining but owing to abundance of insects they might linger in banks to prey upon them and thus tended to become terrestial which they could do during the Carboniferous and Permian times.

EVOLUTION OF AMPHIBIA

Changes undergone by Amphibia to become terrestrial.

Let us briefly summarize the various main changes that the amphibians have undergone in acquiring terrestrial life from an aquatic one. The following are the main changes :

(i) The exoskeleton has been lost in many of the forms, and to keep the skin moist, skin glands have developed.

(ii) Gills have been lost in most cases, and lungs developed to enable the animals to breath atmospheric air.

(iii) The nasal passages extendedto form internal nares for ingulf of air when the mouth is closed.

(iv) Development of tetrapod type of limbs for locomtion on the land. The lobed fins of the Crossopterygii could easily became the tetrapod limbs by :

(a) The elongation of the bones of the basal lobe

(b) The loss of the expanded fin blades and

(c) The modification of the radials into the digits.

(v) The connection of the pectoral girdle to the skull by means of supraclthrum is lost.

(vi) Pelvic girdle acquired an attachment with the vertibral column serving to anchor the animals firmly during locomotion.

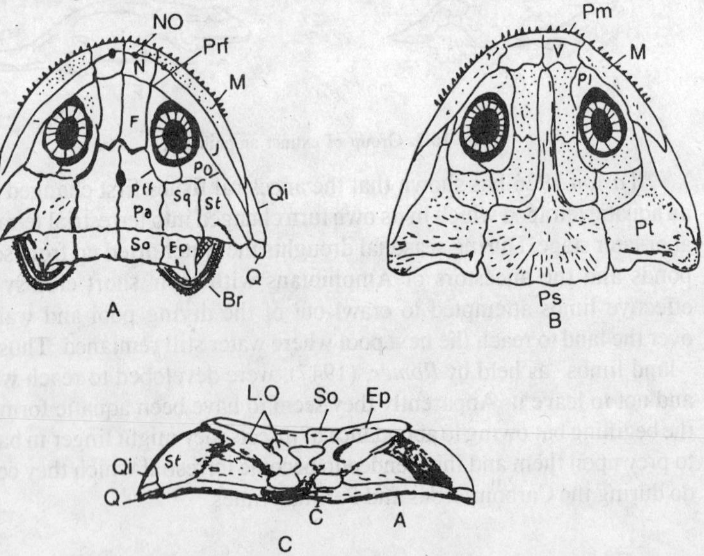

Fig. 16.4. Palaeozoic amphibian skulls.

(vii) For supporting the weight of the body on land the limb girdles were strengthened by the addition of an interclavicle joining the two halves of the shoulder girdle together.

(viii) Corresponding to the new mode of life a modification of sense organs has been brought about. The lateral line system was rendered useless. The auditory, optic and olfactory sense organs gain prominance to keep in line with the terrestrial mode of life.

Correlated with the acrial mode of respiration a number of modifications occured in the vasular system. They are as given below:

(a) The heart has come to posses two auricles and a ventricle, the deoxygenated blood is kept separeate in one auricle and sent to the lungs directly.

(b) Presence of the eustachian valves in the veins to regulate the flow of blood to the various branches.

(c) Of the six pairs of aortic arches only the fourth pair (systemic) of arches form the dorsal aorta, the third pair becomes the carotids, the 1st, 2nd and fifth pairs disappear and the six pair is modified into the pulmocutaneous trunks which have lost their connections with the dorsal aorta.

Besides the above mentioned changes adapted to a terrestrial life, modern amphibians show other characteristics, some of which are the followings:

(i) The nacked skin (except in Apoda)

(ii) The presence of two occipital condyles.

(iii) The absence of lateral line system in the adult.

Despite these modifications to Piscine descent of Amphibia are still proclaimed by the following features :

(i) The presence of a long *conus arteriosus* provided with valves (Apoda)

(ii) Strictly symmetrical arrangement of aortic arches.

(iii) The three chambered heart is still like that of the lung fishes.

(iv) The occurence of as many as four or even five branchial skeletal arches in the larval stage.

(v) The glottis is suported by cartilages which are the derivatives of posterior visceral arches.

(vi) The development of the vertebra (*Stegocephalia* and *Urodela*) form four paired units.

(vii) The existance of the hypoglossus nerve outside the cranium.

(viii) The presence of lateral line sense organs atleast in the larval stage.

(ix) The possession of external gills which occur in fishes like the lung fishes and the crossopterygians.

(x) The presence of cycloid scales (Apoda)

THE MODERN AMPHIBIA

The Amphibia living today are only the remnants of a large group which lived in abundance in former days, but they are specialised in some respects and degenerate in other. (i) The adult frogs and toads have short tailess bodies and long hind limbs modified for leaping. (ii) The caudates (Salamanders and Newts) retain the larval tail throughout life and have short legs useful in walking but not for running. They have adapted secondarily to aquatic life, developing even median fins supported by fin rays. (iii) The Gymnophiona or Caecilians are worm like, burowing creatures of the tropics with a very short tail and without any indication of limbs.

The amphibians called Labyrinthodonts gave rise to the other lines of amphibian development from which our modern Salamanders, Caecilians and Frogs descendants. Along and other parts of modifications the Labyrinthodonts produced the ancestral reptiles the Cotylosaurs. It has already been referred that with Labyrinthodonts there lived Phyllospondyls and Lepospondyls. From the Phyllospondyls have arisen the frogs and Salamanders of today. The primitive frogs were placed closely with the salamanders in the vertebral column and skull pecularities and this seems certain that they have a common origin.

Branchiosaurs among the Phyllospondyls resembles closely the Salamanders in body form and thus shows that the Salamanders have arisen from Branchiosaurs. The ribs, limbs, pelvic girdle and vertebral colomn of Branchiosaurs closely resemble those of Urodeles. Thus it appears that salamander and frogs have arisen from Branchiosaurs of the order Phyllospondyli.

Together with Phyllospondyls and Labyrinthodonts there lives the members of the order Lepospandyli. The best known genus of this order is *Diplocaulus* which resembles which the Caecilians closely in the characters of the skull. Although Leponspondyls resemble Urodeles in many points yet the differences are also numerous and also show different lines of ancestory. Caecilians are believed to have evolved from Lepospondyls that is to say they have adapted a different line of evolution from the lower *Carboniferous* time.

17

Courtship and Mating in Amphibians

It is in spring that the average person is most conscious of the amphibian. The Spring Peeper, *Hyla crucifer,* is considered by many to be more reliable harbinger of warm weather than is the robin. One old saying is that there will be but three more freeze-ups after the peepers are heard calling. This is akin to the superstition that if a gound hog sees his shadow on the second of February, there will be six more weeks of winter. Though the peepers are weather prophets far superior to our finest meteorologists, unfortunately they are not so expert that they can forecast just how many more frosts will occur before it is safe to set out the tomato plants.

A great many amphibians breed in the spring, but by no means all of them do. Some breed in the summer, some in the fall, some in the winter. However, in the North we are most apt to notice the breeding activity in the spring. Spring must be interpreted very loosely, for sometimes the peepers and Wood Frogs are calling before March 21st even as far north as New England. The nights are often cold and forsty, and you may wonder why these little creatures have come out of hibernation so early.

We do not begin to recognize all the conditions that cause the amphibians to emerge from hibernation and to commence courtship and mating, any more than we understand all the reasons behind bird migration. But though there is much to be learned on this subject, it is interesting helpful to discuss a few of the factors that have an important bearing on the matter.

The prime factor governing the amphibian's emergence from hibernation is the weather. If the ground is frozen solid, the animal hibernating beneath the frost line would not be able to breakthrough the forzen crust, even should he so desire, which he does not. For those that hibernate in the detritus of pond bottoms, ice on top prevents their escape. But the amphibian is a cold-blooded creature, whose internal temperature is nearly the same as his external surroundings, and very cold surroundings make him sluggish and incapable of the violent movement necessary to burrow out of hibernation. Therefore, until the temperature of the earth or pond water rises to a certain level, the amphibian remains in the dormant condition known as hibernation, where heart beat and respiration are slowed to be minimum.

All amphibians are extremely sensitive to temperature changes, and notice the slightest gradations that are imperceptible to us. Furthermore, each amphibian has a temperature at which he must live for optimum comfort and activity. This varies from species to species, and helps to explain why the Spring Peeper emerge form hibernation and begins to breed earlier than the toad.

The temperature of the water is important not only because it must be warm enough to arouse those sleeping beneath it to activity but also because it must be warm enough so that any eggs laid in it will not be frozen and killed.

Humidity also plays a tremendous part in determining courtship and mating time. You will always find that the peak of breeding activities in all species occurs on evening of high humidity—the choruses of peepers, toads, treefrogs, and frogs are at their loudest on rainy overcast days and especially nights. Naturally, the humidity of the air has more influence on those amphibians who are more terrestrial than on those who are partially or completely aquatic. But it affects them all to some extent. Perhaps there is considerable truth in the fresherman's adage that fish bite better on a rainy or dull day. Certainly it would be true if one fished for amphibians.

The weather does not, of course, completely govern courtship and mating. It is also regulated by the animal's ductless glands—especially the anterior lobe of the pituitary gland. The secretions of this gland stimulate the sexual glands, which in turn rouse the animal to mate.

We usually think of ponds and lakes as being the place where amphibians congregate to mate and lay their eggs. It is true that the great majority of all amphibians do deposit their eggs in water. The salamanders may choose a quiet pond, as do the Newt and many Mole Salamanders. They may perefer the swift-running water of a brook, as do many Lungless Salamanders. Or they may select a moist place in the woods or in the mud. Doubtless, this dry-land laying is a surprise to many. And no wonder, for it is far more difficult to find a few eggs under a stone or log in the woods than it is to see the thousands upon thousands clustered in various parts of the pond. It may be even more of a surprise to learn that some salamanders lay their eggs in trees.

Frogs and toads lay in much the same places as do the salamanders. There are pond layers, river layers, and even tree layers, though none of our native frogs lay in trees. With the frogs and toads, coutship is always conducted very close to the place where mating and egg laying will occur. How do they court one another ? Let us take a specific example, the Spring Peeper.

The peeper hibernate in the woods, beneath the earth. When the ground becomes thawed, they emerge from their winter burrows and head for ponds and swamps. On dull afternoon and in the evenings, the male sits on the bank of the pond and utters his sweet birdlike call. He takes air into his lungs and closes his mouth and nostrils. He sends the air into the vocal sacs located in the throat region. They balloon out into a glistening bubble that is almost as large as the body of the peeper. The air is sent back and forth between lungs and vocal sacs, causing the vocal chords to vibrate. An enormous sound for so small a creature emerges: *Preep, peep, peep..* he sings sweetly. Other males join in, and soon there is a deafening chorus of pepers all calling to the females. A female approaches one of the singing males. She is silent, for only the males sing in the breeding season. But the male senses her approach. He turns towards her, climbs on her back, and embraces her, placing his arms just behind hers in her "armpits." The couple are now ready to enter the pond and lay the eggs. Courship in frogs and toads consists mainly of the male's calls. The female approaches the calling male. He may be so intent on his singing that she may even have to touch him to make him aware of her. Female toads frequently nudge males, though in other species of frogs and toads, movement in the vicinity of a calling male is sufficient to make the male cease his calling and turn to embrace the moving object.

Since the peak of the breeding activities are carried out at night, sight plays no part in the recognition of a mate. Sound and hearing and feeling are the things that count. The females are guided to the males by their calls. The males hear or feel a nearby female. "But," you may ask quite reasonably, "how do the males know they are embracing a female and not another male ? And how can they be sure that they have a mate of their own species, and not a female of another species, if they cannot see her ?"

First of all, the males distinguish the females by their silence. Should a male embrace another male—and this happens quite frequently—the male who is thus treated squeaks or croaks in protest, and struggles to free himself or such unwanted attentions. The female, however, is completely silent during the breeding season. Some female frogs can call at other times of the year, but when the breeding season comes they are mute.

Second, different species breed at different times. They are not all in or around the ponds at once. However, there are several separate species there at the same time. The males of like species tend to congregate in groups apart from others. Since each species has its own distinct song, the females naturally go toward the sound of their own kind calling.

Should the male embrace a female of a different species, however, he can tell by feel that she is not of his own kind. She must be the correct size— larger than he, and swollen with unlaid eggs, but not so large that she is of a different species. The way she moves when he embraces her may also tell him whether or not she is of his own kind.

It sometimes happens, however, that mistakes are made in the excitement of the moment. Toads, whose nuptial embrace is strong, have been known to grasp a fish and not let go until the fish was crushed to death. This is rare, but it is probably due to the fact that there weren't enough females to go around and that the urge to reproduce was so strong that the male seized the first object that nudged him.

About the only romantic part of the courtship of frogs and toads from a human standpoint are their songs. These may be as sweet as are the calls of birds, and many people mistake the trill of the American Toad and some of the treefrogs for birds. They may be plaintive, as is the lamb-like bleating of the Narrow-mouth Toad. They may be insect-like, as are the calls of the Cricket Frogs. They may be squirrel-like, or like the noise of riverters; they may sound like a banjo, like a snore, or like a foghorn. It all depends upon the species, and there is but one male frog in all the world that, so far as we know, lacks a voice with which to call to his mate. This curious exception, which we shall discuss more fully later, is the Tailed Frog, *Ascapus truei*, found in parts of the northwestern United States.

When we look at courtship in the salamanders, we perceive an altogether different picture. In the first place, because the salamanders lack vocal chords they are silent. Not for them are the pleasures of serenading a lady love on a warm humid night. Neither have they any ears; they "hear" through their front legs or, in certain aquatic species, the lower jaw, which are especially adapted to receive vibrations from the ground. So even if the males could sing, neither the singer nor the one sung to could hear the sounds. They are like the forgs and toads in that sight plays no part in the recognition of a mate. How then do the salamanders find their mates, and recognize them ? So far as we know, scent is the main factor in recognition of sex and species. Females and males smell differently, and each species evidently has its own distinctive fragrance. We humans with our dull sense of smell cannot detect most of the odorus that attract the salamanders to one another. The salamanders have their own built-in perfume factories. The *hedonic glands*, as these "factories" are aptly named, are located mainly at the base of the tail and on the underside of the head on the males. Though the females lack any readily differentiated glands, their skin secretions evidently possess the odour that enable the males readily to identify them as to species and sex.

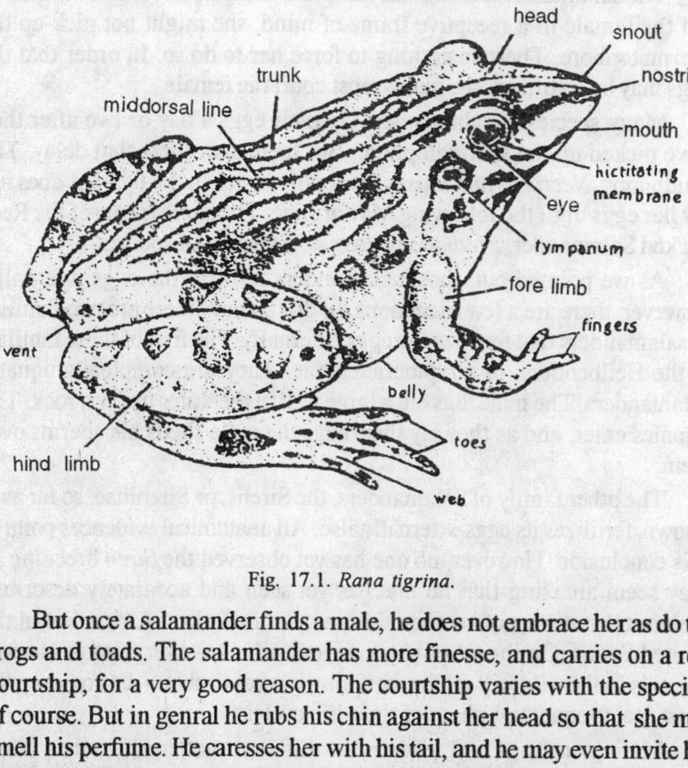

Fig. 17.1. *Rana tigrina.*

But once a salamander finds a male, he does not embrace her as do the frogs and toads. The salamander has more finesse, and carries on a real courtship, for a very good reason. The courtship varies with the species, of course. But in genral he rubs his chin against her head so that she may smell his perfume. He caresses her with his tail, and he may even invite her to dance if that is the accepted thing with his particular species. The dance may consist of her transporting her on his back, or of many other "engaged" couples joining together and making various figure eights around each other. In certain species the female may straddle the male's tail, placing her head on the base of the tail, and the two will then waddle off together in this position. It is the male's object to make himself irresistible to the female, and to excite her so that mating may take palce.

In most salamanders the eggs are fertilized internally, but internal fertilization is accomplished in a manner for different from that employed by mammals. When the male salamander feels that the female is sufficiently excited, he deposits, either on land or in the water, according to the habits of his species, a small jelly-covered package. This is known as the spermatophores, and each one contains the male's sperm. Next, the female comes and picks up one of these spermatophores with the lips of her cloaca, and it is placed inside her body in a special receptacle, known as the spermatheca, where the sperms remains to fertilize the eggs before they are laid.

The salamander has such an elaborate courship because if he did not put the female in a receptive frame of mind, she might not pick up the spermatophore. There is nothing to force her to do so. In order that the eggs may be fertilized, the males must court the female.

Many species of salamanders lay their eggs a day or two after they have picked up the spermatophore. But there are others that delay. The Mudpuppy, *Necturus maculosus,* generally mates in the fall, but does not lay her eggs until the following May or June. The same is true of the Red-backed Salamander, *Plethodon cinereus,* a terrestrial species.

As we pointed out, most salamanders fertilize the eggs internally. However, there are a few exceptions. In this country there are two families of salamanders that fertilize the eggs externally. The first of these families is the Hellbenders, or Cryptobranchidae. They are completely aquatic salamanders. The male digs out a large nest in the water under a rock. The females enter, and as they lay their eggs the male sheds his sperms over them.

The other family of Salamanders, the Sirens, or Sirenidae, so far as is known, fertilizes its eggs externally also. All anatomical evidences point to this conclusion. However, no one has yet observed the *Siren* breeding. It may seem amazing that no one has yet seen and accurately described these vital statistics of an animal found, not in darkest Africa, but in the United States. On the other hand, anyone who has ever tried to observe animals in the wild will realize how long it takes to obtain data on even the most inconsequential phase of their life cycles.

Mating in frogs and toads is an different matter altogether. Most frogs and toads fertilize their eggs externally. The male frog mounts the female, puts his arms around her, and grasps her firmly either just in back of her arms or in her groin. "Firmly" is a mild word for this nuptial embrace. If you catch a mated pair of toads, you will find it almost impossible to separate them, so tight is the male's grasp and so strong is the clasping reflex. However, it does not seem to bother the female in the least. Possibly, she enjoys this bear hug. In any case, if the pair mate on land they soon enter the water.

The female does not, however, always lay her eggs immediately. She may lay them anywhere from 3 to 26 days after pairing, the couple remaining in amplexus all during this time. What is it that govern when the eggs shall be deposited? Is it some physiological factor? Do some species require prolonged clasping in order to lay? Or does the length of time between coupling and laying depend mainly on the weather? Perhaps all of these have some bearing on the matter.

As the female lays her eggs, the male sheds his sperms on top of them. After all the eggs are laid, the female is considerably slimmer, for she may have had as many as 20,000 eggs inside her body. As soon as she no longer feels so pleasingly plum, the male releases her. Does he return to the bank and recommence his calling in the hope of attracting another female? According to one authority, frogs and toads fertilize the eggs complement of but one female each year, but this may be wrong, at least for some species. It is an extremely difficult thing to prove either way.

What of the female who finds no mate? Does she lay her unfertilized eggs just the same? Evidently not. As with many unmated birds, the eggs of the female are gradually resorbed into the body. A few may emerge from the oviduct, but they are never deposited in the characteristic mass of the species as they are when the male clasps the female.

There are several outstanding and interesting exceptions to the way most frogs and toads mate. We shall discuss three of them.

The first example is the primitive aquatic Surinam Toad known as *Pipa pipa.* This large flat-bodied creature lives in the ponds of South America. The mating call is a rapid clicking. This metallic sound is not produced by air vibrating the vocal chords, as in all other frogs, but by the cartilaginous disks of two bones "cracking" as the bones are moved. In much the same manner, some people can "crack" the joints of their fingers, jaws, or knees.

Clasping before laying is prolonged, and lasts at least 24 hours and sometimes longer. During this period the skin on the female' back becomes swollen and puffy. For many years it was believed that *Pipa* had a protursile oviduct that was everted when laying began. However, it has recently been proved that this is not true. When the couple are ready to lay, the pair roll over and, while they are in an upside-down position, three to five eggs emerge and are fertilized. The pair then right themselves. The entire roll and righting take about 11 to 14 seconds, and the pair is upside-down for about one second of this entire time. When the female is ready to lay more eggs. the pair once more roll over, until, after many such turns, the entire complement of from 40 to 114 eggs are laid. The eggs are pressed into the spongy skin on the female's back by the male's ventral surface; the first eggs are placed near the anus, later ones successively farther forward toward the female's shoulders. One day after deposition, the eggs are half buried in the skin of the female, and by the tenth day the top membranes of the eggs are level with the skin of the back.

Our own Tailed Frog, *Ascapus truei* is voiceless. Since he does not seem to be able to hear, and spends most of his time in swift-running mountain streams, a voice would be of little use to him anyway. He possesses something far more valuable, namely, a tail. Actually, it is not a real tail, though it certainly looks like one. It is an organ for copulation. The male crawls along the bottom of the stream searching for a mate. When he finds a female, he embraces her and then inserts his "tail" into an extension of her cloaca, and thus her eggs are fertilized internally.

The Tailed Frog alone possesses an intromittent organ because of his habitat. External fertilization of eggs would be precarious, to say the least, in the fast—flowing water where the Tailed Frog makes his home. No sooner would the sperm be shed than the water would carry it downstream before it could possibly fertilize all the eggs of the female. So in order that the species may continue to reproduce. Nature has provided the Tailed Frog with a "tail" so that he may fertilize his eggs internally.

There are two African toads with the jawbreaking names of *Nectophrynoides vivipara* and *Nectophrynoides tornieri.* These toads also fertilize their eggs internally. But the mystifying thing in their case is how they go about it. They have no copulatory organ as has the Tailed Frog. Scientists have long been puzzled as to how the sperms are introduced into the female's body. Do they, like the female salamanders, pick up a spermatophore which the male deposits. There is no indication that they do. But scientists know that the eggs are fertilized internally because both species give birth to fully transformed young. The entire larval period is spent in the mother's body and when the young are born they are miniatures of their parents. *Nectophrynoides vivipara* and *Nectophrynoides tornieri* and the only two known species of frogs and toads that are ovoviviparous, though there are several salamanders that are normally ovoviviparous and several that are occasionally so when existing conditions, such as extreme cold or high altitude, make egg laying impractical.

Let us look at some of the external differences between the sexes. With the sole exception of the Tailed Frog, these differences are secondary sex characteristics in frogs and toads. They are to a frog what a beard is to a man. With the Tailed Frog, the male is easily distinguished from the female by his longer "tail". Her "tail" is an extension of her cloaca, and is much shorter and more blunt than is his.

With the rest of the frogs and toads, we find great variety in secondary sex characteristics. About the only socondary sex characteristics that most male frogs and toads possess in common are their vocal sacs— and even here there are one or two exceptions that we shall examine in a movement. These vocal sacs are of different sizes and shapes, according to the species. They may be in throat region and when in use swell out to a glistening bubble, as is true in the peepers and many toads. They may swell out in kidney-shaped masses on the side of the head, as in the Lepoard Frog. Or there may be no localized swelling, but a general enlargement of the throat, as in the Bullfrog.

Vocal sacs might seem absolutely necessary to the male frog, as without them he would be unable to call the females in the breeding season. But that is evidently not so, for some of our frogs, such as the California Toad, *Bufo boreas halophilus,* and a few others, lack vocal sacs altogether. The Tailed Frog lacks them also, but he is believed to be silent. However, the California Toad is known to have a voice—a trill, similar in character to that of our northeastern American Toad, *Bufo americanus americanus,* but lower pitched. Neither does the sound carry so well, but whether this is because of the lack of vocal sacs, as one eminent scientist believes, or because lower-pitched sound do not seem to carry so well as those that are shrill, has not been proved.

The vocal sacs, even through they are usually present, are not very helpful to us when we pick up a frog and want to know whether or not he is a male. Unless we see his vocal sacs swelled up, we would not even known he had them. The females of some species lack vocal sacs, and in others they are greatly reduced in size. And, as we have said, the females are silent during the breeding season, though at other times of the year they may make calls similar to the males of their kind, but not so loud or so resonant.

Size is a factor in sex recognition of frogs and toads. The female as a general rule, larger than the male. It is just as well that she is, because she must carry him about on her back during mating and egg laying. In the water, though the additional weight does not matter so much, the female nervertheless does the swimming for both. Many males keep their hind legs drawn up on the female's back, while others allow their legs to float out behind. In a few species, if the couple is alarmed, the male may try to aid the female by using his feet in swimming motion, but their efficiency is impaired by his position on top of her. Many, however, like the American Toad, make no attempt at all to help the female in her race to escape. It seems curious to us that the male refuses to release his hold on the female and that each does not go its separate way when threatened with danger. But such is not their habit. Some species separate more easily than others, but none does it voluntarily, and often it is almost impossible to force the mated pair apart without injury, so strong is the embrace of the male.

Whereas the female is usually larger in over-all size, the male may have much larger and heavier forelegs. Perhaps, he has need for powerful arms the better to grasp the female. The male toad, *Bufo boreas,* found in the Northwest and in California, has enlarged forelimbs. These are insignificant, however, compared with a south American frog, *Leptodactylus ocellatus* whose arms are fully three times the size of those of the female!

In some species of frogs, the eardrum or tympanum, of the male is considerably larger than the eye whereas in the female it is the same size. A male Bullforg can easily be distinguished from a female by this characteristic. Why the male should need a larger ear than the female has never been explained. You would think that if either of them should have a larger one, it would be the female that would have most use for it. And why, of all species, should the Bullfrog, with his tremendous foghorn cry that can be heard from a distance of half mile or more, need a larger ear. The answer probably lies in the Bullfrog's evolution. At one time male perhaps did need larger ears, and through they are no larger useful they have not as yet been discarded

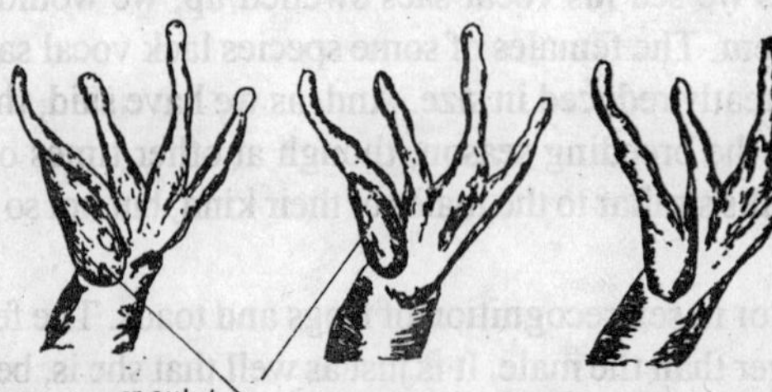

Fig. 17.2. A, Foot of frog showing web, B, Hand of male frog showing nupial or amplexusory pad.

In certain species of frogs and toads, the males have much larger thumbs. These may be swollen at the base or at tip. This enlargement of the thumb gives the male better gripping power. Does it also help to cushion the female's skin from being overly bruised by the male amphibian's as a

reason—it would probably be considered rank sentimentality by most scientist—but we can see no reason why it should not be so.

There is also a difference in the shape of the toe webbing of the two sexes in certain species. A male Wood Frog can be distinguished from a female in the breeding season by his convex toe webs. The female's are concave. Of course, you have to catch the frog and spread his hind toes apart in order to see this. It can't be observed from a distance.

Some reptiles and many birds present striking color dimorphism between the sexes. This is not true of frogs and toads. Colour differences, when they exist, are usually confined to the underparts, and especially the throat region. Some males have darker or more brightly coloured throats than the females of the same speices.

Of all the secondary sex characteristics exhibited by the frogs and toads, none is more startling than those developed by the male Hairy Frog. *Astylosternus robustus,* of Africa. All male frogs and toads need a great deal more oxygen during the breeding season than at any other time. This is due in part to their vociferous calls, and in part to the fact that their metabolic rate is heightened. Most male frogs, land toads, therefore, have larger lungs to satisfy the necessary requirements of their bodies for oxygen. But the Hairy Frog is an aquatic frog with very small lungs. Since he is a lage fellow, he needs a great deal more oxygen in the breeding season than his diminutive lungs can supply. Therefore, he broadens his skin area at that time, so that he will have a greater surface through which to absorb the extra oxygen needed, by growing long "hair" on his hind legs and lower sides. Of course, they are not really hairs, any more than gills and feathers, which they resemble at times. Scientists call these "hairs" vascular villosities. Be that as it may, they look like hair and they work like gills, enabling the Hairy Frog to obtain the additional oxygen necessary during the breeding season.

All in all, the secondary sex characteristics of frogs and toads are not very useful to us in helping us to tell whether our frog is male or female. It is unfortunate, but in this case there is no short cut. In order to distinguish between the sexes, you must know the secondary sex characteristics of each species.

Fortunately, the same state of affairs does not exist in the salamanders, in the breeding season. There are the larger over-all size of the females, the enlarged hind legs and or tail of the male, differences in the colours of the two sexes, and differences in the teeth. These correspond to those secondary sex characteristics in frogs and toads. But in almost all salamanders, there are differences around the vent, especially during the breeding season, though at other times these may be negligible. The male's vent is large, protuberant, and has tiny nipple-like projections. The female's vent is smooth or in folds.

Before we go on to eggs. Let me urge you to choose a warm humid overcast night in May for an outing. Wear a pair of galoshes, take a strong flashlight, and head for the nearest pond or swamp. You should have an experience that you will not soon forget. Peepers, treeforgs, toads, and forgs will be calling from all sides. You should be able to approach them easily, for they depend mainly on sight to warm them of enemies, and at night they cannot see you. Look in the water. There you will see mated pairs, salamanders and frogs, calling under the water. You will notice species you never knew existed, and species that you rarely if ever catch a glimpses of during the day. You have read how the forgs, toads, and salamanders court and mate but there is nothing that can compare with the thrill of actually witnessing these things with your own eyes and ears. Even if you aren't a keen field naturalist, you will be amazed at all you will discover, and will be very glad that you went. Perhaps you may even be so impressed and enthusiastic that will want to repeat the experience.

Index

A

Acetabulum, 50
Acoelous, 47
Acoustic ridge, 125
Acrodont, 64
Acromian process, 49
Aestivation, 1, 25
Aistopod, 4
Ambystoma, 5, 14, 177
Amphicoelous, 47
Amphiuma, 5, 11
Amplexus, 25, 135
Amplexary pads, 28
Antebrachium, 28
Alytes, 6, 18, 177
Archenteron, 148
Articular pads, 29
Arytenoid cartilage, 78
Ascaphus, 6
Autodax, 173

B

Bidder's canal, 129
Blastocoel, 142
Blind spot, 122
Bombinatu, 6
Bowman's capsule, 127
Brachium, 28
Branchiosauridae, 180
Brown spot, 28
Brucke, 88
Buccopharyngeal cavity, 63
Bufo, 6, 21

C

Calcaneum, 53
Camouflage, 25
Capitosaurus, 3
Capitatohamatium, 52
Cartilage bones, 39
Cauda equina, 112
Cavum aorticum, 87
Choroid, 119
Chordae tendineae, 86
Chief cells, 68
Chiromantes, 170
Cnemial crest, 53
Coccygeal nerve, 112
Coelomic fluid, 36
Columnae carneae, 87
Columella auris, 41
Condyle, 52
Conjunctiva, 119
Convergence, 149
Corpora bigemina, 103
Cricoid cartilage, 78
Cryptobranchus, 5, 16, 173
Cyclotosaurus, 3

D

Deltoid ridge, 52
Depressor mandibulae, 56
Dermal bone, 39
Dermal plicae, 26
Dicondylic, 1
Diplocaulus, 4
Dorsal mesentery, 37

E

Endocardium, 85
Endomysium, 55
Eogyrinus, 3
Epiboly, 147
Epicardium, 85
Epimysium, 55
Eryops, 3
Eustachian tube, 123
Excitation, 100
Exoccipitals, 39

F

Fasciculi, 55
Fenestra ovalis, 41, 123
Fibrinogen, 96
Filum terminale, 105
Foraman magnum, 39
Foxon, 89
Fringed lips, 167
Frontoparietals, 40
Fungiform papillac, 116
Funiculi, 106

G

Gall bladder, 70
Gastrocnemius, 61
Gastric glands, 66, 68
Gastric pits, 66
Genioglossus muscles, 65
Glands of Swammerdam, 110
Glenoid cavity, 49
Glomerulus, 129
Glutaeus, 60
Gregory, et. al., 182

H

Hallux, 29
Harderian glands, 119
Heparin, 72
Hepatopancreatic duct, 70
Hibernation, 25
Homodont, 64
Hump, 28
Huxley, 186
Hyla, 6, 20, 1668
Hylodes, 170
Hypodactylus, 169
Hypoglossus muscles, 57, 65
Hypophysis, 102
Hypothalamus, 102

I

Ichthyophis, 5, 7, 174
Infundibulum, 102
Inhibition, 100
Invagination, 147
Involution, 148
Iris, 119
Islets of Langerhans, 73

J

Jacobson's organ, 119

L

Laryngotracheal chamber, 78
Lateral sub-rostral fossa, 63
Latissiumus dorsal, 56
Levator bulbi, 57
Linnaeus, 185
Longissimus dorsal, 59
Lysorophus, 4

M

Macula lutea, 122
Mcromere, 140
Maculae, 125
Malpighian body, 127
Marshall, 129
Masseter, 56
Median subrostral fossa, 63
Megalobatrachus, 5
Megalophyrs, 7
Membranous labyrinth, 124
Meninges, 100
Mesethmoid, 41
Mesonenephric, 2
Mesorchium, 131

Mesovarium, 132
Metacrosis, 32
Micromeres, 140
Mylohyoid, 57
Myocardium, 85

N

Neoteny, 16, 176
Nephrons, 127
Nephrostome, 129
Neural crest, 152
Neural tube, 152
Neurentric canal, 152
Nictitating membrane, 27
Notorema, 172

O

Obturator, 61
Omenta, 37
Otolith, 125
Optic chiasma, 102
Optic thalami, 102
Otic capsule, 124
Otoconia, 125
Oxyntic cells, 66

P

Pacemaker, 88
Paedogenesis, 16, 176
Palaeogyrinus, 3
Palatines, 43
Parasphenoid, 40
Pars basilaris, 124
Pars neglacta, 125
Parotid gland, 33
Pelobates, 7
Pericardial fluid, 84
Pericardium, 84
Perimysium, 55
Peritoneum, 37
Peroneus, 61
Petrohyal, 78
Phyllomedusca, 169
Phyllospondyli, 180
Pineal stalk, 102
Pipa, 6, 19, 171
Plaudicola, 169
Poikilothermal, 25
Poison glands, 33
Postzygapophyses, 47
Procoelous, 46
Prezygapophyses, 46
Prootic, 41
Proteus, 6, 10
Pseudobranchius, 6
Pulmocutaneous valve, 88
Pylangium, 87

Q

Quadratogugal, 43

R

Respiratory tract, 77
Retractor bulbi, 122
Rhacophorus, 7, 22, 172
Rhinatrema, 5
Rhinocoel, 101
Rhyacotriton, 5

S

Salamandra, 6, 13
Salamandrella, 173
Sartorius, 60
Sauropleura, 4
Scapula, 49
Sciatic plexus, 112
Sclerotic, 119
Semilunar valves, 87
Semitendinous, 61
Sinuatrial aperture, 86
Sirin, 6, 17
Sphincter muscle, 119
Spiral valve, 87
Squamosal, 43
Stapideal plate, 41, 123
Stegocephalia, 180
Sternohyal muscle, 77
Suspensorium, 42
Synangium, 87

T

Tele choroidea, 101
Temporalis muscle, 57
Thrombin, 96
Trapezium, 52
Trapezoid, 52
Triton, 6, 12, 170
Truncus arteriosus, 87
Tuberculum prelingule, 80
Tympanium, 2, 27
Typhylonectes, 5

U

Uralotyphlus, 5, 8
Ureotelic, 129

V

Valvulvae conniventes, 67
Vitreous chamber, 120
Vitreous humour, 121
Vertebral line, 26
Vomerine teeth, 64
Vomeronasal organ, 119

W

Watson, 186
Williston, 186
Wintiebert, 188

X

Xenopus, 170